dBase IV

Up to and including version 2.0

PRISMA Computer Courses are structured, practical guides to mastering the most popular computer programs. PRISMA books are course books, giving step-by-step instructions, which take the user through basic skills to advanced functions in easy to follow, manageable stages.

Now available:

Excel 4.0 for Windows
Lotus 1-2-3 2.4
MS-DOS 3.3 to 5.0
UNIX
Windows 3.0 and 3.1
WordPerfect 5.1
WordPerfect for Windows

Peter Freese, Friedrich Müllmerstadt

dBase IV

Up to and including version 2.0

PRISMA **COMPUTER**
COURSE

Prisma Computer Courses first published in Great Britain 1992 by

McCarta Ltd
P.O. Box 2996
London N5 2TA London

Translation: George Hall
Production: LINE UP text productions

© Rowohlt Taschenbuch Verlag GmbH, Reinbek bei Hamburg
For the English translation
© 1993 Uitgeverij Het Spectrum B.V. Utrecht

ISBN 1 85365 375 6

British Library Cataloguing-in-Publication Data.
A catalogue record for this book is available from the British Library.

Contents

9.7.1   Procedure files 248
9.7.2   Procedures with parameters 252
9.7.3   Error procedure with the error number as
        parameter 256
9.8   Saving memory variables 257
9.8.1   Saving memory variables 257
9.8.2   Loading memory variables 259
9.9   Commands and programs for printer output . 261
9.9.1   Printer protocol 261
9.9.2   Protocol file 262
9.9.3   Printer operation 262
9.9.4   Displaying the contents of the screen on the printer 264
9.9.5   Output to the printer using the TO PRINT option 264
9.9.6   Output to the printer using @-SAY 265
9.10   Writing programs using the application generator 281
9.10.1 The DEFINE commands 301
9.11   Creating reports using the report generator . . 303
9.11.1 Modifying a report 312
9.12   Creating forms using the form generator . . 312

10   Working with several files 318
10.1   A sample system for contribution administration 318
10.2   Collecting data for the CONTRIBA file using
        CONTRIB 321
10.3   Access to several files 327
10.4   Linking records from two files 331
10.5   Entering and booking contributions using
        CONTRPAY 336
10.6   Contribution administration using CONTRAD . 338
10.6.1 Use of the contribution administration system . 341
10.7   Creating a new file from two existing files . . 344
10.8   Placing sums in a new file 346
10.9   Updating a main file using a mutation file . . 349
10.10   Linking records from three files 354

11   Converting files to a different file format . . 358
11.1   Importing and exporting files in dBASE . . . 358

12   Installing dBASE 369

13   Configuring dBASE 371
13.1   Setting the parameters for the current session . 371
13.2   Editing the CONFIG.DB configuration file . . 375

Appendices
A   List of dBASE commands 378
B   dBASE-related files 400
C   ASCII table 403
Index   404

Foreword

The use of database management software has increased greatly over the last few years. Application of this type of administration occurs chiefly in the following areas:

- management and interpretation of business information,
- storage of, and access to, knowledge.

Database management software has a number of attractive features:

- fast and effective searching procedures,
- efficient use of the storage medium,
- easy modification of the stored information.

Not all that long ago, it was only possible to manage databases on very large computers (mainframe). The necessary programs were extremely costly, and only specialists were able to work with these. Nowadays there are extensive and cheap database programs for mini and micro computers, which do not require expert know-how. This makes them suitable for small companies and personal users.

One of the most well-known database programs is dBASE which runs on personal computers with an MS-DOS operating system.

This book provides a basic course in the operation and use of dBASE. This is suited to everyone who wishes to manage business or other data on a PC and it is a supplement to the manuals which are supplied along with the package. We shall give explanations of the commands and deal with the mutual cohesion and background of the concepts in the area of data management. We do not presume that you are already familiar with databases.

In order to help clarify the text, a large number of figures, diagrams and program examples are included which you can also reproduce on your computer. All examples have been developed on an 80386 computer.

The book consists of thirteen chapters:

■ Chapters 1 to 7 deal with the operation of dBASE and the direct construction and interpretation of data files using the computer.
■ Chapters 8 and 9 discuss programs for automatic mutation and interpretation of data.
■ Chapter 10 deals with relationships between databases.
■ Chapter 11 discusses the import from, and export to, other program packages.
■ Chapters 12 and 13 deal with the installation of dBASE on your computer and the adjustment to specific circumstances (configuration).

We have chosen to deal with the dBASE IV package in the light of instructions which can be specified directly, instead of via the facilities provided by the *Control Center*. Although the Control Center makes working with dBASE IV easier (although not true of all procedures), it tends to conceal the way in which the procedures are implemented. This is fine if you are not at all interested in the procedures, however, the disadvantage is that the Control Center menus provide fewer possibilities than the *Command Mode*. In addition, the program runs more slowly due to the extra procedures required by the screen layout.

In the case of commands which have an equivalent in a menu option in the Control Center, we shall always state how you can implement the procedure via the Control Center.

At some places in this book, a lengthy line of text does not fit into one line, although it does fit into one line on the screen. Accordingly, you should type these on one screen line when you are trying out the examples.

1   Introduction

A collection of data is called a **database** when these data are stored in such a way that they can be retrieved and interpreted quickly. A filing cabinet in which the documents are ordered chronologically or alphabetically satisfies this description.

An **electronic database** is a collection of data which is stored in the computer. In comparison to a common filing cabinet, this provides a number of important advantages:

- rapidity of the searching process,
- possibility of applying search criteria,
- large storage facilities in a small space.

We shall deal with electronic databases.

In a database, the data are stored in an external memory medium. This is done not only for reasons of space, but also for security considerations and commercial interests. An external memory medium should fulfil the following requirements:

- high transmission speed,
- large storage capacity,
- maximum reliability in transmission and registration.

Disks with a magnetic layer are extremely suitable for this. Nowadays there are also storage media which are able to read and write data optically. dBASE has been developed for magnetic disks: floppy disks and hard-disks.

Databases are only usable with corresponding programs which lend themselves to all kinds of data applications. These are referred to as the **database software**. The database software, in conjuction with the database, form the database system. The application programs are able to create, modify and delete data

files, to link files to each other according to logical criteria and to transmit data. All these procedures are part of
the function package of dBASE IV.

Structured and unstructured databases

There are databases in which the data are registered in
logical units with a fixed structure (records). These are
called **structured** databases. There are also databases
without a fixed structure, in which, for example, snippets
of text are gathered. These are referred to as **unstruc-
tured** databases.

There are different types of structured databases, according to the way in which the software manages the
information: databases with a network structure and a
hierarchical structure on the one hand, and relational
databases on the other.

Network structure and hierarchical structure

Data files with a network structure or a hierarchical
structure are so labour-intensive in terms of management that they can only be used on large computers.
With these types of files, the system retrieves the files
via predefined routes called **pointers**. This provides the
benefit of high working speed due to the quick access,
however the system is inflexible because of the fixed
structure.

A great deal of experience is needed to design a structure which satifies the demands here. Experts, referred
to as database administrators, are also required for the
file maintenance.

Databases with a fixed structure, monitored by experts,
provide more protection against non-authorized access
to the data and loss of information than systems in
which the user is able to alter the structure personally.

Relational databases

In a relational database, all data are accessible regardless of the starting point. Various data categories are
linked to one another in records within a file in the same

way. You decide at the moment you request the data, just how that is to be done. This makes the system very flexible, but also very open. Accordingly, a relational database requires special measures to protect the data against loss due to ineptitude or non-authorized use. However, a database manager is not needed for this.

Relational databases are very suitable for personal computers owing to the open structure and the straightforward management.

The dBASE database system
The dBASE package manufactured by Ashton Tate (taken over by Borland) is the most well-known of all the database systems which are on the market. Two different versions are currently in common use on personal computers: dBASE III+ and dBASE IV. Both can also be installed in a special network version.

The versions dBASE II and dBASE III are obsolete in comparison to the greatly extended packages dBASE III+ and dBASE IV.

This book will deal mainly with the 1.5 and 2.0 versions of dBASE IV, which are the successors to version 1.1. It is obvious that the new packages provide a much larger assortment of functions and that the capacity has also greatly increased. In the case of version 2, the improvements are to be found largely in the more technical areas, behind the scenes. It runs faster than the other versions and the new Virtual Memory Manager (VMM) is a technique which uses disk space to augment RAM, lifting the restrictions of the computer's physical memory on your program.
In addition, versions 1.5 and 2.0 support the use of a mouse, so that windows and pull-down menus can now be fully exploited, as was the intention with version 1.1.

The dBASE IV package contains a query language for databases and a programming language.

■ The *SQL* (structured query language) behaves as a
separate mode in dBASE IV: using much fewer commands you can achieve the same result more simply
and quickly than in the standard mode of dBASE IV.

In addition to the SQL commands, you can also construct search structures, preconditions and logical
procedures by activating the required elements of the
files using the cursor. The general command is created
by giving an example with concrete information: Query
By Example (QBE). Using a kind of filter (View), you
can search in a structured way for data and combine information in order to produce conclusions. Using a mutation filter, you can make a systematic choice from a
file in order to make automatic and selective alterations.

■ The *programming language* provides the possibility
of automizing all kinds of procedures with the data files. You can write a program (application) yourself
line by line, or you can assign this to the application
generator which links the standard modules to each
other to carry out the procedures which you have selected from the menus.

The query language consists of commands and functions. You can create, for instance, a new file using
these functions and enter, alter, remove and sort data
and construct logical relations between the data.

By means of the query language operating instructions,
you can combine the procedure commands with the database to produce a program which automatically executes the procedures. dBASE IV automatically uses
the application generator when you have designed a
form letter, a report or a label.

In the following chapter, we shall discuss in more depth
the ways in which you can operate dBASE IV:

■ via the command mode (at the dot prompt) using direct instructions on the command line,
■ using the menus in the *Control Center*. This mode is

also referred to as the ASSIST mode.

dBASE IV also has an in-between form of individual commands and programs: *macros*. These are fixed ranges of commands which can be registered in a library and activated by means of a function key.

In addition to the help provided via the dBASE IV Control Center in the form of the application generator and the three generators for forms, reports and labels, the package also contains an extensive help function which can be activated by HELP <dBASE key word>. We shall deal with this further in section 2.4.

In the Control Center, context-related help appears when you press the function key F1.

2   Operating dBASE IV

2.1   Preparing dBASE IV

If you have not previously worked with dBASE IV on your computer, it will first have to be adjusted to the hardware. This procedure is outlined in chapter 12.

2.2   Starting up and closing down dBASE IV

Entering commands

Commands in dBASE IV may be written using small letters, capitals or a random combination of capital and small letters. In this book, in order to make things clear, we shall write the keywords (commands, functions and options) in capitals and the names of variables and other parameters in small letters.

Note: The dBASE IV set of commands has been constructed in such a way that the first four letters of lengthy commands are sufficient. Thus, if the printer is the output destination, the command TO PRIN can be given instead of TO PRINTER. This is particularly convenient in cases of direct input. In programs, the legibility of the command is of more importance than the ease of abbreviated input.

The computer only carries out an instruction when you have confirmed it by pressing Enter. We shall not state this explicitly in the future.

2.2.1   Activating dBASE IV

You should place the dBASE directory in the *search*

path of your computer. If that has been done, you can start up dBASE by giving the command:

```
DBASE
```

An opening screen appears with registration information. The program continues almost immediately. Just how this takes place depends on the settings used by the DBSETUP program to configure the dBASE work environment. The current settings are located in the CONFIG.DB file.

We shall presume that the program opens on the Command Mode: the dot prompt, with the blinking cursor behind it, is located on the third line from the bottom. In older versions, the line above it will remind you that the help function is available. This is activated by the command HELP.

If the program marches on to the Control Center, you can use the *Exit* menu and the *Exit to dot prompt* option to switch to the command mode. Activate this menu by pressing Alt-E, or F10 and the cursor keys, or click on Exit using the mouse.

In all cases where you mark an option using the cursor keys and then confirm it by pressing Enter, the mouse can also be used. We shall not state this explicitly in every case in the future.

A much shorter way to discontinue a procedure in dBASE uses a method which is applicable in all facets of dBASE IV: press the Esc key. The program will then ask whether you really wish to abandon the operation. Pressing Enter or No will leave the situation as it was; Yes will discontinue the current activity.

In both cases, the program is in the command mode. The word *Command* is shown in the first field of the status line.

If you wish to switch to the Control Center from the command mode, press F2 or type ASSIST.

2.2.2   Ending dBASE IV

The program is closed from the dot prompt by means of
the instruction:

QUIT

This command removes the variables used from memory, closes all opened data files and then returns to the
operating system.

Caution: If you just switch the computer off, you take
             the risk of making unclosed files inac-
             cessible, leading to the loss of important
             data.

Exercise

Clear the screen using the command

CLEAR

Only the status line remains.

Activate the program a couple of times using the commands mentioned and clear the screen each time.

2.3   Specifying dBASE settings

In the Control Center, you can give a number of general
SET instructions using the *Tools* menu and the *Settings*
option.

The *DOS utilities* option opens a new menu bar. Pay attention to the first field of the status line; the current
directory is shown in the second field. In the *DOS* menu,
you can activate another drive and/or directory by
means of the option *Set default drive:directory*. First
change the drive and then the directory. Although the
dialog box does not indicate this, you can use the key

combination Shift-F1 (PICK function) to display the directory tree. Activate the required directory of the current drive using the vertical cursor keys. Confirm the choice by pressing Enter.

In section 13.2, we shall deal with how you can store settings in the CONFIG.DB file, so that they are automatically activated when dBASE is started up.

2.4   The help function

You can use the HELP command at any moment to request help concerning a specific command or function.

If you give this command without any other indications, dBASE IV generates a menu with six options (seven if you are working in a network, five if you are using version 1.1). The information then supplied depends on the context in which you request it.

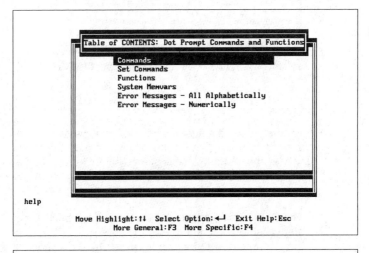

In the Control Center, the function key F1 is used to request help related to the current menu option.

Request specific help using the command:

```
HELP command/function
```

Example:

The CLEAR command can effect much more than just clearing the screen. Request information about the command and the syntax by giving the command:

```
HELP CLEAR
```

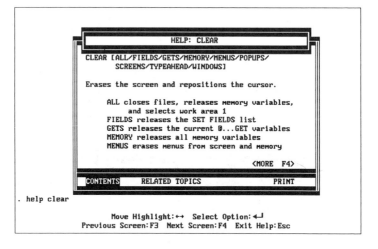

The help text no longer fits into one window all at once. Browse further using F4. In the final screen, the menu line at the bottom of the screen contains the option BACKUP. Activate this option using the cursor keys and return to the beginning of the text by pressing Enter.

The CONTENTS option produces an alphabetical list of all available commands. Use the cursor keys to select the command about which you wish to know more. If you type a letter, the highlight bar will jump to the first command which begins with that letter.

The PRINT option only sends the *current* help window

to the printer. Cancel the print command using Esc and discontinue the output using Ctrl-S (the printer first empties its buffer).

Instead of doing this, you can print the entire screen contents without having to refer to dBASE IV: pressing Shift-PrSc will send a copy of the screen to the printer.

Quit the help function using Esc.

2.5 Repeating previous instructions

dBASE IV stores the previous twenty commands which you have given in a buffer: the HISTORY buffer. Press the Cursor Up key to draw the previous command to the dot prompt. You can move through the list using the vertical cursor keys:

up   scroll backwards through the HISTORY buffer

down   scroll forwards through the HISTORY buffer

The commands are shown behind the dot prompt as you scroll. Press Enter in order to execute a displayed command again.

You can change a command in the buffer before it is implemented. Using the horizontal cursor keys and the edit keys, you can delete, alter and insert letters.

left   cursor leftwards

right   cursor rightwards

Backspace   delete one character to the left of the cursor position

Del   delete one character at the cursor position, close up text

Ins   insert one character at the cursor position,
               shift text rightwards

You can display the entire contents of the HISTORY
buffer on the screen or print it on the printer:

```
LIST/DISPLAY HISTORY [LAST number]
                     [TO PRINTER]
```

Using the *LAST number* option, you restrict the number
of commands which is shown. The *TO PRINTER* option
sends the screen display to the printer.

You can increase the size of the HISTORY buffer sub-
stantially: theoretically, there is capacity for 16,000
commands. Define the size of the command buffer
using a SET command:

```
SET HISTORY TO 16000
```

Exercises

1   Retrieve the previous commands from the HIS-
    TORY buffer using the Cursor Up key. If you have
    followed the examples, these are HELP, CLEAR
    and HELP.

2   Using the Cursor Down key, move to the blank line
    behind the dot prompt and type the command LIST
    HISTORY in order to examine the list of old com-
    mands. (This command is also part of the list!)

2.6   Displaying a list of files

dBASE IV has an instruction which shows a list of the
files in the current directory on diskette or harddisk.

A file name consists of three components: the name itself with a maximum length of eight characters, a point
and an extension of maximum three characters. You

may use letters, numbers and the underlining character in the name and extension. Some characters are explicitly forbidden, others cause problems for some versions of the operating system. Accordingly, you should choose simple but clear names for new files.

In principle, you can choose the extensions yourself, but this may give rise to difficulties since dBASE IV reserves many extensions for all sorts of files. Data files automatically receive the extension .DBF (DataBase File). The program file of an application receives the extension .PRG. The extension .MDX is used for a multi-index file and .NDX for a single index (see section 4.1).

If you only request database files (by typing 'dir' without any options), the list shows behind each file name the number of records, the date of the last modification and the number of bytes used. If you also request other files, the command shows the files in four columns on the screen.

The two commands below produce the same result:

```
DIR [options]
LIST FILES [LIKE options]
```

In both cases you can specify the command with:

```
[LIKE [drive][path][file pattern][{TO
 PRINTER | TO FILE}]]
```

Note:	In the syntax of a command, the square brackets [...] mean that the parameter is optional. The braces {...} mean that you must choose one of the options given.
drive	the letter of the diskdrive or harddisk
path	the full name of a (sub)directory
file pattern	name of a specific file of group of files, indicated by the wildcards * and ?. Normally,

the list of files only consists of the .DBF files.

TO PRINTER or TO FILE

transports the output to the printer or text file instead of to the screen.

```
. dir
Database Files    # Records     Last Update     Size
ONE.DBF                 32      18/05/93          738
TWO.DBF                  6      05/01/93         5164
THREE.DBF                5      04/01/93         1573
FOUR.DBF                 4      18/05/93         1278

    8753 bytes in      4 files
1921024 bytes remaining on drive

. dir *.*
Z_1.SCR            Z_2.SCR         CATALOG.CAT     ONE.DBF
TWO.DBF            THREE.DBF       FOUR.DBF        UNTITLED.CAT

   25706 bytes in      8 files
1921024 bytes remaining on drive

.
```
`Command`   `Num`

Examples:

`DIR *.*`   All files in the current directory
`LIST FILES LIKE *.*`   of the current drive.

`DIR B:*.*`   All files in the current directory
`LIST FILES LIKE B:*.*`   of drive B:.

`DIR B:*.PRG`   All files in the current directory
`LIST FILES LIKE B:*.PRG`   of drive B: which have the ex-
                                   tension .PRG.

`DIR DB??????.*`   All files in the current directory
`LIST FILES LIKE DB??????.*`   of the current drive, whose
                                   names begin with the letters
                                   DB along with 1 to 6 further
                                   random characters and a ran-
                                   dom extension.

```
DIR C:\DBASE                    All files in the directory DBASE
LIST FILES LIKE C:\DBASE        of the harddisk C: which have
                                the extension .DBF.
```

In the Control Center, you open the menus for editing files by
means of the command Alt-T, D. The window normally gives a
summary of all files (*.*) in the current directory of the current
drive. Switch to another directory and/or drive using the *Files*
menu and the *Change drive:directory* option, or limit the amount
of files displayed by applying the menu option *Display Only*.

2.7   Implementing DOS commands from dBASE

The RUN command from dBASE IV makes it possible
to implement a DOS command without having to quit
dBASE.

A command using the RUN instruction has the following
syntax:

```
RUN <DOS command>
```

Example:

```
RUN DIR A:                      Show the list of files of the disk-
                                ette in drive A: on the screen.

RUN COPY A:begin.prg            Copy      the      program
     A:start.prg                BEGIN.PRG on the diskette in
                                drive A: under the new name of
                                START.PRG on the same
                                diskette.

RUN REN A:begin.prg             Give the program BEGIN.PRG
     A:start.prg                on the diskette in drive A: the
                                new name of START.PRG.
```

In the Control Center, you will find the equivalent of the RUN in-struction via the command *Tools, DOS utilities, DOS, Perform DOS command, Enter*. In abbreviated form this is: Alt-T, D, Alt-D, P, Enter. Type the DOS command as you are accustomed, in the special window.

This is not even an exaggerated example of the detour which has to be made in order to bore through the shell which the Control Center forms around dBASE IV. Although you can open the menu at the extreme left-hand side of the menu bar by pressing F10 (in that case in will save a couple of keystrokes), it remains a roundabout manner of working with the program. The Control Center is, in fact, only really handy if you have a mouse. The figure below illustrates the last part of this procedure.

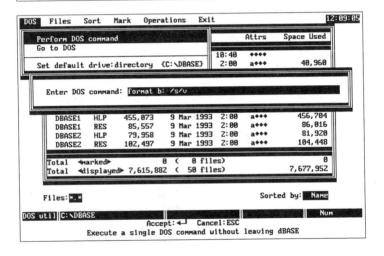

Exercises

1 Display the list of files of the directory containing the dBASE IV program files using both dBASE com-mands (DIR C:\DBASE*.* and LIST FILES LIKE C:\DBASE*.*).
   Display the list of files using the DOS command DIR

(RUN DIR). Pay attention to the differences in screen output which the DIR command produces with dBASE IV and MS-DOS.

2   Make another directory the current directory via a detour using the MS-DOS operating system (for instance: RUN CD \DBASE\LABELS).

3   Examine the other options provided by *DOS utilities* in the *Tools* menu:

Sort   This sorts the file list according to a criterion other than the name: this is either the extension, the last update, or size of the file.

Mark   This marks, unmarks or switches the marking. This is important for the editing in the *Operations* menu. Caution: in lengthy file lists not all applied marking is visible. The individual files are marked by pressing Enter and also unmarked by repeating the procedure.

Operations This enables you to remove, copy, relocate, examine, modify or rename files. Examining and modifying is only meaningful in the case of files with legible texts (ASCII files).

Exit   The option *Exit to Control Center* is self-evident.

3   Setting the dBASE IV work environment

The original situation

dBASE IV is configured by the manufacturer to fit standard situations. The configuration which suits you best can be specified every time you work with the program (depending on the work aspects), or it may be wholly or partially saved in CONFIG.DB which is the configuration file for dBASE.

Display the configuration using the command:

```
LIST STATUS [{TO PRINTER | TO FILE <file
   name>}]
```

Since the output consists of more than fits onto one screen, you should transfer the data to the printer or to a text file with the standard extension .TXT. This may result in the following, for example:

```
File Search Path :
OS Working drive/directory: C:\DBASE
Default disk drive : C:
Print destination : PRN:
Margin =        0
REFRESH count =    0
REPROCESS count =    0
Number of files open =    3
Current work area =    1
Separator: .
Currency: £

ALTERNATE  - OFF   DELIMITERS - OFF
   FULLPATH   - OFF   SAFETY - ON
AUTOSAVE   - OFF   DESIGN     - ON
   HEADING    - ON    SCOREBOARD - ON
BELL       - ON    DEVELOP    - ON
   HELP       - ON    SPACE - ON
```

```
CARRY      - OFF    DEVICE     - SCRN
   HISTORY    - ON     SQL - OFF
CATALOG    - OFF    ECHO       - OFF
   INSTRUCT   - ON     STATUS - ON
CENTURY    - OFF    ENCRYPTION - ON
   INTENSITY  - ON     STEP - OFF
CONFIRM    - OFF    ESCAPE     - ON
   LOCK       - ON     TALK - ON
CONSOLE    - ON     EXACT      - OFF
   NEAR       - OFF    TITLE - ON
DEBUG      - OFF    EXCLUSIVE  - OFF
   PAUSE      - OFF    TRAP - OFF
DELETED    - OFF    FIELDS     - OFF
   PRINT      - OFF    UNIQUE - OFF


Programmable function keys :
F2        - assist;
F3        - list;
F4        - dir;
F5        - display structure;
F6        - display status;
F7        - display memory;
F8        - display;
F9        - append;
F10       - edit;
CTRL-F1   -
CTRL-F2   -
CTRL-F3   -
CTRL-F4   -
CTRL-F5   -
CTRL-F6   -
CTRL-F7   -
CTRL-F8   -
CTRL-F9   -
CTRL-F10  -
SHIFT-F1  -
SHIFT-F2  -
SHIFT-F3  -
SHIFT-F4  -
SHIFT-F5  -
SHIFT-F6  -
SHIFT-F7  -
```

```
SHIFT-F8 -
SHIFT-F9 -
```

The list contains all settings, including those of parameters which have not been altered during the installation procedure. The SET command activates a menu-operated utility which enables you to modify all aspects of the dBASE work environment during the current session: *Options*, *Display*, *Keys*, *Disk drive*, *Files*.

The following points are worth considering:

■ redefining the function keys,
■ removing the automatic specification COMMAND = ASSIST,
■ adjusting the screen colours,
■ specifying the default drive for the data files during activation,
■ activation of your own word processor instead of the dBASE editor, by means of the instruction MODIFY COMMAND. You should, in that case, register the word processor in the CONFIG.DB file using the command TEDIT=... (a full-screen editor) or WP=... (a word processor for memo fields).

Settings can be *temporarily* changed using the SET menus, or by means of a separate SET command, for instance:

```
SET FUNCTION F10 TO "CLEAR; USE sale;
  DISPLAY STRUCTURE;"
```

Permanent changes are made using an editor in the CONFIG.DB file. We shall deal with this more extensively in chapter 13.

Using the Control Center, you can make temporary changes to the work environment using the *Tools, Settings* option. You then have access to the settings in the *Options* and *Display* categories. Compare the number of options provided here with that provided by the SET utility (see above).

If you wish to change the CONFIG.DB file permanently when in
the Control Center, open the *Tools* menu and select *DOS utilities*.
Now open the *DOS* menu to check whether the C:\dBASE
directory is the default directory. (If not, highlight *Set default
drive:directory*, press Enter and specify **C:\dBASE**. Press Enter
to confirm. Now quit this list using Esc and by choosing Yes. You
will return to the Control Center. Start up the process again by
opening the *Tools* menu.) In the file list, highlight the CONFIG.DB
file and open the *Operations* menu. Select *Edit*. The file is loaded
in the dBASE IV word processor.

```
 Layout   Words   Go To   Print   Exit                        12:17:08
[]....▾1.....▾..2....▾....3..▾.....4▾......▾5.....▾..6....▾....7..▾......
*
*       dBASE IV Configuration File
*   Written by Install.exe on 13/5/93
*
COLOR OF NORMAL      = N+/BG
COLOR OF HIGHLIGHT   = RG+/W
COLOR OF MESSAGES    = W/B
COLOR OF TITLES      = W+/BG
COLOR OF BOX         = W+/B
COLOR OF INFORMATION = BG+/B
COLOR OF FIELDS      = W+/N
DISPLAY              = VGA25
COMMAND              = ASSIST
EXCLUSIVE            = ON
STATUS               = ON
SQLDATABASE          = SAMPLES
SQLHOME              = C:\DBASE\SQLHOME
CURRENCY             = "£"
DATE                 = DMY
HOURS                = 24
DOS util C:\dbase\CONFIG          Line:11 Col:1              Ins
```

Exercise

Add two lines to the CONFIG.DB file, in which the separators for decimals and thousands are specified. For
the decimals, the *point* variable is used (see figure
above):

```
POINT = .
```

The *separator* variable is used for the thousands:

```
SEPARATOR =  ,
```

The point and the comma are often applied differently in various countries in Europe, thus alteration may be very useful in certain work situations.

Save the new version using the *Layout* menu. Select *Save this file*.

If you have followed the proposals for the installation of your own word processor, save the text as a DOS file, or ASCII file.

4   Creating files

4.1   dBASE-related files and field types

File types

The dBASE program creates and uses various sorts of files. The most important file type you will deal with now is the one with the extension DBF. This is the file type in which your data will be stored.

We shall discuss the other sorts of file in conjunction with the commands and the generators which create them. In appendix B you will find a complete list of all the dBASE-related files.

Field types

A data file consists of *records* which are constructed out of a fixed range of *fields* in which the different categories of data are stored. Each field has a *field name*, a *field type* and a certain *width*. In the case of numeric fields, you can specify the number of figures after the decimal point (*Dec*). You can also specify a field as a sort criterion (*Index*, standard: N).

dBASE IV has the following types of fields:

Character

In character (also known as text) fields, you may enter all letters, numbers and special characters, to a maximum of 254 characters.

Numeric

Numeric fields may contain numbers, the decimal sign and the pre-signs + and -, to a maximum of 20 characters. This type of field is necessary if calculation has to be performed using the contents of the field. A telephone number should be stored in a character field.

Float

In a field for numbers with a floating point, the position of the point is not fixed (maximum 20 characters).

Date
A date field automatically has a length of eight characters. The way in which the date is displayed depends on
the DATE parameter in the CONFIG.DB file.

Logical
A logical field can only have one of two values, either
true (.T.) or false (.F.). This field automatically has a
length of only one character, which means that, for instance, the value .T. should be entered as T (only the
letter).

Memo
A memo field contains a reference (which can only be
internally interpreted by dBASE) to a text belonging to a
record. The text itself is located in a separate file with
the extension .DBT. The memo field has a formal length
of 10 characters, which are, however, not usable in the
'normal' database.

4.2 Creating the ADDRESS.DBF file

At various points in this book, we shall use a file containing address data in the examples. This file can be
used to record the membership of a club or for the registration of details concerning staff, customers or sup-
pliers to a company.

The ADDRESS file structure
A file can only be filled with data when the categories of
these data are known. In other words, you must con-
sider in advance which elements are going to make up
a record: the number of fields, and the names, types
and widths of these fields.

The ADDRESS file has ten fields with the following features:

field name	field type	width
MEMBERNR	character	3 characters

NAME	character	15 characters
FIRST_NAME	character	15 characters
STREET	character	20 characters
PCTOWN	character	20 characters
C_STATUS	character	1 character
SEX	character	1 character
CONTR	numeric	6 positions, of which one comma and two decimal
BTH_DATE	date	8 characters
NOTE	memo	10 characters

Most field names are self-evident. (C_STATUS = civil status, **m**arried, **s**ingle, **d**ivorced. CONTR = contribution.) In this version of the address file we shall take the postal code and town as being one unit for the moment. In later exercises we shall split the contents of that field into fields for the postal code and the town.

Define the file using the command:

```
CREATE <file name>
```

The instruction activates a dialogue in order to define the fields. The program skips superfluous items and gives error messages in the case of invalid input.

4.2.1   The CREATE process in dBASE IV

Open the input template by means of the command:

```
CREATE address
```

The input template is shown on the screen with the menus *Layout, Organize, Append, Go To* and *Exit*.

Fill in the list according to the record structure outlined above. dBASE automatically writes the field names in capital letters. Proceed to the next column using Enter or Tab and select the required type by pressing the first letter or by pressing the spacebar until the appropriate type appears. Go to the next field and type the required field size.

If you select a character field, the program automatically
skips the *DEC* column and jumps to the *Index* column.
We shall not use an Index for the time being: confirm
the N by pressing Enter. The cursor then moves to the
next line to specify the next field. dBASE automatically
increases the number of the field. The maximum number of fields is 255 and the maximum number of characters in the record structure is 4000. A counter in the
upper right-hand corner registers how many bytes are
still available.

The bottom line of the screen provides a concise explanation of the highlighted field and its current contents.

Using the cursor keys, you can always return to an element which you may wish to alter.

Save the file structure using the command *Layout, Save
this database file structure.* The complete file name is
displayed in a small box: drive:\path\address.dbf. If a
lengthy name does not fit into the box, you can display
the entire name above the status line by means of the
zoom function (F9). Confirm the name by pressing
Enter. While the structure is being written, the statement
'Please wait' will be shown on the bottom line.

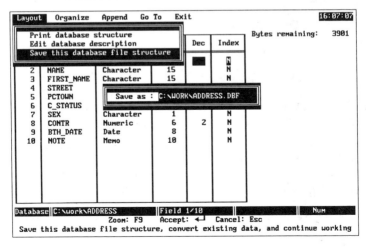

You can also alter the file structure later and then decide whether to save the alterations or not: *Exit, Save changes and exit* or *Exit, Abandon changes and exit.*

When in the Control Center, the input template is activated by placing the cursor on the word *Create* in the *Data* box. Confirm the action by pressing Enter. The input template in the Control Center is identical to that produced by the CREATE command.

In order to keep an orderly survey, it is advisable to put all files which belong to the same project into one catalog. Open an input window to specify the name by choosing the menu *Catalog*, and then select the option *Modify catalog name*. Change the name of the default catalog UNTITLED.CAT to a name which gives an indication of the project. Also give a description of the aim of this catalog by means of the command *Catalog, Edit description of catalog*. This description will be displayed when you browse through the catalogs using the instruction *Catalog, Use a different catalog*.

In addition, give a description of the current file which you have just created. Use the command *Catalog, Change description of highlighted file* to do this.

4.3   Opening and closing a file

You can only work with a data file if it has been opened. dBASE IV has one command to open a file (USE) and different commands to close a file in differing ways.

A command using USE has the following syntax:

```
USE <file name>
```

Example:

```
USE address
```

The closing commands are:

```
USE [file name]
CLEAR [ALL]
QUIT
CLOSE {file type | ALL}
```

If you apply the USE command with a new file name, that file will be opened and the previous active file closed. USE on its own only closes the current file.

CLEAR ALL closes all open files, clears all variables which are dependent on the data files in memory, clears the screen, switches to the first work area and to the command mode. Instead of applying the ALL option, you can also close the various named elements one by one using separate options (see the manual).

The QUIT command does the same but also closes dBASE IV itself and returns to the operating system.

CLOSE closes all files (ALL) or a named type of file: ALTERNATE, DATABASES, FORMAT, INDEX, PROCEDURE. The DATABASES option also refers to relevant format and index files, in addition to the opened data files. The CLOSE command does not influence the contents of memory. If you only wish to end the current file, it is better to apply the USE command.

In the Control Center, you can open a file by highlighting the name of the file using the cursor keys and then pressing Enter. In the *Data* frame, the file name is then shown above the line.

If the file already contains data, you can examine these immediately by means of the Browse function (F2). If you press Enter once more instead of doing this, a dialog box is opened providing the following options:

■ *Close file*, just as in the command mode.
■ *Modify structure/order* of the current file. This option is identical to the *Design* function (Shift-F2) in the opening screen in the Control Center.

■ *Display data.* This option is identical to the above-mentioned
function F2 in the opening screen in the Control Center.

If there are no data in the file as yet, you can only browse in the
edit mode. Otherwise, you can switch to the browse mode using
F2 in order to view a range of records simultaneously.

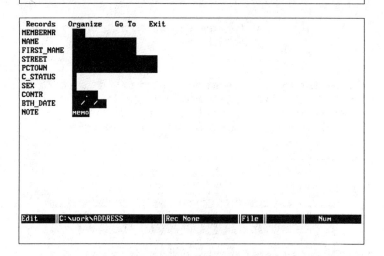

4.4   Examining the file names and file structure

Examining the file names
Imagine you wish to check if the file structure really has
been saved on the disk. Display the files:

```
DIR address.*
```

The * wildcard represents any group of characters. In
the example, the DIR command looks for all files with
the name ADDRESS and any extension. The file pattern *.* covers all files.

The program discovers two files with the name AD-
DRESS: ADDRESS.DBF and ADDRESS.DBT, the
data file and the file containing the texts in the memo
fields. If you also wish to examine file data, request the
list of files via the Control Center (see below) or by
means of the command

```
RUN DIR address.*
```

Since both files are still empty, they only occupy a
couple of hundred bytes.

In the Control Center, open the *Tools* menu and select *DOS
utilities*. All files in the current directory are placed in the list. If you
wish to view only those files which belong to this database, open
the *Files* menu and select *Display only*. Type the filter AD-
DRESS.* and press Enter.

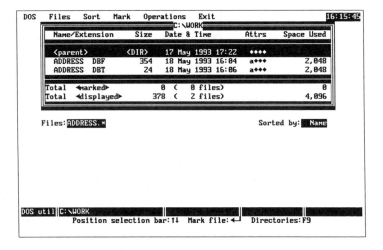

Examining the file structure

You can display the file structure of the opened file at
any time:

```
{LIST | DISPLAY} STRUCTURE [{TO PRINTER |
  TO FILE <file name>}]
```

Display the structure on the screen using the command:

```
LIST STRUCTURE
```

```
. list stru
Structure for database: C:\WORK\ADDRESS.DBF
Number of data records:      0
Date of last update   : 18/05/93
Field  Field Name  Type       Width   Dec   Index
    1   MEMBERNR    Character      3             N
    2   NAME        Character     15             N
    3   FIRST_NAME  Character     15             N
    4   STREET      Character     20             N
    5   PCTOWN      Character     20             N
    6   C_STATUS    Character      1             N
    7   SEX         Character      1             N
    8   CONTR       Numeric        6      2      N
    9   BTH_DATE    Date           8             N
   10   NOTE        Memo          10             N
** Total **                      100

Command   C:\work\ADDRESS          Rec None          File
```

4.5   Altering the file structure

We shall extend the file structure by adding three fields:

■ INTRO, a text field containing ten characters
■ RED, a logical field (one character)
■ WHITE, a logical field (one character).

Activate the alteration program using the command:

```
MODIFY STRUCTURE [<file name>]
```

If no file name is specified, the command applies to the
current file.

INTRO should be placed under MEMBERNR. The
fields for the categories should be in front of the memo

field. This order of sequence is preferable because it is easier and quicker to work when the most well-used fields are foremost.

Highlight the field where the new field is to be located (on NAME in the case of INTRO) and press Ctrl-N to create a blank line for a new field. Define the new field by means of:

INTRO, Enter, Enter, 10, Enter

Highlight NOTE and define the other new fields in the same way:

Ctrl-N, RED, Enter, L
Ctrl-N, WHITE, Enter, L

A logical field automatically acquires the width of one character. The type of field can also be chosen by first examining the the various possibilities using the space-bar. Press Enter to confirm the selection.

```
 Layout   Organize   Append   Go To   Exit                        16:22:04

                                                     Bytes remaining:   3889
  ┌─────┬────────────┬────────────┬───────┬─────┬───────┐
  │ Num │ Field Name │ Field Type │ Width │ Dec │ Index │
  ├─────┼────────────┼────────────┼───────┼─────┼───────┤
  │  1  │ MEMBERNR   │ Character  │   3   │     │   N   │
  │  2  │ INTRO      │ Character  │  10   │     │   N   │
  │  3  │ NAME       │ Character  │  15   │     │   N   │
  │  4  │ FIRST_NAME │ Character  │  15   │     │   N   │
  │  5  │ STREET     │ Character  │  20   │     │   N   │
  │  6  │ PCTOWN     │ Character  │  20   │     │   N   │
  │  7  │ C_STATUS   │ Character  │   1   │     │   N   │
  │  8  │ SEX        │ Character  │   1   │     │   N   │
  │  9  │ CONTR      │ Numeric    │   6   │  2  │   N   │
  │ 10  │ BTH_DATE   │ Date       │   8   │     │   N   │
  │ 11  │ RED        │ Logical    │   1   │     │   N   │
  │ 12  │ WHITE      │ Logical    │   1   │     │   N   │
  │ 13  │ NOTE       │ Memo       │  10   │     │   N   │
  └─────┴────────────┴────────────┴───────┴─────┴───────┘

 Database C:\work\ADDRESS            Field 13/13
              Enter the field name.  Insert/Delete field:Ctrl-N/Ctrl-U
 Field names begin with a letter and may contain letters, digits and underscores
```

Save the new structure using Ctrl-End or *Exit, Save changes and exit* (Ctrl-W). The program asks for confirmation as a security measure. Press Y or Enter.

Check the new structure using the command LIST
STRUCTURE.

A new data file has come into existence due to the alteration in the structure. dBASE automatically adopts the
data from the old file in the new file and states the number of records copied.

Caution: The data are not adopted in the new file if
              you change the field name or the type of
              field. If a field is extended, the previous
              contents are supplemented with spaces. If
              the field is shortened, the contents are
              pruned to the new length.

4.6   Entering data

Input command
dBASE IV presumes that you will add data to a file
where the structure has already been defined. Activate
the address file using the command:

USE address

It makes no difference whether records have been previously added or not.

APPEND

The APPEND command adds a new empty record. In
our case, that is the very first record in the file. The
status line displays: Rec None. The program is running
in the edit mode and this is shown in the status line:
Edit. The status line also displays the current file
(C:\dbase\data\ADDRESS) and indicates that this is a
data file (File).

As soon as you have completed the last field of a record
and have concluded it by pressing Enter, the program
proceeds to the next record. Close the data input and
save it using one of the key combinations Ctrl-End or
Ctrl-W.

You can also do this using the menu *Exit, Exit* (F10, E or Alt-E, E).

The input template

The APPEND command generates an input template with the field names of the opened file listed under one another. The type of field is not shown. However, an acoustic warning signal is given if inappropriate input is specified, such as letters in a numeric field.

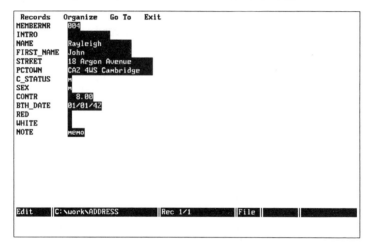

Entering data in the fields

The input template takes over a number of jobs: as soon as a field is full the APPEND command leaps to the following field, giving an acoustic signal at the same time (assuming that the BELL is ON). Use abbreviations if necessary, or make a field longer using the command MODIFY STRUCTURE. If the input is shorter than the field, move to the following field by pressing Enter or Cursor Down. Using the cursor keys, you can move back to a field in order to make alterations (in the overwrite mode). The Ins key is used to switch the command to the insert mode.

Text in the NOTE memo field

We have added the NOTE memo field to the file in order

to store information which does not fit into the fixed structure of the records. Actually, a field like this is only really necessary when this text is longer than 254 characters: for any smaller amount, a normal text field will suffice. As long as a memo field remains empty, the word 'memo' is written with small letters, otherwise it is shown in capitals.

The texts in memo fields are stored in a parallel file of the same name, but with the extension .DBT. The text is entered and stored via the dBASE internal word processor, unless you have defined another (see section 13.2).

Place the cursor in the memo field and activate the word processor using the key combination Ctrl-Home. The system switches to the editor which fills the entire screen.

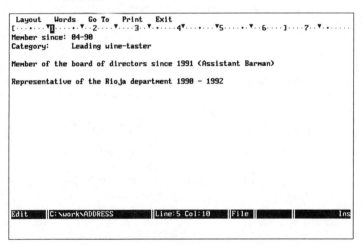

```
 Layout   Words   Go To   Print   Exit
[ . . . • . . . .▼▮. . . . . •▼. .2. . . .▼. . . .3. .▼. •. . . .4▼. . . • . . .▼5. . . . •. .▼. .6. . . .] . . .7. .▼. •. . . .
Member since: 04-90
Category:     Leading wine-taster

Member of the board of directors since 1991 (Assistant Barman)

Representative of the Rioja department 1990 - 1992








Edit    C:\work\ADDRESS            Line:5 Col:10    File                     Ins
```

Save the text using the command *Layout, Save this memo field* (Alt-L, Enter). You can also conclude the input by pressing the key combination Ctrl-End. You then return to the edit mode of APPEND. You will recognize that the text has been saved by the capital letters shown.

For each memo field, dBASE IV has a capacity of 512 Kb available for entering text. However, the internal word processor cannot handle texts which are larger than 64 Kb. For larger texts, other methods have to be applied.

Exercise

In the following chapter, a completed file is required in order to be able to interpret data. Adopt the examples shown below. Type the data without separators, since dBASE does that for you. Type the decimal point in the contribution field; dBASE then knows that decimals will follow and places the number at the right-hand side of the field. We shall use the INTRO, RED and WHITE fields later.

Load the address file and activate the input screen:

```
USE address
APPEND
```

RecNr	MEMBERNR	NAME	FIRST_NAME	STREET
	PCTOWN		C_STATUS SEX CONTR	BTHDATE NOTE

1	004	Rayleigh	John	18 Argon Avenue				
	CA1 4WS Cambridge	m		m	8.00	01-01-42	-
2	003	Sklodowska	Marya	34 Radium Road				
	CU1 2MC Currie	m		f	8.00	02-02-67	-
3	015	Bragg	William	42 Crystal Crescent				
	LD1 3WH Leeds	m		m	8.00	03-03-62	-
4	008	Rutherford	Ernest	37 Charge Court				
	MA1 2HE Manchester m		m	8.00	04-04-71	-
5	057	Todd	Alexander	1 Vitamin View				
	CA1 2BB Cambridge	m		m	8.00	07-07-07	-
6	058	Sanger	Frederick	1 Insulin Isle				
	CA4 8NB Cambridge	m		m	4.50	05-05-18	-
7	064	Hodgkin	Dorothy	9 Pepsin Park				
	OX2 1XR Oxford	m		f	8.00	10-10-10	-
8	002	Ross	Ronald	17 Malaria Mews				
	LV1 4IN Liverpool	s		m	8.00	06-06-52	-

```
9      023      Macleod     John         35 Diabetes Drive
  AB3 2CT Aberdeen   s           m    8.00  07-07-76 -
10     083      MacClintock Barbara     Translocation Tower
  CO1 6DN Cornell    s           f    8.00  02-02-02 -
11     026      Deledda     Grazia       36 Sardinia Slopes
  LE1 7IT Lands End  s           f    4.50  17-01-71 -
```

Quit the input mode using the command *Exit, Exit* (Alt-E, Enter).

When in the Control Center, you open a file by highlighting its name in the *Data* panel using the cursor keys. Subsequently press F2 (do this twice if dBASE IV is in the browse mode). The input module is identical to that in the APPEND command.

Enter the data as described above and save them using the command Alt-E, Enter.

Examining the fields
The contents of a file, or of named fields, can be displayed using the LIST command. For example:

```
LIST intro, first_name, name, red, white OFF
```

Note that the order of sequence of these fields is different to that in the record structure.

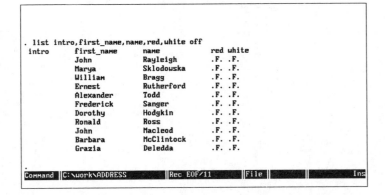

```
. list intro,first_name,name,red,white off
  intro      first_name      name          red white
             John            Rayleigh      .F. .F.
             Marya           Sklodowska    .F. .F.
             William         Bragg         .F. .F.
             Ernest          Rutherford    .F. .F.
             Alexander       Todd          .F. .F.
             Frederick       Sanger        .F. .F.
             Dorothy         Hodgkin       .F. .F.
             Ronald          Ross          .F. .F.
             John            Macleod       .F. .F.
             Barbara         McClintock    .F. .F.
             Grazia          Deledda       .F. .F.
.
Command   C:\work\ADDRESS          Rec EOF/11       File                        Ins
```

The OFF option ensures that the record numbers are not displayed. Instead of LIST, you can also use DIS-PLAY. The latter command has the advantage that the display is halted with every full screen and is continued by pressing a random key. In this case too, you can transport the output to a file or to the printer.

A column remains empty for a new field. This does not apply to logical fields since they may not be empty: the value is either .T. or .F., a space is not possible.

When dealing with the instruction BROWSE in section 6.2, we shall discuss the quickest way to add any missing data and to remove incorrect information.

As mentioned, in the Control Center you are able to select what you wish to do with a file when it has been opened: examine the data (F2), which is equivalent to LIST <field list>, or modify the file structure using Shift-F2 (Design) which is equivalent to MODIFY STRUCTURE.

This choice is also presented if you apply the detour USE (Enter) in the opening Control Center screen: _Modify structure/order_ or _Display data_. If no data are recorded in the file as yet, only the edit mode is available in the latter option.

5 Displaying and searching for records

5.1 General

This chapter deals with the display of records. If you do this using numeric data, this can be done for:

- all records,
- a given interval of record numbers,
- specific records.

You can display the contents of a record in two ways:

- using the record number by which dBASE IV manages the records,
- based on the contents of one or more fields using conditional commands (FOR, WHILE, SET FILTER TO).

In actual practice, the second method of selecting information is more important.

5.2 Displaying all records of a file

As you know, the commands LIST and DISPLAY differ in the way they react when the screen is full (maximum 20 records consisting of one screen line). Display only proceeds when you press a key to continue. With LIST, the display scrolls over the screen until the last record is shown on the screen.

The ALL option displays all records in the order of the record numbers:

```
DISPLAY ALL
```

Example:

You wish to examine all records in the ADDRESS.DBF file. The commands are:

```
USE address
DISPLAY ALL
```

```
Record#  MEMBERNR INTRO    NAME         FIRST_NAME     STREET
PCTOWN                 C_STATUS SEX  CONTR BTH_DATE RED WHITE NOTE
    1  004                      Rayleigh     John           18 Argon Avenue
CA2 4WS Cambridge      M        M    8.00 01/01/42 .F. .F.  MEMO
    2  003                      Sklodowska   Marya          34 Radium Rd
CU1 2MC Currie         M        f    8.00 02/02/67 .F. .F.  MEMO
    3  015                      Bragg        William        42 Crystal Crescent
LD1 3WH Leeds          M        M    8.00 03/03/62 .F. .F.  MEMO
    4  008                      Rutherford   Ernest         37 Charge Court
MA1 2HE Manchester     M        M    8.00 04/04/71 .F. .F.  MEMO
    5  057                      Todd         Alexander      1 Vitamin View
CA1 2BB Cambridge      M        M    8.00 07/07/07 .F. .F.  MEMO
    6  058                      Sanger       Frederick      3 Insulin Isle
CA4 8NB Cambridge      M        M    4.50 05/05/18 .F. .F.  MEMO
    7  064                      Hodgkin      Dorothy        9 Pepsin Park
OX2 1XR Oxford         M        f    8.00 10/10/10 .F. .F.  MEMO
    8  002                      Ross         Ronald         17 Malaria Mews
LV1 4IN Liverpool      s        M    8.00 06/06/52 .F. .F.  MEMO
    9  023                      Macleod      John           35 Diabetes Drive
AB3 2CT Aberdeen       s        M    8.00 07/06/76 .F. .F.  MEMO
   10  083                      McClintock   Barbara        Translocation Tower
Press any key to continue...
Command  C:\work\ADDRESS            Rec 1/11          File                    Ins
```

The display on the screen is rather chaotic. Each record occupies two screen lines. On the one hand, this is the consequence of the fact that the record is longer than the number of characters on a screen line. On the other hand, dBASE uses space to register a complete field name, even if the field itself only requires one character. In addition, there is a space between two adjacent fields and there is also the column with the record number *Record#*.

The NOTE field only contains the word 'memo'; capital letters are used in the first record since this memo field is filled in.

Text in a memo field is not directly visible. We shall return to this topic in section 5.5.

In the Control Center, a survey of the data is displayed by pressing F2 (Data). When you open a file, the program places the cursor on the first record (see the counter in the status bar: Rec 1/11). You can also move to the first record by giving the command *Top field* in the *Go To* menu (Alt-G, Enter). In the browse mode, a clear overview is given of the first part of the records whose fields are displayed on the screen. The remaining fields can be examined by pressing Tab to move through the columns. In the penultimate visible column the survey springs to the left.

```
 Records   Organize   Fields   Go To   Exit

 PCTOWN            C_STATUS SEX CONTR  BTH_DATE RED WHITE NOTE

 CAZ 4WS Cambridge    M      M    8.00 01/01/42            memo
 CU1 2MC Currie       M      f    8.00 02/02/67            MEMO
 LD1 3WH Leeds        M      M    8.00 03/03/62            memo
 MA1 2HE Manchester   M      M    8.00 04/04/71            memo
 CA1 2BB Cambridge    M      M    8.00 07/07/07            memo
 CA4 8MB Cambridge    M      M    4.50 05/05/18            memo
 OX2 1XR Oxford       M      f    8.00 10/10/10            memo
 LU1 4IN Liverpool    s      M    8.00 06/06/52            memo
 AB3 2CT Aberdeen     s      M    8.00 07/06/76            memo
 C01 6DN Cornell      s      f    8.00 02/02/02            memo
 LE1 7IT Lands End    s      f    4.50 17/01/71            memo

 Browse   C:\work\ADDRESS          Rec 2/11        File              Ins
```

5.3   Displaying only some of the fields

Generally, you will not need all fields in a record to deal with a certain problem. If you merely wish to know when the members of a club have their birthdays, you will only require the fields containing the names and the dates of birth.

With a list of fields, you can restrict the output given by LIST and DISPLAY to the specified fields.

```
{LIST | DISPLAY} ALL fieldX, fieldY, ...
```

Example:

In all records in the ADDRESS file, you wish to view the
fields MEMBERNR, NAME, and BTH_DATE.

```
. list membernr, name, bth_date off
membernr name              bth_date
004       Rayleigh          01/01/42
003       Sklodouska        02/02/67
015       Bragg             03/03/62
008       Rutherford        04/04/71
057       Todd              07/07/07
058       Sanger            05/05/18
064       Hodgkin           10/10/10
002       Ross              06/06/52
023       Macleod           07/06/76
083       McClintock        02/02/02
026       Deledda           17/01/71
.
```
```
Command  C:\work\ADDRESS          Rec EOF/11      File
```

In addition to the requested data, dBASE IV also states
the record number. This can be suppressed by giving
the OFF option:

```
LIST membernr, name, bth_date OFF
```

5.3.1   Saving a standard field list

From dBASE III+ onwards, it is possible to temporarily
switch off one or more fields. This is done using the
command:

```
SET FIELDS TO field list
```

Only those fields specified in the field list remain accessible. It appears as if the other fields no longer exist.
This list exists as it is until you specify another list or
until you give the command SET FIELDS TO. Switch
the list off using:

```
SET FIELDS OFF
```

Activate the list using:

```
SET FIELDS ON
```

Example:

```
. SET FIELDS TO name, membernr, contr
. LIST OFF TO PRINTER
```

NAME	MEMBERNR	CONTR
Rayleigh	004	8.00
Sklodowska	003	8.00
Bragg	015	8.00
Rutherford	008	8.00
Todd	057	8.00
Sanger	058	4.50
Hodgkin	064	8.00
Ross	002	8.00
Macleod	023	8.00
MacClintock	083	8.00
Deledda	026	4.50

Check if the other fields are now inaccessible:

```
LIST pctown
```

dBASE IV generates a dialog box containing an error message: Variable not found: PCTOWN. Under this, the erroneous command is shown along with three option fields: *Cancel*, *Edit* and *Help*.

Remove the restrictions by giving SET FIELDS OFF (or definitely using SET FIELDS TO).

In the Control Center, there is no equivalent to SET FIELDS TO. The generators for output, *Forms, Reports* and *Labels* do make internal use of this command (in combination with SET FIELDS ON and SET FIELDS OFF).

Using the following procedure, you can reduce the records in the browse mode in such a way that the result resembles that produced by SET FIELDS TO, to a certain extent.

Highlight the file in the *Data* column and press F2 (Data). If required, press F2 once more to switch to the browse mode. Then place **one** field at the left-hand side of the table using the command *Lock fields on left* from the *Fields* menu.

Using Tab, move to the right until the NAME field jumps to the second column (the MEMBERNR field remains, the INTRO field disappears). Then go back to NAME using Shift-Tab. Narrow this field and all subsequent fields using the command *Size field* from the *Fields* menu: press Cursor Left and the column becomes narrower on the screen. When you have chosen *Size field* the mouse pointer is located at the right line of the column. Instead of using the cursor keys, you can use the mouse to drag the line to a new position.

The minimum width of the column is determined by the field name (thus, for narrow fields, use short names). Adjust the width of the columns until the CONTR field becomes visible. Now all important fields fit onto the screen, but the order of sequence of the fields is fixed.

The Control Center is not designed to handle this kind of round-about procedure. However, this is amply compensated by the ease with which you can make attractive frameworks using the *Reports* generator.

5.4   Requesting specific records

In this section, we shall discuss the commands which display particular records by means of specified numbers.

If you know exactly which record you wish to examine, give the following command:

```
DISPLAY RECORD record number
```

In each opened file, dBASE IV remembers the current working position in the file by means of a *pointer*. This pointer indicates the current record (see the counter in the status line). The current record can be displayed using the DISPLAY instruction without any parameters.

When you open a file, the pointer is always located on the first record. This remains so until a command, for instance LIST, is applied to another record. The following commands move the record pointer:

■ To a specific record:

```
GOTO record number
GO record number
record number
```

The commands all have the same effect.

■ To the first or last record:

```
GO TOP
GO BOTTOM
```

■ Move a number of records forwards or backwards:

```
SKIP [number]
```

If you do not specify an amount, the record pointer moves to the following record. A negative number moves the pointer backwards by the specified amount.

In all cases, dBASE IV states the number of the current record, for instance:

```
. GO TOP
ADDRESS: Record No        1
```

Movements in the edit mode also produce alterations in the pointer position.

Examples:

The examples illustrate various ways of displaying a specific record. We shall switch off the display of the field names in advance: this is not necessary when two fields are displayed, and it saves space on the screen.

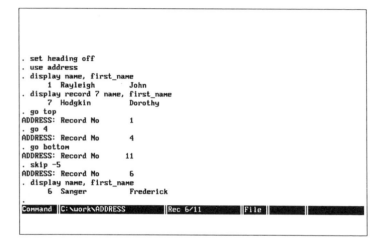

```
. set heading off
. use address
. display name, first_name
        1  Rayleigh       John
. display record 7 name, first_name
        7  Hodgkin        Dorothy
. go top
ADDRESS: Record No      1
. go 4
ADDRESS: Record No      4
. go bottom
ADDRESS: Record No      11
. skip -5
ADDRESS: Record No      6
. display name, first_name
        6  Sanger         Frederick
.
Command  ||C:\work\ADDRESS          ||Rec 6/11        ||File ||
```

(1) *SET HEADING OFF*
   Suppresses the display of the field names.

(2) *USE address*
   The ADDRESS.DBF file is opened and the pointer is positioned on the first record.

(3) *DISPLAY name, first_name*
   Without the parameters ALL or RECORD, DISPLAY shows the specified fields in the current record (in this case the first one).

(4) *DISPLAY RECORD 7 name, first_name*
   This one command places the pointer on the seventh record and displays the specified fields.

(5) *GO TOP*
   Moves the pointer back to the first record.

(6) *GO 4*
Places the pointer at record 4. The command may also be written as GOTO 4 or merely as 4.

(7) *GO BOTTOM*
Places the pointer at the last record.

(8) *DISPLAY name, first name*
The command displays the specified fields of the current record.

(9) *SKIP -5*
Moves the pointer five places backwards, for instance from record 11 to record 6. The DISPLAY command shows the record.

5.4.1   Functions for record numbers

dBASE IV has three functions which produce information about the position of the record pointer: RECNO(), BOF() and EOF(). These terms represent, respectively, 'record number', 'beginning of file' (before the first record) and 'end of file' (after the last record).

The first function produces the the current record number. The others register by means of a logical value whether the pointer is located at the first or the last record, respectively. In combination with the question mark, you can request the function value. If required, open the ADDRESS file.

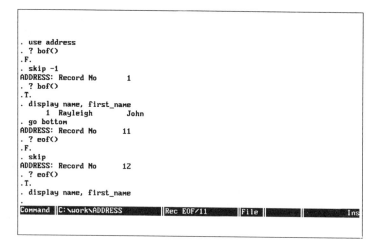

```
. use address
. ? bof()
.F.
. skip -1
ADDRESS: Record No       1
. ? bof()
.T.
. display name, first_name
       1 Rayleigh       John
. go bottom
ADDRESS: Record No       11
. ? eof()
.F.
. skip
ADDRESS: Record No       12
. ? eof()
.T.
. display name, first_name
.
Command  C:\work\ADDRESS         Rec EOF/11      File                    Ins
```

(1) *? BOF()*

Examines whether the pointer is located in front of the first record. When the record is opened, that is not the case: the pointer is *on* the first record (logically false .F.).

(2) *SKIP -1*

Moves the pointer one record backwards. The BOF() function states that the pointer is now at the beginning of the file.

(3) *GO BOTTOM*

Places the pointer *on* the last record.

(4) *? RECNO()*

The function states the current record number (11).

(5) *? EOF()*

The pointer is not located at the end of the file, but at the beginning of the last record (logically false .F.).

(6) *SKIP*

Moves the pointer one record onwards. The instruction registers that this is record 11, the end of the file (see also the status bar). The EOF() function produces the value .T. in this case.

(7) *DISPLAY name, first name*
Since there is no record, this command will have no effect.

In the Control Center, you can move the pointer by means of the *Go To* menu when in the Data panel browse mode. The *Record number* command is analogous to the RECNO() function; the result can be seen in the status line. When you highlight the menu option and press Enter, you can enter a different value in a template. The program places the pointer on the specified record and writes the value between the braces.

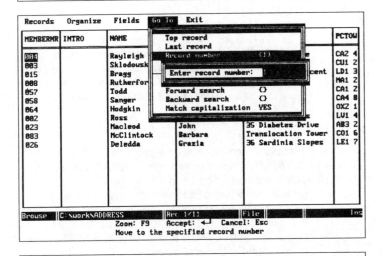

The BOF() and EOF() functions are not available as in the command mode. Also in contrast to the command mode, *Skip* (comparable to the SKIP command) normally jumps 10 records forwards. This number can be altered.

5.5   Displaying text in a memo field

Both methods of moving to a record, outlined in the previous section, can be used to display the contents of a
memo field. First activate the required record and then
display the contents of the named memo field. Both
stages can be combined:

Examples:

```
USE address
GO 1
DISPLAY note
```

or

```
USE address
DISPLAY RECORD 1 note
```

Normally, the contents of a memo field are stored using
50 characters per line. On the screen, you can adjust
the display width of memo fields, varying from a minimum of 8 to a maximum of 32,000 characters per line.

```
SET MEMOWIDTH TO number
```

It would seem obvious to assign the value 80 to the
NUMBER parameter, but the DISPLAY command re-
gards sections of text between two Returns (para-
graphs) as being a field with the standard width: it is
fully reproduced even if the text is shorter. In addition,
the instruction only begins to count at the right of the
Record# column. Thus, a display line of 80 characters
wraps round to the next screen line:

```
. set memowidth to 80
. display note
Record#  note

    1  Member since: 04-90

       Category:    Leading wine-taster


       Member of the board of directors since 1991 (Assistant Barman)


       Representative of the Rioja department 1990 - 1992

.
Command  C:\work\ADDRESS          Rec 1/11          File
```

In the Control Center, when the required memo field is high-lighted, you can switch from the browse mode to the edit screen by means of the Zoom function (F9). The memo text is then shown in the word processor. You have already seen the result in section 4.7. (The square brackets in the layout ruler indicate the margin positions, the standard values of which are 0 and 65.)

5.6   Displaying groups of records

Beginning with the current record, dBASE IV can display a specified number of all subsequent records. Supplement the display command using the option:

```
NEXT number
```

The last group of records is displayed using the option:

```
REST
```

Examples:

Imagine you wish to examine two records, beginning
with number 3. Subsequently, you request the last part
of the file:

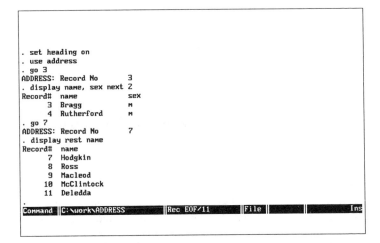

```
. set heading on
. use address
. go 3
ADDRESS: Record No      3
. display name, sex next 2
Record#  name            sex
     3   Bragg           M
     4   Rutherford      M
. go 7
ADDRESS: Record No      7
. display rest name
Record#  name
     7   Hodgkin
     8   Ross
     9   Macleod
    10   McClintock
    11   Deledda
.
Command  C:\work\ADDRESS        Rec EOF/11      File              Ins
```

In the Control Center, there is no means of displaying a specific
number of records from a certain number onwards.

You can specify a *Record number* in the *Go To* menu, and this
will be placed at the top of the list. Since the layout of the browse
screen provides a good overview, it is generally not a problem to
have records which you are not using simultaneously on the
screen.

If, for example, you wish to examine the last five records, specify
Record number {7} in the *Go To* menu.

5.7 Selecting records according to a criterion

One of the most important tasks of a data management system is the gathering of information from a data file according to criteria which you have specified. The commands FOR and WHILE implement one or more commands when the criterion has been fulfilled.

```
FOR condition
```

The FOR command carries out commands in each record which satisfies the specified condition. When the command has been implemented, the record pointer is located on the last record of the file.

```
WHILE condition
```

The WHILE command implements instructions in a group of successive records, *as long as* the specified condition is satisfied. As soon as a record appears which does not fulfil the criterion, the command is discontinued (even if there are other records further on which do satisfy the condition). At the conclusion of the command, the record pointer is generally *not* located on the last record of the file.

Search instructions and display commands using FOR and WHILE are only in force for as long as they are being implemented. As soon as another command is given, the FOR and WHILE commands are dropped, which means they have to be specified in full once more if you wish to repeat the same procedure.

From dBASE III+ onwards you can save the conditions in memory to avoid having to repeat the entire procedure. A *filter* selects the records which satisfy the criterion:

```
SET FILTER TO condition
```

Subsequent to this command, dBASE IV works with only those records which satisfy the criterion. The filter remains in force until you specify a new filter or cancel the current filter using:

```
SET FILTER TO
```

In the Control Center, you can permanently save one or more filters as *Query*. See section 5.12.

You can also regard a selection instruction as a search routine. It is often less work to create a .PRG file using the selection instruction and then activate this program using the DO command when you need the filter. In this way, you can save a whole series of filters under a convenient program name (see chapter 9).

Conditions are mainly instructions which compare the contents of a field with the contents of another field, or with an expression or a constant. The comparisons are made by operators.

Relational operators

=	equal to
<	smaller than
>	larger than
<> or #	not equal to
<=	smaller than or equal to
>=	larger than or equal to

Logical operators

.AND.	logical and

.OR.	logical OR
.NOT.	logical NOT
()	parentheses for grouping

String operators

+	Links two text fields.
-	Links two text fields and moves any existing spaces at the end of the first field to the end of the second field.
$	Checks whether the specified string is present in a text field.

With conditions, text fields and numeric fields are treated differently. When comparing text fields, arguments must be placed between string characters. Distinction is made between capital and small letters. dBASE recognizes three types of string characters: single and double inverted commas and square brackets.

```
name = "Grazia"
naam = 'Grazia'
naam = [Grazia]
```

When the contents of numeric fields are being compared, the arguments should be typed without inverted commas, for example:

```
number = 10
```

Examples with FOR:

Imagine you wish to examine records which satisfy a given criterion. In order to have a clear survey, you omit the field names and you restrict the display to the NAME field alone. (You will save a great deal of typework and help eliminate errors if you repeat the previous command by moving the cursor upwards and altering the command.)

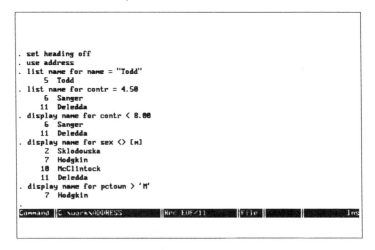

```
. set heading off
. use address
. list name for name = "Todd"
      5  Todd
. list name for contr = 4.50
      6  Sanger
     11  Deledda
. display name for contr < 8.00
      6  Sanger
     11  Deledda
. display name for sex <> [m]
      2  Sklodowska
      7  Hodgkin
     10  McClintock
     11  Deledda
. display name for pctown > 'M'
      7  Hodgkin
.
Command  C:\work\ADDRESS          Rec EOF/11      File              Ins
```

(1) *SET HEADING OFF*
Suppresses the field names.

(2) *USE address*
Opens the ADDRESS file.

(3) *LIST name FOR name = "Todd"*
Selects the records in which the name Todd appears in the NAME field and displays the contents of the NAME field from these records. In the example, the name only occurs in record 5. Thus, the display consists of only one record.

(4) *LIST name FOR contr = 4.50*
Displays the contents of the NAME field of those records in which the CONTR field is 4.50.

(5) *DISPLAY name FOR contr < 8.00*
Displays the contents of the NAME field of those records in which the CONTR field contains a value less than 8.00. Only in the case of large files, the difference between DISPLAY (information per screen)

and LIST (all information in one go) becomes obvious. With this small file, you can use them indiscriminately.

(6) *DISPLAY name FOR sex <> [m]*
Selects the records in which the code "M" or "m" is not located in the SEX field; thus the female members.

(7) *DISPLAY name FOR pctown > 'M'*
Searches for records in which the PCTOWN field contains a string of which the ASCII value of the first character is greater than that of 'M'.
Since the ASCII values of numbers are smaller than those of letters, the following comparison is true (see the ASCII table in Appendix C):

```
"CA4" < "CU1"
```

This principle makes it very easy to sort the PCTOWN field in the correct way according to postal code. In fact, the name of the town is then not important.

Caution: The command PCTOWN="CA" produces an error message. See the Control Center variant at the end of this section.

Examples using SET FILTER TO:

We shall now implement a number of commands using the instruction SET FILTER TO, making use of the previous examples.

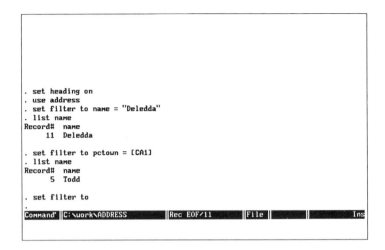

```
. set heading on
. use address
. set filter to name = "Deledda"
. list name
Record#  name
     11  Deledda

. set filter to pctown = [CA1]
. list name
Record#  name
      5  Todd

. set filter to
.
```

Command' C:\work\ADDRESS   Rec EOF/11   File   Ins

(1) *SET HEADING ON*
Activates the field name display.

(2) *SET FILTER TO name = "Deledda"*
Defines a criterion in the filter. From this moment onwards, you can only examine record 11. Cancel this filter by applying another filter: type SET FILTER TO without parameters, or quit dBASE.

(3) *SET FILTER TO pctown = [CA1]*
The new filter instruction assumes the place of the previous one. Here too, the command only compares the ASCII values of the first three characters.

(4) *SET FILTER TO*
Cancels the current filter. All records are again accessible.

Selection using logical fields
When selecting records based on the contents of a logical field, it is not necessary to specify the value of the argument behind the operator since there are only two possibilities: true and false. The criterion is fulfilled if the field has the value .T. (true). The absence of a value is interpreted by dBASE as .F.

Example:

You wish to know the name and address of members who are registered in category RED:

```
LIST name, pctown FOR red
```

The command has no effect whatsoever: the RED field is still empty in all records and thus produces the value .F., so that no name is shown.

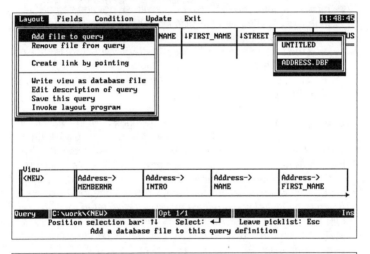

In the Control Center, a selection from the source file is created in the *Queries* generator screen. There are two procedures:

■ Highlight *create* in the *Queries* panel and press Enter. Open the *Layout* menu and select *Add file to Query* in order to inform the system which file is the source file. A survey of the current catalog and its data files appears on the screen. (We shall later learn that it is possible to gather fields from different source files into one view filter.)

In our example there is nothing to choose as yet. If you have linked a description to the file name, this description is shown in a

separate window. This makes it easier to select the proper file.
Press Enter. The file skeleton is shown under the menu bar.
Open the *View* standard frame using F5 (Add/Remove all fields).
The View filter does not yet have a name: <NEW>. As soon as
you have saved the filter using *Layout, Save this Query*, the spe-
cified name is displayed there (with the extension .QBE, repre-
senting Query By Example). Switch to the other frame using F3 or
F4.

■ Instead of this, you can also begin with an opened source file.
In that case, after the *Query* generator has been activated, the
design screen appears immediately, along with the current record structure. In addition, the standard *View* structure is shown
at the bottom of the screen. These are all the fields currently in
the source file. Switch between the source file frame and the
View frame using F3/F4.

Use the command Alt-L, E to enter a description of the view filter
you are about to create, for example 'Members in Cambridge'.
We shall work through the example with just one condition in the
PCTOWN field. Switch to the View frame using F3. Place the cursor on a superfluous field and press F5: you will see the field fly-
ing back over to the source file. This indicates that this field is not
going to be included in the new record. Press Tab to move to the
following field. Only save the fields Address->NAME, Address-
>STREET and Address->PCTOWN by removing the other fields
one by one using F5.
Save the provisory result under the name 'Cambridg' by means of
the commands *Layout, Save this Query*. The extension .QBE is
automatically assigned. Press Enter. The program states 'The
Query has been saved to disk' on the bottom line.
The result of a selection can be seen by pressing F2 in the
browse mode. The program states: 'Processing Query'. Since
nothing has been selected as yet, the View is still identical to the
whole source file, even although only the chosen fields are displayed. This also applies to the edit mode, to which you can
switch using F2.

Caution: If you now make alterations when in the edit mode, do
this in the source file!

Choose *Exit, Transfer to Query Design* and press Shift-F2 to quit
the edit screen again. Use *Layout, Write View as database file* to
save the result in the form of a complete data file (view file). The
program normally allocates the same name as the View filter, but
with the extension .DBF.

Give the command *Condition, Add condition box* and press Shift-
F1 to display the field options list, the operators and the functions
to be used in the condition. Create the condition by highlighting
and confirming the selections consecutively: the PCTOWN field
and the = operator. Conclude the condition by specifying the
postal code "CA" (remember the string signs). In the case of
lengthy conditions, you can enlarge the condition box using F9
(Zoom).

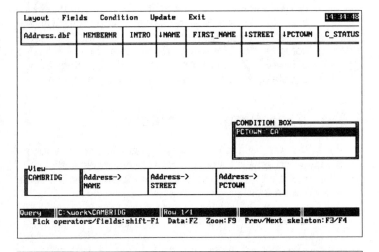

Examine the result using F2. The program states that there is no
record which satisfies the condition PCTOWN="CA". This seems
remarkable at first but it is of course true: the fields consist of
more than the two postal code characters. Thus, there can never
be an exact match. Change the condition by first deleting the
Condition Box using Alt-C, D, and creating a new condition using
Alt-C, A: :

```
PCTOWN > "CA" .AND. PCTOWN < "CB"
```

Now request the selected data once more by pressing F2. The status line indicates that the data have been found by means of a view filter.

If you return to the Control Center, you will see that the View filter 'CAMBRIDG' is available in the *Queries* panel. Shift-F2 directly activates the edit generator in order to subsequently modify the CAMBRIDG.QBE file.

You will have seen that the solution of a simple problem can be executed much more quickly in the command mode than in the Control Center. The Control Center provides the advantage that dBASE IV automatically interprets a normal legible command in a menu with the correct syntax. This becomes more important the more complex the commands are; for example, in the linking of files via *Queries*, form letters via *Forms*, interpretation of data files via *Reports* and sorted labels via *Label*.

5.8   Searching for a record

It is not always necessary to actually display a record which satisfies a condition. It is sometimes sufficient to place the record pointer on that record by means of the command:

```
LOCATE FOR condition
```

The system shows an error message if no record is found which fulfills the condition: 'End of LOCATE scope'. The status line shows Rec EOF/11.

Each LOCATE instruction searches thoroughly from the first record onwards, even if the record pointer is located in the middle of the file, except when you specify the command for a limited interval (see the notes concerning example 5).

If you suspect that there are more records which satisfy
the criterion, repeat the command using

CONTINUE

The CONTINUE command always applies to the most
recent LOCATE instruction which you gave.

Examples:

In the ADDRESS file, you wish to look for all records
which fulfil a certain condition. Because you have
opened the file first, the record pointer is located at the
beginning of the file.

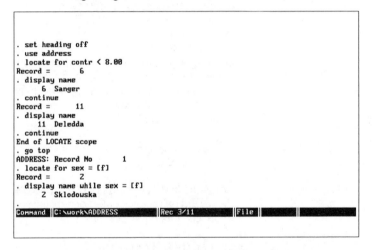

```
. set heading off
. use address
. locate for contr < 8.00
Record =       6
. display name
       6  Sanger
. continue
Record =        11
. display name
      11  Deledda
. continue
End of LOCATE scope
. go top
ADDRESS: Record No      1
. locate for sex = [f]
Record =       2
. display name while sex = [f]
      2  Sklodowska
.
Command   C:\work\ADDRESS        Rec 3/11        File
```

(1) *SET HEADING OFF* and *USE address*
Suppresses the field names in order to save space.
The second command opens the ADDRESS file.

(2) *LOCATE FOR contr < 8.00*
Searches for the first record in which a value less
than 8 is located in the CONTR field. The sixth
record satisfies this condition.

(3) *DISPLAY name*
Displays the NAME field in the current record.

(4) *CONTINUE*
Repeats the search instruction using the condition given in (2) above. Record 11 is found.

(5) *CONTINUE* and *End of LOCATE scope*
Repeats the search instruction once more. From record 11 onwards, there are no further records which fulfil the criterion. Normally dBASE IV looks through all records from the beginning to the end of the file.

Note: The complete LOCATE syntax allows you to search through a part of the file from the current record onwards (NEXT number), or through the remaining records to the end of the file (REST). The WHILE search option also begins at the current record and stops at the first record which no longer satisfies the criterion. This is convenient when looking for the next alteration in the contents of a field in a sorted file.

```
LOCATE [number] [FOR condition]
  [WHILE condition]
```

When the instruction has been carried out, the record pointer is located on the last record which has been examined.

(6) *GO TOP* and *LOCATE FOR sex = [f]*
Places the record pointer at the beginning of the file. This is unnecessary since LOCATE FOR always begins searching at the beginning of the file, even if the the record pointer is located at the EOF as a result of the previous command (see example 5).
The second command looks for the first record registering a female: that is record 2. Beginning at this (current) record we wish to see all names as long as the records fulfil the criterion. Since there is just one, we only see Sklodowska.

To search in the Control Center, the *Go To* menu is used in the browse mode. Place the cursor in the column through which you wish to search and select *Forwards search* or *Backwards search*. Enter a search string in the dialog box. Here you do not have to specify the text between inverted commas. You can determine whether the program should pay attention to the letter style by applying *Match capitalization YES/NO* (switch using Tab).

The program gives an error message if you look for a record with the code K, for example, in the C_STATUS field.

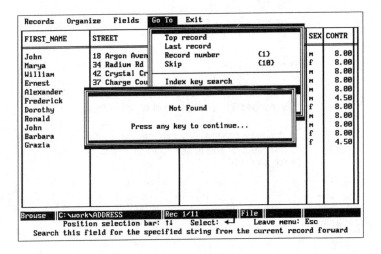

5.9 Matching capitalization in search commands

In section 5.7, we have seen that a search string (text) is written between inverted commas. Search strings for numeric fields do not have inverted commas.

When searching for text, it is important that the letter style regarding small or capital letters exactly matches:

"Bragg", "BRAGG" and "bragg" are all different. dBASE IV normally looks for the letters as they have been entered in the search instruction. In the example file, the program will not find any men in the SEX field if you look for the string "M".

If you no longer know in which style the data have been saved, you can avoid the problem by applying functions which recognize the letters in both capitals and small letters. These are respectively the variables:

```
UPPER(variable)
LOWER(variable)
```

These functions are valid for both output and input commands.

Examples:

1   You wish to display the contents of the NAME field in record 9 in capitals and small letters.

2   You wish to display the names of the women, regardless of the letter style of the code letter in the SEX field.

```
. use address
. 9
ADDRESS: Record No      9
. ? upper(name)
MACLEOD
. ? lower(name)
macleod
. display name for sex = "F"
. display name for lower(sex) = "f"
Record#  name
      2  Sklodowska
      7  Hodgkin
     10  McClintock
     11  Deledda
. display name for upper(sex) = "F"
Record#  name
      2  Sklodowska
      7  Hodgkin
     10  McClintock
     11  Deledda
.
Command  C:\work\ADDRESS            Rec EOF/11       File
```

(1) *USE address*
Opens the ADDRESS file and places the pointer in front of the first record.

(2) *9*
Places the pointer at record 9.

(3) *?UPPER(name)* and *?LOWER(name)*
These commands will produce consecutively the contents of the current NAME field entirely in capitals and entirely in small letters.

(4) *DISPLAY name FOR sex="F"*
Searches for records in which the code "F" is located in the SEX field. Since this code has been entered in small letters, the result of the search instruction is negative.

(5) *DISPLAY name FOR LOWER(sex) = "f"*
Searches in the SEX field for a value which corresponds to "f" when converted to small letters.

(6) *DISPLAY name FOR UPPER(sex) = "F"*
Searches in the SEX field for a value which corresponds to "F" when converted to capitals.

The search function is regulated differently in the Control Center. In the browse mode, you may choose to pay attention to, or to disregard, the letter style by using the menu option *Match capitalization YES/NO* (switch by pressing Tab). Choosing NO covers both examples 5 and 6.

5.10   Searching using a substring

The contents of a character (text) field are referred to as strings (see also section 8.8).

Up until now, we have searched using conditions which apply to the entire contents of a field or the first part of it.

In addition to this possibility, dBASE provides a number of functions which can be used to look for selected substrings in a field.

5.10.1 The comparison operator $

If the string which is being sought is located at a random position in a field, the $ operator shifts the search string through the field from left to right in order to examine whether the string occurs there. The syntax is as follows:

```
"search string"$field name
```

Examples:

Although you do not have much information, you wish to examine the complete data in the ADDRESS file; for instance, you wish to find a street name in which you think that the letters 'ar' occur.

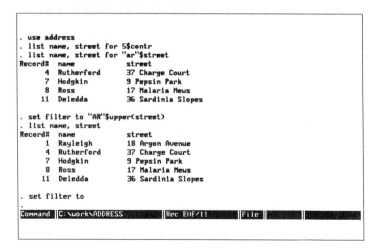

(1) *USE address$*
Opens the ADDRESS file.

(2) *LIST name, street FOR 5$contr*

Searches for records in which the CONTR field contains the number 5. However, this field is not a character field. The system then states that the types do
not match: an error message appears - 'Data type
mismatch'. Cancel the command by pressing Enter
or the C from Cancel.

(3) *LIST name, street FOR "ar"$street*

Searches for the string "ar" at any position in the
STREET field. This combination occurs in four addresses.

(4) *SET FILTER TO "AR"$UPPER(street)*

Selects a string at any position in the STREET field,
which corresponds to "AR" after conversion to capitals. Subsequent to this filter, only those records
which were found by the search instruction 3 remain
available, *plus* record number 1 (Argon Avenue).

(5) *SET FILTER TO*

Makes all records accessible again.

Note: In dBASE it makes no difference whether
or not you have a space between the components of an instruction. If the syntax is
correct, the system will recognize the commands, operators and functions even without separators.

5.10.2   Searching at a specific position: the SUBSTR() function

Occasionally, the string which is being sought may
occur at only a certain position in the field in order to
gain the required information. By means of the SUB-
STRING() function, you can indicate which *substring* of
the field contents is to be used in the comparison according to the criterion.

```
SUBSTR(field,starting position,number of
   characters)
```

The function selects a substring with the specified number of characters in the specified FIELD, beginning at the given starting position. For instance:

```
LIST name, pctown FOR SUBSTR(pctown,1,2) =
   "CA"
```

In this way, only addresses with the postal code "CA" will be selected.

RecNr	NAME	PCTOWN
1	Rayleigh	CA2 4WS Cambridge
5	Todd	CA1 2BB Cambridge
6	Sanger	CA4 8NB Cambridge

5.10.3　Searching in date fields

The SUBSTR() only applies to character fields. If you wish to search in another field type, you will have to convert it to a *character* field first.

In order to enable you to look for data according to date, dBASE provides the conversion function:

```
DTOC(date field)
```

The name is an abbreviation for 'date to character'. Include this conversion function in a command to look for information which carries a certain date, for instance.

Examples:

You wish to display various pieces of information involving dates from the ADDRESS file.

```
. use address
. display bth_date
Record#  bth_date
      1  01/01/42
. display dtoc(bth_date)
Record#  dtoc(bth_date)
      1  01/01/42
. list name, bth_date for substr(dtoc(bth_date),7,2) > [70]
Record#  name              bth_date
      4  Rutherford        04/04/71
      9  Macleod           07/06/76
     11  Deledda           17/01/71

. list name, bth_date for bth_date > ctod("01/01/70")
Record#  name              bth_date
      4  Rutherford        04/04/71
      9  Macleod           07/06/76
     11  Deledda           17/01/71

. display name, substr(dtoc(bth_date),7,2)
.
Command  C:\work\ADDRESS          Rec EOF/11        File                    Ins
```

(1) *USE address*
Opens the ADDRESS file and places the pointer before the first record.

(2) *DISPLAY bth_date*
Displays the contents of the BTH_DATE field in the current record.

(3) *DISPLAY DTOC(bth_date)*
Converts the BTH_DATE field in the current record from a date field to a character field and displays the result. The display is identical to that in example 2.

(4) *DISPLAY SUBSTR(DTOC(bth_date),7,2)*
Record 1 is still the current record. The command converts the date to a string and selects the seventh and eighth characters (the year).

(5) *LIST name, bth_date FOR SUBSTR(DTOC(bth_date),7,2) > [70]*
Displays the name and date of birth of members born later than 1970. The last two numbers in the date of birth are greater than 70.

(6) *DISPLAY name, bth_date FOR bth_date >
CTOD("01/01/70")*
This instruction produces the same result as
example 5. Here, we are using the reversed conversion function CTOD(), character to date. The date
string "01/01/70" is converted to information of the
Date type and then compared to the contents of the
BTH_DATE field. In this way, you can display data
according to day or date.

(7) *DISPLAY name, SUBSTR(DTOC(bth_date),7,2)*
Displays the NAME field from all records and a part
of the BTH_DATE field.

5.10.4   Searching using numeric fields

The conversion function STR() enables you to search in
numeric fields using the strings search function. The
syntax is:

```
STR(field, number of positions [,decimal
  positions])
```

This function is used in the same way as the conversion
functions for date fields. In section 8.8, we shall deal
more extensively with editing using text fields.

In the Control Center, you can create search instructions in the
Query screen by means of the *Condition* menu. A selection is
made from the current file by specifying the conditions in a *Condition Box*. You can make use of the field names, the operators and
functions from the list of options (Shift-F1).

5.11 Linking conditions to a logical operator

In general, the result of a search using one condition is not quite accurate enough. The information often has to conform to a number of features at the same time. If, for example, you wish to have the names of all the unmarried men, this can be done by applying the filter SET FILTER TO "m"$(sex) and one criterion, DISPLAY name FOR c_status="s". There are no further possibilities of specifying extra criteria with the functions which we have currently available.

Using logical operators, you can link an unlimited number of conditions in such a way that only the required data remain.

logical operator	example	effect
.AND.	A .AND. B	The criterion is fulfilled if both basic conditions are satisfied at the same time.
.OR.	A .OR. B	The criterion is fulfilled if one of the two basic conditions is satisfied.
.NOT.	.NOT. A	The criterion is fulfilled if the basic condition is not satisfied.
()	(A.AND.B).OR. (C.AND.D)	The brackets alter the order of sequence in which the conditions are processed: the arguments between brackets are executed first and then the other processes, from left to right.

Length of the instructions

In principle, instructions should be specified after the dot prompt on the command line. A command which is longer than the screen line moves leftwards off the screen. The maximum length is 254 characters. An edit screen for the command line can be opened using Ctrl-Home. This provides room for a maximum of 1024 characters. Confirm the lengthy command using *Layout, Save this command*.

As soon as you have pressed Enter, dBASE breaks off the command at column 80 and places the rest on the next line.

You can save space in two ways:

■ you can omit spaces between the components of a command,

■ you can abbreviate the names of commands, operators and functions to four letters. In this case, you are obliged to use spaces.

Examples:

```
. list name for (c_status = "s" .and. "Li"$pctoun)
Record# name
       8 Ross

. list name, sex, c_status for (sex = "f" .AND. c_status = "m") .OR. (c_status =
"s" .AND. contr = 4.50)
Record# name            sex c_status
       2 Sklodouska       f   m
       7 Hodgkin          f   m
      11 Deledda          f   s

. list name, sex, c_status for (sex = "m" .AND. (c_status = "m" .OR. c_status =
"d") .AND. contr = 8.00) .OR. (sex = "f" .AND. c_status = "m" .AND. contr = 4.50
)
Record# name            sex c_status
       1 Rayleigh         m   m
       3 Bragg            m   m
       4 Rutherford       m   m
       5 Todd             m   m

.
Command  C:\work\ADDRESS          Rec EOF/11        File              Ins
```

(1) *LIST name FOR (c_status = "s" .AND. "Li"$pctown)*
Selects members who are *single* AND in who live in Liverpool. In this uncomplicated linkage of conditions, brackets are not obligatory. They do make the command easier to read.

(2) *LIST name, sex, c_status FOR (sex = "f" .AND. c_status = "m") .OR. (c_status = "s" .AND. contr = 4.50)*
Displays the name, sex and the civil status of female members who are married OR members who are single and pay a contribution of £4.50.
In this example, the two possibilities regarding the civil status must be placed between brackets since they have to be coupled as one unit to the other conditions by means of the AND operators.

(3) *LIST name, sex, c_status FOR (sex = "m" .AND. (c_status = "m" .OR. c_status = "d") .AND. contr = 8.00) .OR. (sex = "f" .AND. c_status = "m" .AND. contr = 4.50)*
Displays the name, sex and civil status of *male* members who are *married* or *divorced* AND who pay a *contribution of £8, and also* (logical OR) the same data about the *female* members who are *married* AND who pay a *contribution of £4.50*.
Both variations of the male civil status should be placed between brackets. The conditions for the men and the women do not have to be placed individually between brackets, since a *group* of AND conditions is understood as one unit under the OR condition. The brackets do increase the legibility.

Logically linked conditions may be combined with the previously outlined search functions and filters. Shortage of space makes it impossible to give examples.

5.12   Storing filter conditions in a Query file

At the end of section 5.7, we created a simple filter in the Control Center as a variant to the SET FILTER TO command for the address file.

Keep in mind the difference between the *view filter* in which the selection criteria are stored (.QBE file) and a *view file* which is the result of the selection and which thus actually contains records (.DBF file).

The first category of files is registered in the Queries panel, the second category in the Data panel. A view file occupies less capacity than the source file and can be loaded directly, but it has the disadvantage that records which are omitted by the selection are not accessible. The only solution is to alter the selection and save the new version of the view file. A view filter provides the advantage that it is flexible; the disadvantage is that the selection must be made all over again each time you open the file.

In this section , we shall deal more extensively with the Query generator in the Control Center. We shall apply the second example from section 5.11 once again.

Creating a QUERY file

We shall give the name QUERYDEM to the demonstration file which is going to make a selection from the AD-DRESS file. The selection makes the following demands on the records:

- the contribution is £8.00,
- the members are men who are married or divorced,
- or they are women who are single.

In dBASE these conditions are specified as follows, respectively:

```
contr = 8.00
```

```
.AND. (sex = "m" .AND. (c_status = "m" .OR.
  c_status = "d"))
.OR. (sex = "f" .AND. (c_status = "s"))
```

If at the dot prompt, activate the Control Center by pressing F2. Highlight the ADDRESS file in the Data panel and press Enter. Select *Use file*. Subsequently, choose *Create* in the Query panel. The module for designing view filters appears on the screen.

You can directly activate the module from the dot prompt using the command:

```
CREATE QUERY querydem
```

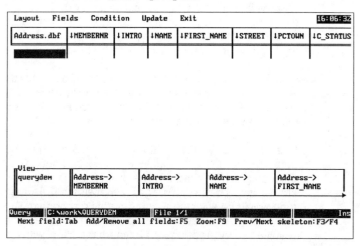

5.12.1   Constructing the filter

There are a couple of rules of thumb when constructing the filter. If you wish to link conditions by means of a logical .AND., place them adjacent to one another on the same line. If you wish to link conditions by means of a logical .OR., place them on separate lines. In terms of the example, this will appear as follows:

```
contr = 8.00 .AND. sex = "m" .AND. c_status
  = "m"
contr = 8.00 .AND. sex = "m" .AND. c_status
  = "d"
contr = 8.00 .AND. sex = "f" .AND. c_status
  = "s"
```

This means: display all records of married men who pay £8 contribution and of divorced men who pay £8 contribution and of single women who pay £8 contribution.

Press the Tab key until the the three fields C.STATUS, SEX and CONTR come into view on the screen. Then highlight the C_STATUS field (press Shift-Tab) and type the first condition for this text field between inverted commas: "m". Press Tab again and type "m" in the SEX field. Press the Tab key and type 8.00 (a numeric value, thus no inverted commas) in the CONTR field.

Check the construction by pressing F2. Four records which fulfil the condition appear in the browse screen. Use *Exit, Transfer to Query Design* to move back to the design module for the view filter.

Use Shift-Tab to move to the C_STATUS column and press Cursor Down to highlight the second line. Type the condition "d" there. The sex and the contribution should also be specified again otherwise all divorced men would be selected. Enter the data for the third line in the same way (see the example below) and check the result again by pressing F2. Compare the effect with the list in the figure at the end of this section.

```
 Layout   Fields   Condition   Update   Exit                      16:09:57
┌─────────────┬───────┬────────────┬─────────┬────────┬──────────┬──────┬────────┬────┐
│ Address.dbf │ ↓NAME │ ↓FIRST_NAME│ ↓STREET │↓PCTOWN │↓C_STATUS │ ↓SEX │↓CONTR  │↓BT │
│             │       │            │         │        │  "m"     │ "m"  │ 8.00   │    │
│             │       │            │         │        │  "d"     │ "m"  │ 8.00   │    │
│             │       │            │         │        │  "s"     │ "f"  │ 8.00   │    │
│             │       │            │         │        │          │      │        │    │
│             │       │            │         │        │          │      │        │    │
│             │       │            │         │        │          │      │        │    │
│             │       │            │         │        │          │      │        │    │
│             │       │            │         │        │          │      │        │    │
┌─View────────┐                                                                       │
│ querydem    │ Address-> │ Address->   │ Address->    │ Address->                     │
│             │ MEMBERNR  │ INTRO       │ NAME         │ FIRST_NAME                    │
└─────────────┴───────────┴─────────────┴──────────────┴───────────────────────────────┘
 Query    C:\work\QUERYDEM     Field 9/13                                          Ins
   Prev/Next field:Shift-Tab/Tab   Data:F2   Size:Shift-F7   Prev/Next skel:F3/F4
```

5.12.2   Saving the filter in a Query file

If you have activated the design module from the dot
prompt, you will have specified the name QUERYDEM
along with the command. In that case, you can save the
view filter using the command *Save changes and exit* in
the *Exit* menu.

If you have activated the design module from the Con-
trol Center using *Create* from the Query panel, the word
<NEW> will still be shown at the bottom of the screen.
When you have chosen *Save changes and exit* from the
Exit menu, assign a name to the filter under which it can
be saved. The design module is closed and the Control
Center appears on the screen once more. The QUERY-
DEM filter is highlighted and active.

5.12.3   Opening a Query file from the dot prompt

Behind the dot prompt, type the command

```
SET VIEW TO <file name>
```

in order to activate a view filter, in this case QUERY-
DEM. You can subsequently examine the records using
the commands BROWSE, LIST or DISPLAY.

```
Layout   Fields   Condition   Update   Exit                      16:09:57
┌─────────────────────────────────────────────────────────────────────────┐
│Address.dbf │↓NAME │↓FIRST_NAME │↓STREET │↓PCTOWN │↓C_STATUS │↓SEX │↓CONTR │↓BT│
│            │      │            │        │        │ "m"      │ "m" │ 8.00  │   │
│            │      │            │        │        │ "d"      │ "m" │ 8.00  │   │
│            │      │            │        │        │ "s"      │ "f" │ 8.00  │   │
│                                                                               │
│                                                                               │
│                                                                               │
│ ┌View────                                                                     │
│ │querydem   │Address->  │Address->  │Address->  │Address->                    │
│ │           │MEMBERNR   │INTRO      │NAME       │FIRST_NAME                   │
└─────────────────────────────────────────────────────────────────────────────┘
Query   │C:\work\QUERYDEM    │Field 9/13                              Ins
   Prev/Next field:Shift-Tab/Tab   Data:F2   Size:Shift-F7   Prev/Next skel:F3/F4
```

5.12.4   Opening a Query file using the Control Center

Highlight QUERYDEM in the Query panel by means of
the cursor keys and press Enter. Select *Display data* in
the dialog box. The selected records appear in the
browse screen.

```
Records   Organize   Fields   Go To   Exit
┌─────────────────────────────────────────────────────────────────────────┐
│MEMBERNR│INTRO│ NAME       │FIRST_NAME │STREET               │PCTOW│
│004     │     │Rayleigh    │John       │18 Argon Avenue      │CA2 4│
│015     │     │Bragg       │William    │42 Crystal Crescent  │LD1 3│
│008     │     │Rutherford  │Ernest     │37 Charge Court      │MA1 2│
│057     │     │Todd        │Alexander  │1 Vitamin View       │CA1 2│
│083     │     │McClintock  │Barbara    │Translocation Tower  │C01 6│
│                                                                          │
│                                                                          │
│                                                                          │
│                                                                          │
│                                                                          │
│                                                                          │
└──────────────────────────────────────────────────────────────────────────┘
Browse  │C:\work\QUERYDEM        │Rec 1/11        │View
```

6   Altering records and fields

6.1   Altering records and fields individually

dBASE IV has a special user-oriented editor, EDIT, to modify data in a file. The program displays the records on the screen one by one, and you are then able to alter the contents of the fields. The altered record is then written to the file once more.

```
EDIT [RECORD record number]
```

If you wish to give the command without specifying a record number, you should place the pointer on the required record in advance. For example:

```
USE address
3
EDIT
```

The combined command has the same effect:

```
EDIT RECORD 3
```

It is also possible to specify the record number in the form of a memory variable (see section 8.2). If a program has assigned the value of the record number to the variable Z, for instance, the variable can then be used as follows:

```
Z = 3
GOTO Z
EDIT
```

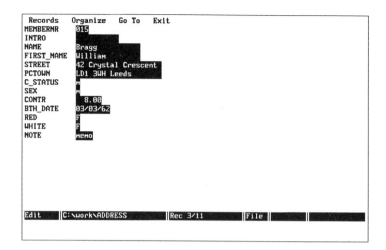

The EDIT menu structure is similar to that in APPEND. Quit the editor using Ctrl-W, Ctrl-End or select *Exit.* The modified records are then saved.

As long as the cursor remains in one record, you can delete changes using the command *Undo change to record* from the *Records* menu.

6.1.1   Browsing through records

If you have specified the EDIT command without parameters, you can move from the current record to the next or previous record by pressing PgDn or PgUp. Normally, you can browse through the entire file. However, you can apply restrictions to the EDIT command by specifying a certain number of records or the rest of the file. Both instructions go to work from the current record onwards. Examples:

```
EDIT NEXT 3
EDIT REST
EDIT RECORD 3
```

In the last case, browsing is not possible.

6.1.2   Activating EDIT with a limited number of fields

By applying the FIELDS option, you can specify which fields may be altered. Only those fields which you name are displayed. This prevents unintentional alterations and keeps the process more orderly. For example:

```
EDIT FIELDS first_name, name, c_status
```

6.1.3   Activating EDIT with a selection

The command to activate EDIT may contain a selection instruction. Imagine that in the ADDRESS file you wish to make alterations to the civil status records because one of the members has recently married. For the complete survey, a list of the members is displayed:

NAME	C_STATUS
Rayleigh	m
Sklodowska	m
Bragg	m
Rutherford	m
Todd	m
Sanger	m
Hodgkin	m
Ross	s
Macleod	s
McClintock	s
Deledda	s

There are apparently four unmarried members. We have seen in section 5.7 that there are two methods of specifying a condition:

```
EDIT WHILE condition
EDIT FOR condition
```

Using WHILE, you can only select a group of records which are consecutive. This is not a suitable option, since the civil status need not always be successively similar. It is better to apply the FOR option, which examines all records from the beginning of the file to see if they satisfy the condition.

In combination with the restrictions on the fields displayed, the command is as follows:

```
EDIT FIELDS name, c_status FOR c_status = "s"
```

EDIT loads the first record; by means of the *Go To* menu and the PgUp and PgDn keys, you can browse through the other records which fulfil the criterion.

6.2   Displaying and altering records and fields per screen

In dBASE you are not only able to examine and modify the records one by one (*edit mode*), you can also do this on the entire screen at one time (*browse mode*). There is a record on each line, as far as that is possible in terms of space. Activate this alteration mode using the command:

```
BROWSE
```

The browse mode screen, which can contain 17 records simultaneously, has only been mentioned in combination with the Control Center up until now. As you see, it can also be activated from the dot prompt.

Tab and Shift-Tab enable you to place the cursor on the next and previous field, respectively. Using Ctrl-Cursor Right you can move the cursor to the end of a word, the beginning of the next word, the end of the field or the next field. Ctrl-Cursor Left does the same but in reverse direction. Ctrl-Z or Home moves the cursor to the first field, and Ctrl-B or End moves the cursor to the last field.

The browse editor opens showing the current record on the first line. If you activate the editor after giving a LIST command, the last record will be located on the first line. The cursor keys (up/down) allow you to browse through the records.

Example of activating the editor:

```
USE address
BROWSE
```

As a result of the defined field lengths, there is only room for the first six fields:

```
 Records    Organize   Fields   Go To   Exit

┌──────────┬───────┬────────────┬─────────────┬───────────────────────┬──────┐
│ MEMBERNR │ INTRO │ NAME       │ FIRST_NAME  │ STREET                │ PCTOW│
├──────────┼───────┼────────────┼─────────────┼───────────────────────┼──────┤
│ 004      │       │ Rayleigh   │ John        │ 18 Argon Avenue       │ CA2 4│
│ 003      │       │ Sklodouska │ Marya       │ 34 Radium Rd          │ CU1 2│
│ 015      │       │ Bragg      │ William     │ 42 Crystal Crescent   │ LD1 3│
│ 008      │       │ Rutherford │ Ernest      │ 37 Charge Court       │ MA1 2│
│ 057      │       │ Todd       │ Alexander   │ 1 Vitamin View        │ CA1 2│
│ 058      │       │ Sanger     │ Frederick   │ 3 Insulin Isle        │ CA4 8│
│ 064      │       │ Hodgkin    │ Dorothy     │ 9 Pepsin Park         │ OX2 1│
│ 002      │       │ Ross       │ Ronald      │ 17 Malaria Mews       │ LV1 4│
│ 023      │       │ Macleod    │ John        │ 35 Diabetes Drive     │ AB3 2│
│ 083      │       │ McClintock │ Barbara     │ Translocation Tower   │ CO1 6│
│ 026      │       │ Deledda    │ Grazia      │ 36 Sardinia Slopes    │ LE1 7│
│          │       │            │             │                       │      │
│          │       │            │             │                       │      │
│          │       │            │             │                       │      │
│          │       │            │             │                       │      │
├──────────┴───┬───┴─────────┬──┴──────┬──────┴───┬──────────┬────────┴──────┤
│ Browse   │ C:\work\ADDRESS │ Rec 1/11 │ File │                      Ins│
└─────────────────────────────────────────────────────────────────────────┘
```

The *Fields* menu has been added to the edit mode menus in the browse screen. The options in this menu will be discussed below.

Using the keys mentioned above, go to the fields which are off-screen at the moment and see how the columns change. The browse screen has a number of utilities to retain a better overview of the records.

Locking fields

In general, the first fields contain information which indicates the type of record, the name for example. It is then convenient to keep that field at the left of the screen while the other fields shift horizontally.

By means of the LOCK [number] parameter, you can hold a number of fields at the left-hand side of the screen. For instance, if you wish to to have the fields MEMBERNR, INTRO and NAME continuously visible, the editor command is then:

```
BROWSE LOCK 3
```

When the file is displayed in the browse mode, you can lock the fields at the left-hand side of the screen using the command *Lock fields on left {number}* from the *Fields* menu.

Limiting the alterations to one field

The parameter FREEZE [field] restricts the freedom of movement of the cursor to the named field. The other fields are visible, but not accessible. For instance, you wish to make alterations to the INTRO field alone:

```
BROWSE FREEZE intro
```

If the file is being displayed in the browse mode, you can block the other fields by means of the commands *Fields, Freeze field {field name}*.

Other options

BROWSE also has a number of parameters which are less well-used, but which are very handy nevertheless. They can be linked to the command behind the dot prompt just as the FREEZE and LOCK options. We shall list them just to be complete:

NOAPPEND   The file cannot be extended with new records.

NOMENU   Blocks the editor menu (see end of this section).

NOFOLLOW   The record pointer does not move if
                a record is relocated in the index
                due to an alteration in a key field.
                The pointer does not receive a new
                value.

WIDTH number   Only the first NUMBER of charac-
                ters of the field contents are visible.

In the Control Center, there are the following equivalents:

NOFOLLOW   *Records, Follow record to new position*, the
                option is only active if you are working with
                index keys.

WIDTH number   *Fields, Size field*

Altering specific fields

Just as in the edit mode, you can limit the display on the
screen to the named fields in the FIELDS list.

Example:

In section 4.5, we added three fields to the ADDRESS
file structure. In fact, you only really need to activate
BROWSE with these three fields, but for the sake of the
exercise, we shall add FIRST_NAME and NAME as
well:

```
BROWSE FIELDS intro, first_name, name, red,
  white
```

Adopt the data from the figure; we shall require these
later in other examples. The logical fields RED and
WHITE can only contain the values .T. or .F.; dBASE
also accepts Y and N respectively as input.

```
 Records   Organize   Fields   Go To    Exit

 INTRO      FIRST_NAME    NAME             RED WHITE

 Dear Sir   John          Rayleigh         Y   N
 Dear Miss  Marya         Sklodouska       N   Y
 Dear Sir   William       Bragg            N   Y
 Dear Sir   Ernest        Rutherford       Y   N
 Dear Sir   Alexander     Todd             Y   N
 Dear Sir   Frederick     Sanger           N   Y
 Dear Miss  Dorothy       Hodgkin          Y   N
 Dear Sir   Ronald        Ross             Y   N
 Dear Sir   John          Macleod          N   Y
 Dear Miss  Barbara       McClintock       Y   N
 Dear Miss  Grazia        Deledda          N   Y




 Browse    C:\work\ADDRESS        Rec 1/11           File
```

After the last record, the program will ask if you wish to add records.

If you activate the editor in the dBASE IV command mode using the parameter NOMENU, the menu will not be shown. Some indication functions remain available, but they are not visible. This option is suitable for those who may read the file but are not permitted to modify it.

6.3   Changing the contents of a field

The REPLACE command replaces the contents of the specified field in the current record. The replace command may apply to all fields or to a given interval. You can also attach a condition to the execution of the command in the same way as in search commands. In its simplest form, the syntax is as follows:

```
REPLACE field WITH expression
```

This instruction is particularly important to numeric fields, since calculations can be made using the field contents. If the result of the calculation does not fit into the field, dBASE IV produces an error message; asterisks are shown in the field instead of the value.

Examples:

You wish to replace the contents of several numeric and text fields in specific records.

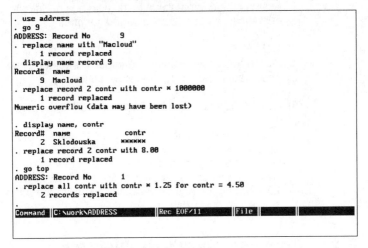

```
. use address
. go 9
ADDRESS: Record No      9
. replace name with "Macloud"
     1 record replaced
. display name record 9
Record# name
     9 Macloud
. replace record 2 contr with contr × 1000000
     1 record replaced
Numeric overflow (data may have been lost)

. display name, contr
Record# name              contr
     2 Sklodowska         ××××××
. replace record 2 contr with 8.00
     1 record replaced
. go top
ADDRESS: Record No      1
. replace all contr with contr × 1.25 for contr = 4.50
     2 records replaced
.
Command  C:\work\ADDRESS          Rec EOF/11        File
```

(1) *USE address* and *GO 9*
Opens the ADDRESS file and places the record pointer at number 9.

(2) *REPLACE name WITH "Macloud"*
Replaces the string "Macleod" in the NAME field of the seventh record with the string "Macloud"; the in-struction states that 1 record has been replaced.

(3) *DISPLAY name RECORD 9*
Checks the new value of NAME in the ninth record.

(4) *REPLACE RECORD 2 contr WITH contr * 1000000*
Forces an error message. The numeric field con-tains six positions including two for the decimal po-sitions and one for the decimal character. Thus, there is only room for three digits before the point.

(5) *DISPLAY name, contr*
Displays the name and the new value of CONTR.
Part of the data may be lost, by rounding off for
example.

(6) *REPLACE RECORD 2 contr WITH 8.00*
Assigns the original value to the field again. Specify
numerical values without inverted commas.

(7) *GO TOP*
Places the record pointer at number 1 (after the previous command it was located at number 2).

(8) *REPLACE ALL contr WITH contr * 1.25 FOR contr
= 4.50*
The GO TOP command is not necessary in this
case, since both the condition FOR contr = 4.50 and
the ALL option ensure that the file is examined from
the beginning onwards. (The options WHILE contr =
4.50 and NEXT number are effective from the current record onwards.)

6.4   Copying records to a new file

Using the COPY command from the operating system,
you can copy a complete file under the same or under a
new name to another storage medium:

```
COPY source file destination file
```

In the Control Center, you can give this command using the menu
Tools, DOS utilities. You can then specify the required command
using the menu *DOS, Perform DOS command.* You can even
leave dBASE IV temporarily (*Go to DOS*).

By means of the *Copy* option from the *Operations* menu, you can
copy one or more marked files in the list of files.

The COPY command in dBASE provides many more
possibilities:

- all records,
- all records with specific fields,
- selected records,
- selected records with specific fields,
- conversion to another file format during copying.

The COPY command always creates a *new* file with the
same structure as the old file, unless you have specified
a field list.

The APPEND command enables you to add records
from another file to the end of the current file:

```
APPEND FROM source file
```

The copy instructions do not have any influence on the
data in the source file.

6.4.1   Copying all records

The following command copies all records in the current
file to the specified destination file:

```
COPY TO destination file
```

6.4.2   Copying all records with specific fields

By applying the FIELDS option, you can copy only specified fields from all records in the current file to the required destination file:

```
COPY TO destination file FIELDS field1,
  field2
```

6.4.3   Copying selected records

A condition along with FOR or WHILE selects records
before they are copied:

```
COPY TO destination file {FOR | WHILE }
  condition
```

The following command copies the first six records from
the current record onwards which fulfil the condition:

```
COPY NEXT 6 TO destination file FOR contr =
  8.00
```

6.4.4   Copying data to another file format

The way in which applications write data to disk has not
as yet been standardized. Even a file which you have
made in dBASE IV cannot just be used in an older version without problems (and vice versa). dBASE has a
copy option for some word processors or spreadsheets
which converts data to the appropriate file format. We
shall deal more extensively with this in chapter 11.

Examples:

You wish to copy various selections from the AD-
DRESS file to the CLUB file.

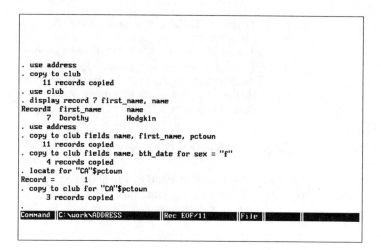

```
. use address
. copy to club
     11 records copied
. use club
. display record 7 first_name, name
Record# first_name      name
       7 Dorothy         Hodgkin
. use address
. copy to club fields name, first_name, pctown
     11 records copied
. copy to club fields name, bth_date for sex = "f"
      4 records copied
. locate for "CA"$pctoun
Record =        1
. copy to club for "CA"$pctoun
      3 records copied
.
Command  C:\work\ADDRESS        Rec EOF/11      File
```

(1) *USE address*

Opens the ADDRESS data file.

(2) *COPY TO club*

Copies eleven records from the ADDRESS file, including the file structure, to the CLUB file.

(3) *USE club* and *DISPLAY RECORD 7 first_name, name*

Opens the CLUB file so that you can check the contents. In order to save room we shall only display record 7.

(4) *USE address* and *COPY TO club FIELDS name, first_name, pctown*

Copies three fields from all records in the AD-DRESS file to CLUB. Since this file aleady exists, dBASE IV generates a dialog box with the message 'File already exists, Overwrite Cancel'. Press Enter to confirm the Overwrite option.

(5) *COPY TO club FIELDS name, bth_date FOR sex = "f"*

Creates a new version of the CLUB file with only the name and date of birth of the female members.

(6) *LOCATE FOR "CA"$pctown* and *COPY TO club FOR "CA"$pctown*
Creates a new version of the CLUB file with only those members who live in Cambridge. The LOCATE command searches for the first record with this postal code. The copy command along with FOR copies all records with the postal code CA.

6.5 Deleting files and records

A complete file can be deleted by the operating system using the DEL (or ERASE) command. dBASE has analogous commands with the same names (DELETE, ERASE). Just as in the copying process, you can restrict the reach of the command to specific records and/or fields.

In all versions of dBASE, deletion is performed in two stages (for safety reasons):

1. mark those records you wish to delete (place an *
   next to the record number);
2. actually delete the records from the file.

Between these steps, you have a chance to reconsider and to remove the marking if required. From version III+ onwards, it is possible to delete all records in one manoeuvre. There are two ways of placing these deletion markings:

1 Placing the marking along with the delete command
The DELETE command is valid for the opened file. If no options are specified, the command applies to the current record. As you already know, the number of records to be deleted can be limited by means of an interval or a condition. The syntax is as follows:

```
DELETE [interval] [RECORD record number]
                {FOR condition|WHILE
    condition}
```

2 Deleting records from the editors

Activate a modification mode using the command EDIT or BROWSE. In the EDIT and BROWSE screens, mark the current record using the command *Records, Mark record for deletion*. You can remove marking by repeating the process. The key combination Ctrl-U has the same effect.

The word *Del* is displayed in the last box in the status line when records are marked for deletion.

6.5.1   Displaying deletion marks

The DELETED() function states by means of .T. or .F. whether or not a record has a deletion mark. If you adopt the function in the search condition, you can display all records which are marked for deletion.

6.5.2   Cancelling deletion marks

The RECALL command removes deletion marks:

```
RECALL [ALL]  [RECORD record number]
              {FOR condition|WHILE condition}
```

From the Control Center, you will find the command under the name *Unmark all records* in the *Organize* menu (first press F2).

6.5.3   Deleting records irretrievably

The following command physically removes records from the file:

```
PACK
```

From the Control Center, you will find this command under the name *Erase marked records* in the *Organize* menu (first press F2).

6.5.4   Deleting records directly

The following command physically removes the records from the file without having to mark them first:

```
ZAP
```

The command has the same effect as DELETE ALL, followed by PACK.

6.5.5   Deleting a file from the disk

You can only delete a file from disk if it is not opened at that moment. There are two commands to implement this:

```
ERASE file name
DELETE FILE file name
```

Examples:

In the CLUB file which we copied from the ADDRESS file in the previous section, we shall apply deletion marks and remove them again.

```
. use club
. ...
. ... <Ctrl-U and Ctrl-W>
. delete record 3
      1 record deleted
. go 6
CLUB: Record No      6
. delete
      1 record deleted
. display name for deleted()
Record#  name
      1 *Rayleigh
      3 *Bragg
      6 *Sanger
. recall record 3
        1 record recalled
. display name record 3
Record#  name
      3  Bragg
. recall all
      2 records recalled
.
Command  C:\work\CLUB              Rec EOF/11        File
```

(1) *USE club*
Opens the CLUB file.

(2) *EDIT 1* and *<Ctrl-U and Ctrl-W>*
Activates the edit screen along with record 1. Delete the current record using Ctrl-U and quit the editor by pressing Ctrl-W. (We have not shown this due to shortage of space.)

(3) *DELETE RECORD 3*
Marks record 3 for deletion. Perhaps an error message will appear ('Record out of range'): The CLUB file still has the format of the previous copying process in section 6.4. Complete the file by giving the command:

```
USE address
COPY TO club
```

Begin at step 1 again.

(4) *GO 6* and *DELETE*
Place the record pointer at number 6 and mark the current record for deletion.

(5) *DISPLAY name FOR DELETED()*
Displays the record which have been marked for deletion.
The output command only displays a record if the DELETED() function for that record has the value .T. An asterisk represents the deletion mark in the display.

(6) *RECALL RECORD 3* and *DISPLAY name REC-ORD 3*
Removes the deletion mark from record 3. The command states the number of records recalled. The following command indicates that record 3 is accessible again.

(7) *RECALL ALL*
Removes the remaining deletion marks.

More examples:

In the following series of examples, we shall mark records according to a certain criterion. Subsequently, these and other records will be removed and finally, we shall remove the CLUB file from the disk.

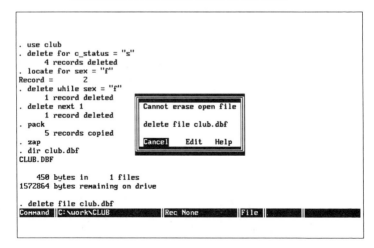

```
. use club
. delete for c_status = "s"
      4 records deleted
. locate for sex = "f"
Record =      2
. delete while sex = "f"
      1 record deleted
. delete next 1              ┌─────────────────────┐
      1 record deleted       │ Cannot erase open file │
. pack                       │                        │
      5 records copied       │ delete file club.dbf   │
. zap                        │ ▐Cancel▌  Edit   Help  │
. dir club.dbf              └─────────────────────┘
CLUB.DBF

    450 bytes in     1 files
1572864 bytes remaining on drive

. delete file club.dbf
Command  C:\work\CLUB                Rec None           File
```

(1) *USE club* and *DELETE FOR c_status = "s"*
Opens the CLUB file.
The second command marks all records of single members for deletion.

(2) *LOCATE FOR sex = "f"* and *DELETE WHILE sex = "f"*
Searches for the first female record.
The second command marks all subsequent consecutive records of the female members for deletion.
The instruction registers 1 record deleted.

(3) *DELETE NEXT 1*
Marks the following record.

(4) *PACK*
Physically deletes the marked records from the storage medium. After the action has been performed, 'Rec 1/5' is shown in the status line. This means that a file has been created consisting of the five records in question.

(5) *ZAP*
Directly deletes the five remaining records physically from the diskette. The command asks if you really wish to delete the file (Zap CLUB.DBF?). This helps protect large data files against unintentional or hasty deletion instructions. Confirm the command using Yes.

(6) *DIR club.dbf* and *DELETE FILE club.dbf*
Checks whether the CLUB.DBF file still exists.
The file structure is still present under the name CLUB.DBF. The instruction registers the size of the file and the capacity still available in the current drive.
If you now attempt to delete the file using the command DELETE FILE, the command will produce an error message. It is not possible to delete an opened file, even if it no longer contains any records (see the status line: Rec none).
Close the file by means of the command USE and

repeat the deletion command for the file, delete file
club.dbf. The program indicates that this time the attempt has been successful: File has been deleted.

7   Sorting and indexing files

7.1   Sorting a file

One of the most important features of a database is the speed with which you can retrieve data from the files. If that takes longer than a few seconds, you often tend to go on the hunt for coffee.

It can be very laborious to search through an unsorted file. Imagine you have to look for a number in a telephone directory which is not arranged in alphabetical order. Accordingly, one of the most important tasks of a database system consists of sorting the data in a file. dBASE contains a program which places the records in a file in ascending or descending order according to the specified field.

The sorting procedure generates a new file, since the source file cannot be both the source and destination file (data would then be easily lost). If you do not explicitly specify otherwise, the new file will have the same structure as the original file, but the data are sorted according to the criteria in the specified field (the *key*).

The procedure sorts as follows:

- according to size in numeric fields,
- according to ASCII value of the characters in text fields,
- chronologically in date fields.

The syntax of the sort command is as follows:

```
SORT TO destination file ON key field
```

It is also possible to sort a file according to more than one field:

```
SORT TO destination file ON field1, field2,
   ...
```

The field first named forms the main criterion. Identical values are then sorted according to the second field etc. In this way, subscribers with the same name are listed in the telephone book according to initials.

The command has a number of options:

ASCENDING   sorting in ascending order (standard). This can be shortened to /A.

DESCENDING   sorting in descending order. Can be shortened to /D.

/C   sorting letters without taking capitalization into account (case insensitive).

NEXT number   copying a specified amount to
REST   the new file.

FOR condition   only records fulfilling the condi-
WHILE condition   tion are sorted and written to the new file.

Examples:

We shall sort the ADDRESS file according to a number of different criteria.

(1) *USE address* and *SORT TO sortfle1 ON name DE-SCENDING*
Opens the ADDRESS file.
The second command sorts the file according to name in descending order and writes the result to the file SORTFLE1. The message line indicates the progress of the process. Finally, the command displays how many records have been copied and that a text file with the memo fields has been copied.

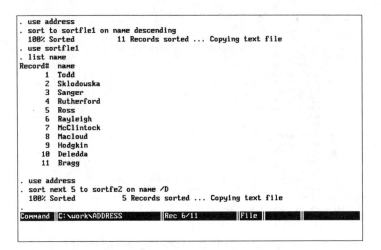

```
. use address
. sort to sortfle1 on name descending
  100% Sorted           11 Records sorted ... Copying text file
. use sortfle1
. list name
Record#  name
      1  Todd
      2  Sklodouska
      3  Sanger
      4  Rutherford
      5  Ross
      6  Rayleigh
      7  McClintock
      8  Macloud
      9  Hodgkin
     10  Deledda
     11  Bragg

. use address
. sort next 5 to sortfe2 on name /D
  100% Sorted            5 Records sorted ... Copying text file
.
Command  C:\work\ADDRESS              Rec 6/11        File
```

(2) *USE sortfle1* and *LIST name*

Opens the sorted file SORTFLE1.

The second command displays the NAME field of all records.

(3) *USE address* and *SORT NEXT 5 TO sortfle2 ON name /D*

Activates the ADDRESS file once more.

The second command sorts the next (in a file just opened, the first) five records and writes them to SORTFLE2. The abbreviation /D produces the same effect as the specification DESCENDING. (We do not show the result here due to shortage of space.)

More examples:

In these examples, we shall sort according to two fields. In the second example we shall also apply a condition.

```
. use address
. set heading off
. sort to sortfle4 on sex, first_name
  100% Sorted          11 Records sorted ... Copying text file
. use sortfle4
. list membernr, sex, first_name
      1  083 f Barbara
      2  064 f Dorothy
      3  026 f Grazia
      4  083 f Marya
      5  057 m Alexander
      6  008 m Ernest
      7  058 m Frederick
      8  023 m John
      9  004 m John
     10  002 m Ronald
     11  015 m William
. use address
. sort to sortfle4 on sex, first_name for membernr >= "064"
  100% Sorted           2 Records sorted ... Copying text file
. use sortfle4
. list membernr, sex, first_name
      1  083 f Barbara
      2  064 f Dorothy
.
```

```
Command  C:\work\SORTFLE4        Rec EOF/2       File
```

(1) *SET HEADING OFF*
    (The ADDRESS file is already opened.)
    Switches the display heading off in order to save
    space on the screen.

(2) *SORT TO sortfle4 ON sex, first_name*
    Sorts alphabetically in ascending order, first accord-
    ing to sex and then according to FIRST NAME.

(3) *USE sortfle4* and *LIST membernr, sex, first_name*
    Opens the sorted file SORTFLE4.
    The second command displays the MEMBERNR,
    SEX and FIRST_NAME fields of all records.

(4) *USE address* and *SORT TO sortfle4 ON sex,
    first_name FOR membernr >= "064"*
    Switches back to the ADDRESS file.
    The second command sorts alphabetically in as-
    cending order, first according to SEX and then ac-
    cording to FIRST_NAME for members whose mem-
    bership number is greater or equal to 064. Since
    MEMBERNR is a character field, the argument in
    the condition is written between inverted commas.

Since SORTFLE4 already exists, the program first
asks if you wish to overwrite the previous data.
Answer YES.

(5) *USE sortfle4* and *LIST membernr, sex, first_name*
Opens the new version of SORTFLE4 and then displays the selected sorted records.

In the Control Center, open the marked ADDRESS source file in
the Data panel by pressing Enter. Then choose the *Modify struc-
ture/order* option by pressing Enter. The structure design screen
opens showing the *Organize* menu. Select the *Sort database on
field list* option. Type in the *Field order* the key fields with descending priority. Select a field from the list which you have displayed by pressing Shift-F1 (in most cases, the first letter is sufficient). Confirm the choice by pressing Enter.

Apart from the ascending and descending orders according to the
ASCII codes, dBASE IV also recognizes an ascending and descending order as in a dictionary. Capitals and small letters are
not sorted separately in this case. (This prevents, for instance,
the name Marylou being sorted to a lower position than MaryLou
in a field.) Using Tab or Enter, go to the *Type of sort* and activate
the sort type by pressing the spacebar as indicated at the bottom
of the screen.

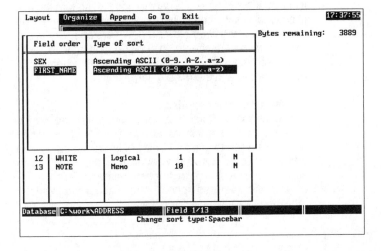

Quit the input template by pressing Ctrl-End or Ctrl-W. dBASE IV
will then ask for the name of the destination file. Enter: SORT-
FLE4. As soon as you press Enter, the program will state the
dBASE command with which the process is being executed (similar to the command which we mentioned previously in this section). The program will then ask for a descriptive text for the new
.DBF file. Finally, it writes the new file to disk and registers the
sorting percentage, the number of records copied and the memo
file.

This clearly illustrates that the Control Center executes the tasks
in a rather roundabout manner in the command mode. Although
this detour is a disadvantage, the operational ease is a benefit.

7.2   Indexing a file

In the previous section, we have seen that each sorted
file results in a new file containing the same data in a
different order of sequence. This is not only space-con-
suming on the disk, it also inherently contains the risk
that different versions will no longer be similar in the
long run when one version is adjusted to new information and not the other.

It is advisable to have the data in one file, so that the applications which alter a file do not have to handle all
kinds of half-modified old and new versions. Sorting is
thus not always desirable. In addition, sorting is relative-
ly time-consuming: the delays can easily extend to a
minute or more in the case of large files.

Advantages of index files
It is much more effective to copy from the database file
only the record numbers and the fields (key fields)
which you wish to use for sorting. The destination file in
this process is called the index file: the key field is
sorted and in a search instruction the record number indicates the required record. You can create various
index files for a source file.

Sorting an index file consumes much less time than sorting a complete data file and the original data are not pluralized: there is no question of *data redundancy*.

Using data via an index file
If you have made an index file for a field, access to the data in the main file is made more rapid.

Imagine you have made an index file for the NAME field in the ADDRESS file, and you have opened the index file at the same time as the database file. If you wish to find data under a specific name, apply a normal search instruction. The system will search automatically in the index file and if the name occurs there, it switches to the database file via the record number. Subsequently, give the display command.

When you have entered or altered data in the database file, the index is no longer accurate: sort the key field once again.

Types of index files
Just as with sorted files, you can also make indices for all types of files:

■ according to size in numeric fields,
■ according to ASCII value of the characters in text fields,
■ according to chronology in date fields.

You can not only make an index on all fields in the main field, but also a part of a field or on combinations of fields (without or without expressions). The maximum length of an index expression is 220 characters, the resulting key may have a maximum length of 100 characters. Using the conversion functions STR() and DTOC() you can also combine various types of fields. With the SUBSTR() function, you can use a part of a field as the index expression. We have used these methods in the examples. If required, first read sections 8.8. and 8.9 concerning manipulations with text and date fields.

7.2.1   Creating an index file

In dBASE III+ and previous versions of dBASE, each index was stored in a separate file which received the extension .NDX. This had some obvious disadvantages. Prior to being able to work with an index, you had to first open the index file (only a few could be open simultaneously). If you altered data in a file, these were only adjusted in the opened index files.

In dBASE IV, an index file has the extension .MDX (multiple index). The difference between both types of index is that in an .MDX file, up to 47 indices can be opened. An index like this is called *TAG*. In dBASE IV, you do not have to create a new file for each index. This saves a lot of work when opening files and there are few restrictions on the number of indices which may be simultaneously opened. In addition, .MDX files are automatically adjusted.

Owing to these developments, it is not really advisable to save new indices as .NDX files. However, we shall give the syntax for the command here since older versions of dBASE are only able to work with these.

Assuming that the database file has been opened, you create an index using the command:

```
INDEX ON index expression TO file [UNIQUE]
   [DESCENDING]
```

The *index expression* is, for example, only the name of the sorted field whose contents are written to the index file along with the record numbers. The UNIQUE option ensures that the index contains no double registration. The command normally sorts in ascending order; the DESCENDING option reverses this.

Every time you open a data file in dBASE IV by means of the USE command, a corresponding multiple index file is opened with the same name but with the extension .MDX. In order to add a new index to that file, apply the following instruction:

```
INDEX ON index expression TAG index name
   [OR file.MDX]
```

Apply the parameter between square brackets if the index has to be written to another index file.

Indexing can also be implemented from the Control Center. Highlight the ADDRESS file in the Data panel, press Enter and select *Modify structure/order*. The design screen is opened along with the *Organize* menu. Select the option *Create new index*. A new window is opened in which you can enter the index data.

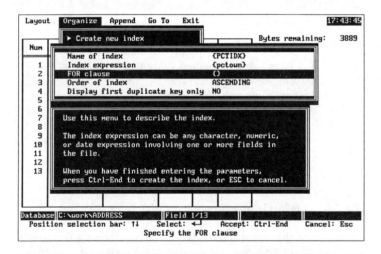

The figure above shows the data for an index according to postal code (ascending). Press Ctrl-End. While the index is being created, dBASE states 'INDEX ON pctown TAG PCTIDX, xxx% indexed, xxx records indexed'. This will probably take place so quickly that you will not be able to read it. When the program has completed the process, press F2. The file is displayed on the screen, sorted according to the new index.

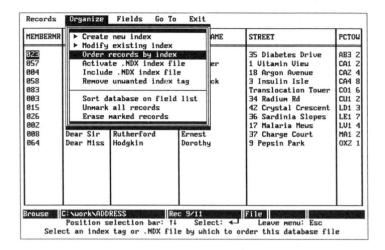

In the figure, you will see that the PCTOWN character field has been sorted in ascending order. When you have created several indices for the file, you can choose another index by means of the *Order records by index* option. All these indices are saved in the ADDRESS.MDX file, without you being aware of this. That which you have specified in *Name of index* functions as a label, in order to be able to distinguish between the various indices.

7.2.2   Using index files

In the command mode, the .MDX index file is normally opened along with the data file. You do not have to perform any special action for this. Of the 47 possible indices, the 'Natural Order' index is active. This is the index according to record number; in other words, the order of sequence in which you have entered the records.

To choose a different order, give the command:

```
SET ORDER TO name of index
```

For the 'name of index', enter one of the index labels: PCTIDX, NAMEIDX etc. The natural order can be restored by using the command SET ORDER TO without giving parameters.

If you wish to use another index file, open the data file along with the following parameter:

```
USE database file INDEX index file
```

Example 1:

In the ADDRESS database file, create an index called NAMEIDX for the NAME field in the standard index file. Examine the result using a display command.

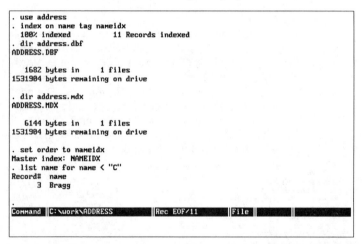

```
. use address
. index on name tag nameidx
  100% indexed            11 Records indexed
. dir address.dbf
ADDRESS.DBF

   1682 bytes in      1 files
1531904 bytes remaining on drive

. dir address.mdx
ADDRESS.MDX

   6144 bytes in      1 files
1531904 bytes remaining on drive

. set order to nameidx
Master index: NAMEIDX
. list name for name < "C"
Record#  name
      3  Bragg

.
Command  C:\work\ADDRESS           Rec EOF/11      File
```

(The heading of the display function is switched off.)

(1) *USE address*
     Opens the ADDRESS file.

(2) *INDEX ON name TAG nameidx*
     Creates an index for the NAME field under the label NAMEIDX in the standard ADDRESS.MDX file.

(3) *DIR address.dbf* and *DIR address.mdx*
Two commands which can be used to compare the
sizes of the database file and the index file. Since
the ADDRESS.DBF example file is rather small, the
difference is not very conspicuous; this difference
only becomes evident with files larger than several
hundred kilobytes.

(4) *SET ORDER TO nameidx*
Activates the new index in the opened data file.

(5) *LIST name FOR name < "C"*
Displays a part of the alphabetical list of members.
The records retain their original number.

Example 2:

In the ADDRESS database file, create a separate single
index file called TNNMIDX.NDX to combine the name of
the town in the PCTOWN field and the entire NAME
field. We isolate the name of the town from the
PCTOWN field using the SUBSTR() function. The postal code consists of eight characters including spaces.
The name of the town begins on the ninth position in
this field of 20 characters. The first field is the main
criterion, the second field the subcriterion.

```
use address
display substr(pctoun,9)
      1 Cambridge
. index on substr(pctoun,9)+name
Enter destination index file: tnnmfle
   100% indexed          11 Records indexed
. use address index tnnmfle
Master index: TNNMFLE
. list name, pctoun
Record# name             pctoun
      9 Macloud          AB3 2CT Aberdeen
      1 Rayleigh         CA2 4WS Cambridge
      6 Sanger           CA4 8NB Cambridge
      5 Todd             CA1 2BB Cambridge
     10 McClintock       CO1 6DM Cornell
      2 Sklodowska       CU1 2MC Currie
     11 Deledda          LE1 7IT Lands End
      3 Bragg            LD1 3WH Leeds
      8 Ross             LU1 4IN Liverpool
      4 Rutherford       MA1 2HE Manchester
      7 Hodgkin          OXZ 1XR Oxford
.
Command  C:\work\ADDRESS        Rec EOF/11      File
```

(1) *USE address*
Opens the ADDRESS file.

(2) *DISPLAY SUBSTR(pctown,9)*
Displays the name of the town located in the first record.

(3) *INDEX ON SUBSTR(pctown,9)+name*
Creates the index file TNNMFLE.NDX with the name of the town as main criterion and the NAME field as second sorting criterion. Because you have not specified the TAG parameter, the program will ask in which index file you wish to save the index.

(4) *USE address INDEX tnnmfle*
Since nothing else has been specified, the AD-DRESS.MDX multiple index file has been opened. Using this command, you open the new index file in addition to the multiple standard index file.

(5) *LIST name, pctown*
Displays the file which has been sorted alphabetically according to town. There is no system in the postal codes (see LE and LD): the order depends on the names of the towns and on the NAME field as the second criterion.

7.2.3   Opening various index files simultaneously

dBASE IV can work with the new .MDX files and the old .NDX files at the same time. In addition to the .MDX file which is normally opened, you can also open ten other index files: type them consecutively, separated by a comma. The first index file regulates the access to the database file (generally; see later in this book). It is advisable to always open the .NDX files which you wish to continue using if you are going to modify the database file using APPEND, EDIT or BROWSE. The indices are then automatically adjusted.

The syntax for opening and closing index files is:

```
SET INDEX TO [indexfile1, ..., indexfile10]
```

If you do not specify an index file, all opened index files
will be closed.

Requesting information concerning indices

If you activate all indices (from single and multiple index
files) of a large database, you will immediately lose
track of what is going on: which index from which file is
active? Using a couple of functions, you will be able to
get clarification of the position. Actually, all opened indices receive a sequence number.

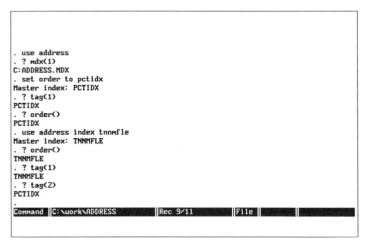

```
. use address
. ? mdx(1)
C:ADDRESS.MDX
. set order to pctidx
Master index: PCTIDX
. ? tag(1)
PCTIDX
. ? order()
PCTIDX
. use address index tnnmfle
Master index: TNNMFLE
. ? order()
TNNMFLE
. ? tag(1)
TNNMFLE
. ? tag(2)
PCTIDX
.
Command  C:\work\ADDRESS              Rec 9/11        File
```

(1) *USE address*
    Opens the ADDRESS file.

(2) *? MDX(1)*
    Requests the standard multilple index file which is
    opened in conjunction with ADDRESS.DBF.

(3) *SET ORDER TO pctidx*
    Selects the index PCTIDX from the ADDRESS.DBF
    file.

(4) *? TAG(1)*
Asks which index is located at the top of the list of opened indices.

(5) *? ORDER()*
Asks according to which index the database has been sorted.

(6) *USE address INDEX tnnmfle* and *? ORDER()*
The first command opens the TNNMFLE.NDX single index file. The second command confirms that this index is now active.

(7) *? TAG(1)* and *? TAG(2)*
The list of opened indices has been adjusted: PCTIDX has been ousted from the first position by TNNMFLE.

7.2.4 Searching for and displaying a record via an index file

Owing to the scant number of fields in an index file, searching for a particular record takes only a few seconds, even in a file consisting of several thousand records. There are two commands for searching in an index file:

```
FIND {string | number}
SEEK expression
```

The commands both produce the same effect, but the syntax shows that they are aimed at differing circumstances.

FIND and SEEK do not recognize the CONTINUE command: in a sorted file, the next similar item is located in the next record.

Searching using FIND
In the FIND instruction, you specify a search string or a number without inverted commas. For example:

```
FIND Radium
FIND 8.00
```

It is not necessary to specify the entire string if less characters also make it clear but it does have to consist of the first characters in the field contents. In addition you will have to inform to the program that the exact search object is not being specified. Give the command:

```
SET EXACT OFF
```

You can now give enter the search string:

```
FIND Rad
```

If there are several records in which the search string occurs, you can display all records by applying a condition (FOR/WHILE). If the search string or field contents begin with spaces, you must type the string between inverted commas:

```
FIND "   Z"
```

Type the search string between other string characters if the string contains inverted commas:

```
FIND ["Grazia"]
```

The FIND instruction can also be used for a search string in a memory variable. This is often used in application programs. The name of the memory variable should be preceded by an & sign.

The first command writes a value in the memory variable, the second searches for the value which has been registered in that variable:

```
STORE "Radium" TO s_name
FIND &s_name
```

The search string is not 's_name' but 'Radium'. The memory variable only serves as a funnel.

You cannot use FIND to look for date fields, not even if assisted by the conversion functions CTOD() or STR().

If the search string does not occur in the index file, dBASE IV states 'Find not successful'. The record pointer is on EOF, the value of the EOF() function is .T. (logically true).

Searching using SEEK

The SEEK command also searches for the first record in which the index field coincides with the search value. In contrast to FIND, SEEK always interprets the search value as a memory variable. This means that strings **must** be specified between brackets:

```
SEEK "Radium"
SEEK "Rad"
SEEK 8.00
STORE "Radium" TO s_name
SEEK s_name
```

The SEEK command has the advantage that it can also be applied in date fields.

The notes concerning an unfound search value and the record pointer in the case of FIND, also apply to the SEEK instruction.

Examples:

You wish to use diverse criteria to search in the AD-DRESS file. We shall presume that you have created an .MDX file by means of the following command:

```
INDEX ON index expression TAG xx
```

This file has the following criteria:

criterion	TAG
name	NAMEIDX
bth_date	BDATEIDX
SUBSTR(pctown,9)	TOWNIDX

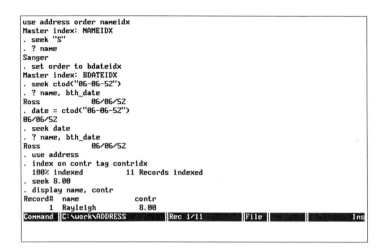

```
use address order nameidx
Master index: NAMEIDX
. seek "S"
. ? name
Sanger
. set order to bdateidx
Master index: BDATEIDX
. seek ctod("06-06-52")
. ? name, bth_date
Ross            06/06/52
. date = ctod("06-06-52")
06/06/52
. seek date
. ? name, bth_date
Ross            06/06/52
. use address
. index on contr tag contridx
  100% indexed        11 Records indexed
. seek 8.00
. display name, contr
Record#  name            contr
      1  Rayleigh        8.00
Command  C:\work\ADDRESS      Rec 1/11      File              Ins
```

(1) *USE address ORDER nameidx*
Opens the ADDRESS file with the index on the names.

(2) *SEEK "S"*
Searches for the first record whose name begins with "S" and places the record pointer on that record.

(3) *? name*
Displays the contents of the NAME field in the current record.

(4) *SET ORDER TO bdateidx* and *SEEK CTOD("06-06-52")* and *? name, bth_date*
The first command activates the index for the dates of birth.
The second command looks for a date. It is not possible to directly specify a date as a search value. The conversion function CTOD() changes the specified string into a dBASE date.
The third command displays the name and date of the found record.

(5) *date = CTOD("06-06-52")* and *SEEK date* and *?*
    name, bth_date
    Writes the sought date in the DATE memory vari-
    able, searches for the value in the memory variable
    and displays this. This is a variation of example 4.

(6) *INDEX ON contr TAG contridx* and *SEEK 8.00* and
    DISPLAY name, contr
    Creates an index, CONTRIDX, for the contributions,
    searches for the first record with a contribution of
    8.00 and displays the record (number 1).

In the Control Center, open the file by pressing *Modify struc-
ture/order* or *Display data*. Select the option *Order records by
index* from the *Organize* menu in order to choose an index (tag)
or to switch over to another tag. *Natural Order* works without an
index, with the unsorted database file.

Alter the sort criterion of an index by selecting the option *Modify
existing index*.

The option *Activate .NDX index file* activates the required .NDX
file alongside the current data file, so that the index file is automatically adjusted.

The option *Include .NDX index file* adds an .NDX file to the present catalog. You can subsequently activate the file.

The last option in this part of the menu removes a superfluous
index from the current .MDX file (*Remove unwanted index tag*).

Under the line, there is the option for sorting to a new data file
(see section 7.1).

The last two menu options have already been discussed in section 6.5.

8   Commands dealing with the contents of fields

8.1   Terminology

File variable

In the previous chapter, we have worked with fields of the type Character, Numeric, Date, Logical and Memo. The file fields were defined for one data file, in our case ADDRESS. A field like this is called a file dependent variable or, in short, a file variable, since the contents of the field are continually being changed by input or by its relation to another field.

Memory variable

In contrast to file variables, the contents of a memory variable are not subject to changes due to switching to another record.

Memory variables mostly serve as temporary storage of data: as long as an application program is running or as long as dBASE IV is active. This type of variable serves as a buffer in calculation and as a funnel for input from the keyboard and for output to the screen or printer.

Memory variables consist of the same types as file variables, except for the Memo type of field. The name with a maximum of 10 characters consists of letters, numbers and underlining. The first character must be a letter. Spaces are not permitted.

You can directly assign a value to a memory variable when in the direct mode (behind the dot prompt) and in programs. The type of value defines the type of memory variable.

Constant

In many places, data with fixed values will be needed: the names of the days of the week or the months, or standard values in calculations, such as 100 and 360 in an interest calculation. The word Constant is self-explanatory. In dBASE you can type a constant as a value in a command, or save that value in a memory variable or a field variable. String constants are typed between string characters, numeric constants are not.

8.2 Declaring memory variables

A memory variable has to be *declared* before it can be used. Declaring means registration in the system. This can be done in two ways: by means of an assignation or by input of data. In both cases, the type of the declared memory variable is only established after the first reference.

8.2.1 Assigning a value to a memory variable

There are two methods of storing data in a memory variable:

```
STORE expression TO (list of) memory
   variable(s)
memory variable = expression
```

EXPRESSION may be:

- an alphanumeric string containing a maximum of 254 characters (also spaces),
- a numeric value,
- a mathematical expression,
- a logical value,
- a date.

By applying the first of the above-mentioned syntaxes, you can assign a value to different memory variables at the same time. In the case of an alphanumeric memory variable, the number of characters in the string determines the length of the field.

The system registers the value which a memory variable has received (the result of the calculation in the case of mathematical expressions). The SET TALK OFF command suppresses these messages (system echo).

Examples:

In dBASE, all text behind an asterisk on a command line has the status of comment. In the examples below, the 'system echo' follows each command.

```
. STORE "wednesday" TO wday
   * save string "wednesday" in WDAY
     wednesday

. STORE 0 TO zero
   * save the number 0 in ZERO
        0

. STORE 88 TO note
        88
. STORE note*1.175 TO vatnote
   * save result in VATNOTE
        103.40

. STORE .T. TO true
   * save logical value .T. in TRUE
.T.
```

You may occasionally require a memory variable which is empty in order to work with other variables. Imagine that you wish to declare an empty variable for a string of ten spaces. This can be done analogous to the examples shown above:

```
. STORE "          " TO empty
   * save ten spaces in EMPTY

   * (nothing visible on this line)
.
   * prompt for the next command
```

You can also use the SPACE() function to directly store the string in the EMPTY memory variable:

```
. empty = SPACE(10)
```

8.2.2   Entering data in a memory variable

dBASE has four commands for entering data. Three of these, which do not display the values in a fixed column and row of the screen, will be discussed in this section. We shall allocate a separate section to the fourth (8.5).

Along with each of the three input commands, you may add comments which are displayed on the screen prior to the input field.

ACCEPT
The command registers alphanumeric data (strings) with a maximum length of 254 characters. The string need not be placed between inverted commas.

```
ACCEPT [comment] TO memory variable
```

By means of the VAL() function, you can convert the input of numbers in a character variable or field to a numeric value (see the subsection concerning macro substitution in section 8.8).

INPUT
The INPUT command is used to save three types of input: numeric, alphanumeric and logical. The memory variable type is only established after the first allocation. You can then use the TYPE() function to display the memory variable type.

With INPUT, the strings have to be placed between inverted commas. A date is first interpreted as a string. If required, use the CTOD() function to create a Date type variable. See the examples below.

The syntax of the command is:

```
INPUT [comment] TO memory variable
```

WAIT

The command is not really meant to be used with input. WAIT discontinues the execution of a program. The next command is only implemented after a random key has been pressed. The key character can, however, be stored in a memory variable. It is not necessary to confirm this input using Enter. This instruction can also display comment:

```
WAIT [comment] TO memory variable
```

Examples:

We shall experiment with the three input commands and check the results. In order to produce a bit more space on the screen, we have switched off the status line by specifying SET STATUS OFF.

```
. accept "Enter name: " to name
Enter name: Hall
. ? name
Hall
. input "Enter a number: " to number
Enter a number: 12345
. ? number
     12345
. ? type('number')
N
. input "Enter a date: " to date
Enter a date: "23-10-57"
. ? type('date')
C
. date=ctod(date)
23/10/57
. ? type('date')
D
. wait "Proceed? " to run
Proceed? j
. ? type('run')
C
Command
```

(1) *ACCEPT "Enter name: " TO name*
Defines an input field for the NAME memory variable with a prompt (comment).

Shows the prompt and registers the input.

(2) *? name*
Displays the contents of the memory variable.

(3) *INPUT "Enter a number: " TO number* and *? number*
Defines an input field for a number. A number need not be entered between inverted commas.
Checks the specified value.

(4) *? TYPE('number')*
Displays the type of the variable which was created in (3) above. The answer is as expected: N (numeric).

(5) *INPUT "Enter a date: " TO date*
Defines an input field for a date. The command either accepts a character string (thus, between inverted commas) or a numeric string (without inverted commas). We have entered a character string.

(6) *? TYPE('date')*
Displays the type of the variable which was created in (5) above. The answer corresponds to the way in which you entered the date: either C or N.

(7) *date = CTOD(date)*
Converts the field to the Date type. The system echo registers the result.

(8) *WAIT "Proceed? " TO run* and *? TYPE('run')*
Demonstrates a WAIT application in a program. In this way, you suppress the system statement 'Press any key to continue...'. The memory variable always has a length of only one character and is of the type C (character), an alphanumeric variable.

8.3   Output of data without a fixed position

The contents (value) of file and memory variables and constants can be shown on the screen or printed out at a position which can be determined. The output command may refer to one or more variables or constants which are in a list (separated by commas) or are joined into a string. Different types of data may only be joined if they have been converted beforehand to alphanumeric characters.

The syntax of the output command is as follows:

```
? list_of_variables/constants
```

A space between the question mark and the list is not absolutely necessary.

When the command has been implemented, the output continues on the next line. If a double question mark is used, the output begins at the current cursor position (in the command mode, this is immediately behind the command).

Remember to switch the printer on if you wish to reproduce data using SET PRINT ON.

Examples:

We shall display variables from the address file and also memory variables, separately, as a list and also linked.

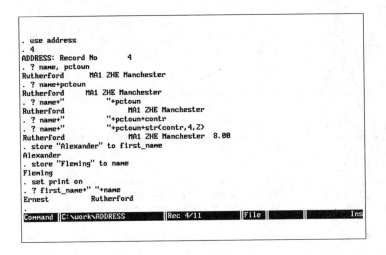

```
. use address
. 4
ADDRESS: Record No      4
. ? name, pctown
Rutherford      MA1 2HE Manchester
. ? name+pctown
Rutherford      MA1 2HE Manchester
. ? name+"    "+pctown
Rutherford          MA1 2HE Manchester
. ? name+"    "+pctown+contr
. ? name+"    "+pctown+str(contr,4,2)
Rutherford          MA1 2HE Manchester  8.00
. store "Alexander" to first_name
Alexander
. store "Fleming" to name
Fleming
. set print on
. ? first_name+" "+name
Ernest      Rutherford
.
Command  C:\work\ADDRESS          Rec 4/11        File                     Ins
```

(1) *USE address* and *4*
Opens the ADDRESS file.
Places the record pointer at number 4.

(2) *? name, pctown*
Displays the NAME and PCTOWN fields in list form.

(3) *? name+pctown*
Displays the NAME and PCTOWN fields linked as one string: the spaces between the name and address are empty positions in the name field.

(4) *? name+"   "+pctown*
Places a string of ten spaces in the linked string consisting of the NAME and PCTOWN fields.

(5) *? name+"   "+pctown+contr*
You attempt to add a numeric field to the output string. The program states in a dialog box that there is a data type mismatch. Press E (Edit) to modify the data. In the insert mode (Ins), type the STR() function in the command. You can also cancel the incorrect command by pressing Enter and recall the line from the command buffer by pressing Cursor Upwards.

(6) *? name+"   "+pctown+STR(contr,4,2)*
Display the data mentioned along with the contribution as a string of 4 characters with 2 decimal
places.

(7) *STORE "Alexander" TO first_name* and *STORE
"Fleming" TO name*
Declares and specifies the memory variables
FIRST_NAME and NAME. (NAME already exists as
file variable.)

(8) *SET PRINT ON* and *?first_name+" "+name*
The first command sends the output to the printer.
The second produces an extra space between the
two variables.
It is perhaps surprising to see the name Rutherford
in the output. This is because the value in the
NAME file variable in the opened file has priority
over the NAME memory variable. Fortunately, the
contents of NAME file field are not lost as a result of
this incorrect name. See the dialogue below:

```
. USE address
. GO 6
. STORE "Crick" TO name
Crick
. name = " "

. ? name
Sanger
```

dBASE still sends the data to the screen as well as
to the printer (see the text behind the arrow). You
cannot suppress this in the command mode. This
can be done if you are in a program: type the command SET CONSOLE OFF in front of the output
command. Input remains possible, but you will not
see what you type on the screen.

8.4   Positioning output using @

dBASE has a special command to place output at a
specified position. This is essential when printing forms
and form letters (or displaying them on the screen). You
also require this command when constructing an input
template.

Since this command is used so often, its name consists
of only one character: the at sign @. The command positions the cursor not only for output, but also for input.
In this section, we shall only deal with output using @.
In the following section, we shall discuss combined applications with input and output.

The output command @ is valid for all types of fields except memo fields. The output command also applies to
variables or constants which have been joined in a
string (but not to a list of variables). Different types of
data may only be joined if they have been converted to
alphanumeric characters in advance.

Positioning on the screen
The screen consists of 24 rows with the numbers 0 to
23 inclusive. Each row consists of 80 characters with
the column numbers 0 to 79. The positioning commands may be given in any order of sequence. They do
not need to be entered in ascending order of rows and
columns.

Rows 0, 22 and 23 are reserved for messages from
dBASE. The *Scoreboard* displays in row 0 the status of
the Ins, NumLock and CapsLock keys. The word Del indicates that there are records marked for deletion. Normally, this information is part of the status line in row 22.
Row 23 contains explanations and other messages
from dBASE IV, or self-defined texts.

If you wish to make the entire screen available for out-
put, suppress these lines using the commands SET
SCOREBOARD OFF, SET STATUS OFF and SET
MESSAGE OFF. (The SET SCOREBOARD ON com-

mand only has effect if SET STATUS is switched to OFF; SET MESSAGE ON only has effect if SET STATUS is switched to ON.)

Positioning on the printer

dBASE cannot operate the printer in such a way that the (imaginary) printhead can be moved backwards, either in terms of a number of rows or of columns. This means that you have to sort the output to the printer according to row and column number. For the printer, the row numbers range from 0 to 32,767 and the column numbers from 0 to 255.

The syntax of the output command is as follows:

```
@ row, column SAY {variable | constant}
```

Enter the required row and column numbers for 'row' and 'column'. If necessary, switch on another output device using the command:

```
SET DEVICE TO {PRINTER | SCREEN | FILE file
   name}
```

If you write data to a file, they are stored there along with the output position. If you give the command TYPE <filename>, the output appears at the specified position by means of the activated device.

Exercises:

We shall display a number of constants and file and memory variables at a specified position.

```
. store 3 to loan
         3
. use address
. set device to file tst.txt
. 2
ADDRESS: Record No       2
. @ 15, 5 say "Miss "+trim(first_name)+" "+name
. 11
ADDRESS: Record No      11
. @ 16, 5 say "Miss "+trim(name)+" was born on "+dtoc(bth_date)
. 5
ADDRESS: Record No       5
. @ 17,5 say "Mister "+trim(name)+" still has to pay £ "+str(contr,4,2)+" contri
bution and £ "+str(loan,4,2)+" loan."
. set device to screen
. type tst.txt
Command ║C:\work\ADDRESS          ║Rec 5/11        ║File ║        ║         Ins
```

(1) *STORE 3 TO loan*
Loads a numeric value in the LOAN memory variable.

(2) *USE address* and *SET DEVICE TO FILE tst.txt* and *2*
Opens the ADDRESS file, sends the output to the TST.TXT file and sets the record pointer at record number 2.

(3) *@SAY "Miss "+TRIM(first_name)+" "+name*
Displays the FIRST_NAME and NAME fields as one string from column 5, row 15 onwards. The TRIM() function suppresses the superfluous spaces in FIRST_NAME. The string containing one space prevents the data being displayed consecutively without any space in between.

(4) *11* and *@ 16, 5 SAY "Miss "+TRIM(name)+" was born on "+DTOC(bth_date)*
Activates record 11 and displays the abbreviated NAME field along with the BTH_DATE field in string constants.

(5) *5* and *@ 17, 5 SAY "Mister "+TRIM(name)+" still has to pay £ "+STR(contr,4,2)+" contribution and £ "+STR(loan,4,2)+" loan."*
The first command activates record 5.
The second command displays the abbreviated NAME field and the numeric fields CONTR and LOAN which have been converted to character fields, along with the string constants. It is of no importance that one variable originated in the file and the other is a memory variable.

(6) *SET DEVICE TO SCREEN* and *TYPE tst.txt*
Sends all subsequent output to the screen and displays the contents of the ouput file TST.TXT. This command clears the screen and displays the output data according to the commands mentioned above.

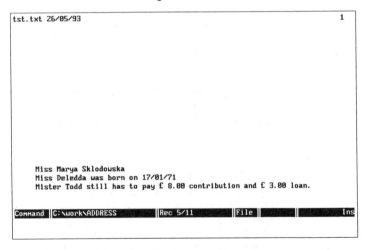

```
tst.txt 26/05/93                                                    1




                             




    Miss Marya Sklodouska
    Miss Deledda was born on 17/01/71
    Mister Todd still has to pay £ 8.00 contribution and £ 3.00 loan.

 Command  C:\work\ADDRESS          Rec 5/11         File               Ins
```

dBASE states the name and date of the file displayed and also the page number in the upper right-hand corner. The output is given on rows 15, 16 and 17.

8.4.1 Defining the output format

The PICTURE option of the output command defines a template for the value to be displayed or transported. In addition to a string with a format, dBASE can also shape the output using a formatting function:

```
@ row, column SAY variable PICTURE
  "{@function | format}"
```

Formatting functions
Each formatting function is coded using a symbol consisting of one character. The functions differ according to the type of field.

Text fields

A	displays alphabetic characters only
!	displays any character and converts letters to uppercase
R	displays literal characters in the template, but doesn't enter them in the field
S(n)	limits the length of a field to *n* characters
I	centres text in @...SAY
J	right-aligns in @...SAY

Numeric fields

C	appends CR to a positive number (credit)
X	appends DB to a negative number (debit)
(	registers negative numbers between brackets
Z	displays zero numeric values as a blank string
B	left-aligns numeric value in @...SAY

Date fields

D	current SET DATE format for dates
E	European date format (DDMMYY)

Examples:

We shall format the contents of memory variables using diverse functions.

```
. store 23.50 to price
        23.50
. store "The price is " to info
The price is
. @ 5,8 say info
. @ 5,21 say price
. @ 6,8 say info
. @ 6,21 say price picture "@B"
. @ 7,8 say info picture "@!"
. @ 7,21 say price picture "@B,@CX"
```
`Command`   `Ins`

```
        The price is        23.50
        The price is 23.50
        THE PRICE IS 23.50        CR




. store 23.50 to price
        The price is        23.50
. store "The price is " to info
The price is
.
```
`Command`   `Ins`

(1) *STORE 23.50 TO price*

Loads the PRICE memory variable with a numeric value and INFO with a string.

Note: dBASE does not scroll the screen as a result of the @-SAY commands. The commands remain available in the HISTORY buffer, but they disappear from sight after confirmation using Enter. For this reason, we have placed the commands in a separate figure.

(2) *@ 5,8 SAY info and @ 5,21 SAY price*
Displays the text in INFO at row 5 from column 8 onwards and the number in PRICE from column 21 onwards. The large space between column 21 and the first number of the price is due to the fact that a numeric field normally has 10 positions before the decimal point and that the value is right-aligned in the field.

(3) *@ 6,21 SAY price PICTURE "@B"*
Displays the price left-aligned in the field. The space between the text and the number is part of the string, see (1).

(4) *@ 7,8 SAY info PICTURE "@!"*
Displays the text completely in capitals. If you omit the at sign, the command only displays one capital: the T (see the format codes).

(5) *@ 7,21 SAY price PICTURE "@B,@CX"*
Displays the price on a separate line with two formatting functions: left-align and with the two bookkeeping appendices.

Template codes
In contrast to the formatting functions, the codes in the template string describe each column of the output field individually.

The codes below also apply to the templates for input fields (see section 8.5).

9   displays only numbers in alphanumeric data;
     with numeric data, displays numbers and pre-sign
displays the numbers, the pre-sign and spaces
$ displays zeroes at the beginning as dollar signs, $
*   displays zeroes at the beginning as asterisks, *
A   displays only letters
N   displays only letters and numbers

X   displays all characters
!   changes the corresponding letter to a capital
,   is shown if the number is larger
     than a thousand, a million etc
     (also at the other side of the decimal point)
L   displays only logical values
Y   accepts only the logical characters Y/y/N/n and
     changes these automatically to capitals
.   is the position of the decimal point

If the template does not contain a point for the decimal
sign, only the numbers in front of the decimal point are
shown. The number is then rounded off to a whole
value.

Examples are given overleaf. The codes X, A and ! are
dealt with in section 8.5.

8.4.2   Relative positioning

In addition to specifying absolute co-ordinates, you can
also position output to the screen or printer by means of
relative co-ordinates which begin counting at the current
cursor position.

The following functions enable you to request the current row and column position:

```
ROW()
COL()
```

The syntax of this relative command is as follows:

```
@ROW()+row_number,COL()+column_number SAY
   ...
```

In this way, you can split a lengthy display command
into two commands without having to count the length
of the output:

```
@ 7,10 SAY "In this way you can easily
```

```
  place the second part "
@ 7,COL() SAY "of the sentence behind the
  first part."
```

Examples:

We shall display numbers and text at absolute and relative positions and also according to a template.

(Since it is almost impossible to construct a figure that correctly shows the effects of these commands, we suggest that you try out the examples yourself.)

(1) *price = 23.50*
    Loads the PRICE memory variable with the number 23.50.

(2) *@ 1,2 SAY price PICTURE "99"*
    Displays the value in a field which is too small; the number is rounded off.

(3) *@ 2,2 SAY price PICTURE "99.99"*
    Displays the value in a suitably sized field with the decimal sign at the correct place.

(4) *@ 3,2 SAY price PICTURE "9999.99"*
    Displays the value in a larger field with a decimal sign (right-aligned is standard).

(5) *@ 4,2 SAY price PICTURE "9999"*
    Displays the value in a larger field without decimal sign, therefore rounded off to a whole number (right-aligned is standard).

(6) *price = 0023.50 and @ 12,2 SAY price PICTURE "##.##"*
    Loads a new value in PRICE. The screen rolls one line upwards, so that the display command can use the same row number (12).

(7) *@ 13,2 SAY price PICTURE "***9.99"*
    Displays the value with pre-zeroes in a large field.

Numbers at the positions shown by asterisks are reproduced normally, except for zeroes at the beginning: these are shown as asterisks. In this way, you
can prevent for instance, a 0 being changed to a 9
on a printed cheque.

(8) *price = 000000.00* and *@ 13,2 SAY price PICTURE
"@Z 999999.99"*
The variable receives the value 000000.00. The formatting function @Z ensures that the display field
remains empty (see the beginning of the row), des-
pite the appropriate template.

(9) *@ROW()+2,COL()+2 SAY "The bill amounts to £ "*
Type the command behind the prompt at row number 21. dBASE IV proceeds from the cursor position
at the moment you press Enter and displays the text
2 positions lower and to the right: just under the
status line. If +1 had been the relative co-ordinate
for the row, the text would be written over the status
line: in this way you can delete the status line.

> *Note:* After the CLEAR command has been
> given, the screen is empty, but the cursor
> is located behind the prompt. The co-ordi-
> nates are (21,0). Using, for example, +10
> as a relative co-ordinate for the row, the
> program gives an error message in a dia-
> log box: 'Coordinates are off the screen'. In
> order to place output (in the command
> mode) at the top left-hand corner of the
> screen, use *negative* relative co-ordinates.

```
@ ROW()-21,0 SAY "Top left"
```

A more convenient method is:

```
@ 0,0 SAY "Top left"
```

8.5 Entering data at a specific position; testing the validity

By means of a self-made template, you can ensure that the values entered in a certain field are automatically assigned to the appropriate variable. The following instruction defines an input field for a variable on the screen:

```
@ row,column [SAY text [PICTURE "template"]]
            GET variable
            [PICTURE "[@function]
   template"]
            [RANGE lower limit, upper
   limit]
 ...
READ
```

Note: If you also wish to keep rows 0 and 22 free for the template, switch off the dBASE IV system messages SCOREBOARD and STATUS (see section 8.4).

The GET <variable> element in the command leads to the current value of the variable being shown first in the field. This presumes that the variable has been initialized.

On the screen, the input field has a different background colour. The field has the same length as the number of characters in the variable. If required, you can place a descriptive text in front of the current value, and then display it using a template. The displayed contents of the variable can be modified using the familiar edit keys. The READ command saves the new value in the variable.

The second PICTURE option defines an *input template*. dBASE checks whether the input conforms to the template. The code signs for the input template are similar to those for the output template (see section 8.4).

The RANGE option defines an interval of acceptable values for numeric fields. If you attempt to enter a value which lies outside these limits, dBASE displays an error message in the bottom line (MESSAGE line). See the examples.

You can define a number of input fields consecutively using @-SAY-GET and thus construct a complete input framework before switching over to the input mode using READ.

In the Control Center, you can activate the *Screen Designer*, which enables you to place fields directly on the screen. See section 9.12.

Examples:

We shall initialize the AMOUNT memory variable in advance. This has the value 000.00. We wish to place this variable as an input field on the screen with a text. Only numbers are valid as input (code 9) and pre-zeroes should be suppressed (format function @Z). The valid input values range from 400.00 to 800.00.

The NAME field is initialized as a string of fifteen spaces.

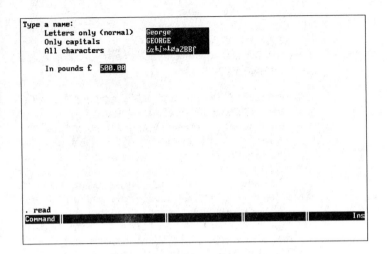

This example contains only the results of the commands. The commands which are necessary for the output in rows 0 to 5, are shown below.

(1) *amount = 000.00* and *name = SPACE(15)*
    Defines two memory variables. Instead of SPACE(15) you can also type fifteen spaces between inverted commas.

(2) *@ 0,0 SAY "Type a name:"*
    Displays a single text at row 0.

(3) *@ 1,5 SAY "Letters only (normal) " GET name PICTURE "AAAAAAAAAAAAAAA"*
    Displays a text constant and the current value in the highlighted NAME field. Since the field is full of spaces, the field on the screen consists of only a bar. Due to the template code A, all small letters and capitals are valid.

(4) *@ 2,5 SAY "Only capitals   " GET name PICTURE "!!!!!!!!!!!!!!!"*
    As in (3), but now small letters are *automatically* changed into capitals. Thus, you do not need to enter the name in capitals.

(5) *@ 3,5 SAY "All characters   " GET name PIC-
TURE "XXXXXXXXXXXXXXX"*
As in (3), but now all characters are valid due to the
X template code.

(6) *@ 5,5 SAY "In pounds £ " GET amount PICTURE
"@Z 999.99" RANGE 400.00,800.00*
Displays a text constant and shows the current
value of the numeric variable AMOUNT in the highlighted field. The template code 9 accepts only numbers.
If the pound sign is not on your keyboard, you can
enter it using the Alt key. (Press the Alt key and
while holding it down enter 156 on the numeric pad
of your keyboard.) You do not have to type the decimal sign. Since the standard value of SET POINT
TO is the point ("."), dBASE IV uses this as the decimal sign.
The RANGE option defines the lower and top limits
of the applicable values as 400.00 and 800.00 respectively.

(7) *READ*
Each @-GET command disappears from the
screen as soon as you confirm it using Enter. The
READ input command is retained. The cursor
moves to the first input field. Enter the required
data. Use Enter or Cursor Down to move to the following field. As long as the cursor is in the last field,
you can move back to the previous fields using Cursor Upwards, to make modifications.
dBASE gives a warning signal in the case of an invalid alphanumeric character. In the case of an invalid number (e.g. 300.00), the system will display
an error message on the bottom line. Press the
spacebar and enter a valid number.
If the field is full, the system also gives a warning
signal. The cursor then proceeds automatically to
the following field. Be especially careful in the last
field here.

8.6 Calculating using numeric fields

In dBASE, you can carry out calculations by means of mathematical expressions with:

- numeric file variables,
- numeric memory variables,
- values which are directly entered.

The results can again be stored in both types of variable or can be directly displayed on the screen using ?.

The calculation command (mathematical expression) can be given directly in the command mode, or you can include the command in a program. In the command mode, the command to display the result of a calculation is as follows:

```
? numerical_expression
```

8.6.1 Basic calculation

The four main calculation processes have the following operators:

+	add
-	subtract
*	multiply
/	divide

dBASE rounds off the result of the calculation to the number of decimals specified in the command SET DECIMALS TO <number>. The standard number is 2; the minimum is 0 and the maximum is 18. Whole numbers are displayed without decimal zeroes, but numbers with digits behind the point are supplemented with zeroes up to the specified number of decimals. See point (4) in the example.

Examples:

We shall make a number of calculations using file variables, memory variables and values which have been entered directly. We shall display the answers directly or via a memory variable.

First open the ADDRESS file and switch the system echo off using SET TALK OFF.

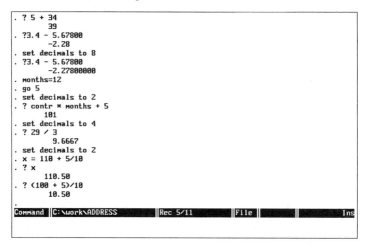

```
. ? 5 + 34
        39
. ?3.4 - 5.67800
        -2.28
. set decimals to 8
. ?3.4 - 5.67800
        -2.27800000
. months=12
. go 5
. set decimals to 2
. ? contr * months + 5
        101
. set decimals to 4
. ? 29 / 3
        9.6667
. set decimals to 2
. x = 110 + 5/10
. ? x
        110.50
. ? (100 + 5)/10
        10.50
.
```
```
Command  C:\work\ADDRESS          Rec 5/11       File              Ins
```

(1) *? 5 + 34*
    Displays the result of the calculation in a standard field with 10 positions in front of the decimal sign.

(2) *? 3.4 - 5.67800*
    Displays the answer with the standard number of decimals. The answer is negative; the pre-sign is placed immediately in front of the first number.

(3) *SET DECIMALS TO 8* and *? 3.4 - 5.67800*
    Displays the calculation once more, but this time with 8 decimals.

(4) *months = 12*
Initializes the MONTHS memory variable with the value 12.

(5) *GO 5*
Places the ADDRESS record pointer at number 5.

(6) *SET DECIMALS TO 2*
Reduces the number of decimals to 2.

(7) *? contr * months + 5*
Performs a calculation using a file variable and a memory variable. In record 5, CONTR has the value 8.00; dBASE understands this as a whole number. Accordingly, the answer is displayed without decimal zeroes. If you nevertheless wish to have the answer with decimals, you require a @-GET command with a template.

(8) *SET DECIMALS TO 4* and *29 / 3*
Rounds off the answer to a recurring fraction to four decimal places.

(9) *x = 110 + 5/10*
Performs a calculation and saves the answer in a memory variable. The value of X remains available during the current session.

(10)*? (100 + 5)/10*
Performs a calculation which is not stored in memory.

8.6.2   Mathematical functions

dBASE has numeric functions for a large number of complicated mathematical calculations.

**	raise to a power
ABS()	absolute value
EXP()	exponential (e^x)
INT()	integer part

LOG()	natural logarithm
MAX()	calculate the greater of two values
MIN()	calculate the smaller of two values
MOD()	remainder of the division
ROUND()	round off
SQRT()	square root

Raise to a power
Raises the BASIS number to the power EXPONENT:

```
answer = basis ** exponent
```

Absolute value
Calculates the absolute value of a number (the value without pre-sign):

```
answer = ABS(expression)
```

Exponential
Raises e to a power:

```
answer = EXP(expression)
```

Integer part
Ignores the numbers behind the decimal point:

```
answer = INT(expression)
```

Natural logarithm
Calculates the power to which the number e should be raised in order to produce the value of the expression:

```
answer = LOG(expression)
```

Calculating the greater/smaller of two values
Calculates the greater/smaller value of two given expressions:

```
answer = MAX/MIN(expression1,expression2)
```

These functions also apply to Character and Date types of expression.

Remainder of the division
Calculates the remainder of the division of two expressions:

```
answer = MOD(expression1,expression2)
```

The function value is a whole number which is positive if expression2 is positive and negative if expression2 is negative.

Round off
Rounds off a number according to the common rules at the specified number of positions:

```
answer = ROUND(expression,positions)
```

A negative number of positions produces a whole number.

Square root
Calculates the square root of an expression with a positive value:

```
answer = SQRT(expression)
```

Examples:

Various calculations using numeric functions.

```
. set decimals to 10
. ? 9**3
        729
. ? 27**(1/3)
        3
. ? sqrt(16)
        4
. ? exp(1)
        2.7182818285
. ? log(2.7182818285)
        1.0000000000
. x = 33/7
. ? x
        4.7142857143
. set decimals to 2
. ? round(x,3)
        4.71
. ? int(x)
        4
.
Command  C:\work\ADDRESS        Rec 5/11        File              Ins
```

(1) *SET DECIMALS TO 10*
Sets the maximum number of decimals to be displayed at 10.

(2) *9**3*
Raises 9 to the power 3.

(3) *27**(1/3)*
Raises a number to a fraction: this is the same as
drawing a root. In this example, this is the cube root.

(4) *SQRT(16)*
Calculates the square root. The answer is 4.

(5) *EXP(1)*
Calculates the number e to the power 1, thus e itself.

(6) *LOG(2.7182818285)*
The natural logarithm is the inverse of the e power.
The answer is rounded off to 1.0000000000 in this
case since the answer in (5) is not exactly the number e (it has been rounded off to ten decimals).

(7) *x = 33/7* and *? ROUND(x,3)*
The output formatting command SET DECIMALS
TO 2 is applied to the answer to the rounding off
command for 3 decimals. Accordingly, the output
has only 2 decimals.

(8) *INT(x)*
Produces the whole number part of the value in the
memory variable. Keep in mind that this is different
to rounding off to a whole number.

8.6.3   Altering the number of decimals

dBASE IV normally displays numbers with two decimals. You can change this for any required instance
using the output, or generally using a SET command:

```
SET DECIMALS TO number_of_decimals
```

dBASE IV normally rounds off the fraction 33/7 to 4.71;
with six decimals the value is 4.714286.

8.6.4   Requesting the variable type

Calculations can only be implemented using numeric
variables. If you do not know which type a variable is,
you can ask:

```
.? TYPE("variable")
```

Imagine you wish to know the type of the CONTR field
in the ADDRESS file:

```
.USE address
.? TYPE("contr")
N
```

If you give this command while the ADDRESS file is not
opened, dBASE will respond U (undefined). The command ? TYPE(contr) produces the error message 'Variable not found'.

8.7   Calculating using numeric values in a file

dBASE can perform calculations with a collection of values in a file field (or part of it):

- calculate the sum,
- calculate the average,
- calculate group totals (compress file).

8.7.1   Calculating totals and averages

The commands SUM and AVERAGE normally apply to all numeric fields and records (as long as they are not marked for deletion). You can restrict the influence of the command to one or more records by applying the parameter   SELECT(RECORD<n>,NEXT<n>,ALL, REST). If you specify a list called EXPRESSION LIST, the command only applies to named numeric fields. The command TO VARIABLES LIST indicates in which memory variables the result should be stored. In addition, the answer appears on the screen. If you omit the TO option, only the answer appears on the screen.

The above also applies to calculating the average.

The syntax of the instruction is as follows:

```
SUM/AVERAGE [select][expression list] [TO
   variables list]
            [FOR/WHILE condition]
```

Example:

You wish to know the total and the average of the CONTR field in the ADDRESS file and you wish to save the answers in CONTRSUM and CONTRAVE.

```
. SET TALK OFF     * no system echo
. USE address      * open the address file
. SUM TO contrsum  * calculate total of all
```

```
* numeric fields and save in CONTRSUM
.? CONTRSUM
       83.26
. AVERAGE TO contrave
  * calculate average of all numeric
  * fields and save in CONTRAVE
.? CONTRAVE
        7.57
```

8.7.2   Counting records

The COUNT command counts all records in the current file:

```
COUNT [select][TO memory variable]
      [FOR/WHILE condition]
```

It is of little use to apply the RECORD <n> and NEXT <n> options for the SELECT parameter in this command: the answer is predictable in both cases. The ALL option is allowed but is superfluous.

The COUNT command counts all records even if they are marked for deletion. The marked records are only ignored if you have specified the command SET DELETED ON. The default setting is SET DELETED OFF.

Example:

```
. SET TALK ON
. USE address
. COUNT TO number
.      11 records
. ? number
.          11
. GO 4
ADDRESS: Record no.     4
. DELETE
       1 record deleted
. SET DELETED ON
```

```
. GO 3
ADDRESS: Record no.        3
. COUNT NEXT 4
       4 records
  * status line: Rec 7/11
. SET DELETED OFF
. GO 3
ADDESS: Record no.         3
. COUNT NEXT 4
       4 records
  * statusline: Rec 6/11
. RECALL ALL
```

8.7.3   Calculating group totals (compressing a file)

If there are double records (identical values in the index field) in an opened or sorted file (source file), you can count the contents of the numeric fields and write the thus compressed file to a new file (destination file).

In the remaining type of fields, only the first record of the set with an identical index is copied to the destination file. The memo fields are not copied at all. Thus, the new file contains fewer records than the source file, and it contains in the numeric fields the totals of double records in the source file.

The syntax of the command is as follows:

```
TOTAL ON index field TO destination file
        [FIELDS field list]
        [FOR/WHILE condition]
```

In this way, you can remove double values for any field in a file. For example, index on the NAME field and give the command TOTAL ON name, in order to reduce the number of people with the name Rayleigh to one. This is only relevant if you are not dealing with a particular Rayleigh, but with a numeric item concerning the group of people with the name Rayleigh. Only the first Rayleigh in the source file survives the compression.

The command copies the entire file structure to the destination file, except when you specify a FIELD LIST by means of the FIELDS option. dBASE automatically assigns the extension .DBF to the destination file. If a file of that name already exists, the system asks if this is to be overwritten.

We shall give an example using TOTAL ON in section 10.8.

8.8 Working with text fields

Strings which may consist of any characters from the ASCII character set are stored in text fields. The contents of a string can be entered directly, or they can be retrieved from a file variable or memory variable. A string must always be entered between string signs: single or double inverted commas or square brackets.

The commands and functions which we shall discuss in this section apply to all these types of strings.

8.8.1 Linking strings

There are two operators to link several strings to form one new string:

+ links strings without changes
- links strings; spaces at the end of the first string are moved to the end of the second string.

Examples:

```
. ? "The World"+" "+"Trade Center"
   * links two text constants
The World Trade Center

. a = "The World Trade Center     "
   * enters text constants in
. b = " "
```

```
  * memory variables
. c = "in New York        "
  * and links these
. ? a+b+c
The World Trade Center     in New York

. USE address
. GO 7
. ? "Good morning "+LOWER(intro)+name
  * links constant and
Good morning dear miss   Hodgkin
  * file variables

. ? "Good morning "+LOWER(intro)-name
  * links, and moves
Good morning dear missHodgkin
  * the spaces in INTRO
```

It is not possible to use the - operator to place a space between two strings:

```
. ? "Good morning "+LOWER(intro)+" "-name
Good morning dear missHodgkin
```

This can be done, however, by means of the TRIM() function.

8.8.2   Shortening the string

The TRIM() removes spaces at the end of a text field or string constant:

```
TRIM(text field/string constant)
```

Example:

You wish to remove the spaces from the INTRO field and enter a space between INTRO and NAME.

```
.? "Good morning "+LOWER(TRIM(intro))+"
  "+name
```

```
Good morning dear miss Hodgkin
```

There are two other shortening functions:

```
RTRIM(text field/string constant)
   * identical to TRIM()
LTRIM(text field/string constant)
   * removes leading spaces

. ? LTRIM("        Demo")
Demo
```

8.8.3   Calculating the length of a string

```
LEN(text field/string constant)
```

The LEN() function calculates the length of a string or a text field. The answer is a whole number.

Examples:

```
. c="The Manchester Olympics"
. ? LEN(c)
        23

. ? LEN("The Manchester Olympics")
        23

. USE address
. ? LEN(name)
        15
```

Since the function value is a numeric type (N), you can perform calculations using the LEN() answer:

```
. ? LEN(c)+5
        28
```

8.8.4   Isolating a part of a string

The SUBSTR() function isolates a substring in a string:

```
SUBSTR(text field/string constant,starting
  position,number)
```

If you omit a number, the substring is the same as the remainder of the original string.

Examples:

```
. STORE "Napoleon" TO c
  * store text constant as C
. ? SUBSTR(c,5)
  * display from position 5 onwards
leon

. ? SUBSTR(c,5,1)
  * one character from position 5 onwards
l

. USE address
  * open the address file
. GO 2
  * activate record 2
. ? SUBSTR(name,1,4)
  * first 4 characters in the NAME field
Sklo
```

The LEFT() and RIGHT() functions isolate the left and right parts, respectively, of the string:

```
LEFT/RIGHT(text field/string
  constant,number)
```

Examples:

```
.? LEFT(name,3)
  * display the first 3 characters in NAME
Skl
```

```
.? RIGHT(name,9)
   * display the last 9 characters in NAME
wska
   * (the field has a length of 15
   characters)
```

8.8.5   Replacing a substring in a string

In a string, you can replace a specified number of characters with another substring; the replacement substring may be shorter or longer than the deleted part of
the original string:

```
STUFF(string,starting
   position,number,replacement string)
```

If the NUMBER argument is 0, this amounts to insertion.
Type the replacement string between inverted commas

Example:

You wish to replace the third and fourth character in
"Rutherford" with "bb":

```
. USE address
   * opens the address file
. 4
   * activates record 4
. ? STUFF(name,3,2,"bb")
   * replaces 2 characters (th)
Rubberford
   * with "bb"
```

8.8.6   Searching for a string in another string

The relational operator $ searches for a substring in a
text field. The answer is a logical type (L):

```
. choice = "1"
   * saves "1" in CHOICE
```

```
. ? choice$"1234"
  * checks if CHOICE occurs in "1234"
.T.

. choice = "456"
  * alters the value of CHOICE
. ? choice$"1234"
  * checks if CHOICE occurs in "1234"
.F.
```

8.8.7 Searching for the starting position of a substring

The AT() function searches for the starting position of a substring in a string constant or a text field.

Examples:

```
. c="The Manchester Olympics"
. ? AT("chest",c)
  * states the first occurrence
        8
  * of the search string

. ? AT("CHEST",c)
  * the search string is not
        0
  * present in capital letters
```

You can perform calculations using the value of the AT() function:

```
. ? AT("chest",c)+5
  * add five to the starting position
        13
```

8.8.8 Small and capital letters

The functions LOWER() and UPPER() change all letters in a string into small and capital letters, respectively.

Examples:

```
. n="Dorothy Hodgkin"
. ? LOWER(n)
dorothy hodgkin

. ? UPPER(n)
DOROTHY HODGKIN
```

8.8.9 Creating a blank string

You can create an empty string by typing spaces between inverted commas, but this can also be done using the SPACE() function. Which method is quicker depends on the length of the required string. The advantage of this function is that the argument may be a numeric expression or a variable.

Examples:

```
. blank1 = "          "
  * 10 spaces

  * (invisible empty string)
. blank2 = SPACE(10)

  * empty string (invisible)
. ? LEN(blank1)
        10
. ? LEN(blank2)
        10
```

Using a memory variable which contains an empty string, you can delete another variable either partially or entirely. For example:

```
. name = "Pearl Buck"
  * loads a variable with 10 characters
. STORE blank2 TO name
  * delete field contents
. ? name
```

```
     * request field contents
     * blank string (invisible)
. ? LEN(name)
        10
     * the field does exist
```

8.8.10 Creating a string consisting of the same characters

Analogous to the SPACE() function, there is a function which applies to all other characters in the ASCII character set:

```
REPLICATE(character, number)
```

Examples:

```
. ? REPLICATE("*",15)
***************
```

Instead of typing the required character, you can also specify it by entering the number of the character in the ASCII table along with the CHR() function:

```
. @ 5,5 SAY REPLICATE(CHR(33),15)
     !!!!!!!!!!!!!!!
   * (row 5, from column 5 onwards)
```

8.8.11 Adopting the system time and date from the computer

The computer clock registers the time and date. These values can be displayed by means of the TIME() and DATE() functions.

Examples:

```
. ? TIME()
17:12:06
. ? DATE()
```

```
07-05-93
```

If your computer does not have a battery-powered clock, the TIME() function will display the time which has elapsed since the computer was switched on. The system clock then starts at 00:00:00 on 01-01-80.

You can set the system clock to the proper time and date using the following commands:

```
. RUN TIME
   * activates the MS-DOS command
Current time is  17:25:21,28
Enter new time: 16:30
   * enter the proper time

   * blank line
. ? TIME()
16:30:17
   * a few seconds later
```

8.8.12   Defining a template for output

Variables and constants can be transported in format using the TRANSFORM() fuction along with the commands ?, DISPLAY, LIST, LABEL and REPORT. The effect is analogous to the PICTURE variable in @ ... SAY. The syntax is as follows:

```
TRANSFORM(variable,"@function template")
```

Examples:

```
. USE address
. GO 2
. LIST TRANSFORM(name,"@R X X X X X X X X
  X X ") NEXT 2
Record#  transform(name,"@R X X X X X X X X
  X X X ")
     2  S k l o d o w s k a
     3  B r a g g
```

```
. number = 1325.75
      1325.75
  * system echo
. ? TRANSFORM(number,'#,###.##')
  * British and American format
1,325.75
. ? TRANSFORM(number,'#.###,##')
  * Continental European format
*,***.**
  * INVALID European format in template;
  * meaningless output in British/American
format
```

In the standard numbers template, dBASE accepts only the British/American convention; the settings can be altered by means of SET POINT TO (for the decimal point) and SET SEPARATOR TO (for the thousands separator). In our example, these are respectively "." and ",".

8.8.13   Replacing data with a memory variable (macro substitution)

Normally, dBASE interprets the name of a variable as being the name of a file variable. This type of variable has higher priority than the memory variable of the same name. However, if the name begins with the & operator, the system always uses the contents of the corresponding memory variable instead of the file variable of the same name, if any.

```
&variable name
```

The term *macro substitution* is derived from the fact that one (memory) variable whose name begins with & can represent an extremely large amount of data.

Example:

The following methods of opening a file have the same effect:

```
. USE address

. file_name = "address"
. USE &file_name
```

8.8.14 Conversion from alphanumeric to numeric and vice versa

The STR() function converts numeric data to the alphanumeric type: the VAL() function performs the reverse:

```
string = STR(number/variable,total_length,
  decimals)
number = VAL(string/variable)
```

The TOTAL_LENGTH is: the pre-sign, numbers in front of the decimal point, the decimal point, the decimal places.

In the display of VAL(), the system adheres to the specified settings (POINT, SEPARATOR, DECIMALS).

STR() Examples:

From type N(umeric) to C(haracter):

```
. y = 256.80
      256.80
. x = STR(y,6,2)
256.80
. ?TYPE("y")
N
. ?TYPE("x")
C
    * the value has been correctly converted
```

The display of STR() begins at the left-hand side of the field. If there is not enough space for all the decimals, the number will be rounded off:

```
. ? STR(y,4,2)
 257
```

If there is not sufficient space for the whole numbers, the system ignores the command and a blank line is displayed along with the message 'Execution error on STR() : Out of range':

```
. ? STR(y,2,2)
.
```

If you do not specify a length for the display field, dBASE adheres to a standard length of 10 characters. The number is rounded off to a whole number (without decimals):

```
. z = 9876543219.123
 9876543219.12
. ?STR(z)
 9876543219
```

VAL() examples:

From C(haracter) to N(umeric).

```
. STORE "256" TO x
256
. ? TYPE("x")
C
. y = VAL(x)
      256
   * (X contains no decimals)
. ? TYPE("y")
N
   * the value has been correctly converted

. STORE "-256.803" TO z
-256.803
. ? VAL(z)
     -256.80
```

A conflict could arise between the British/American and the Continental European method of registration. For example:

```
. STORE "-256,803" TO z
-256,803
. ? VAL(z)
     -256
```

In this case, the system does not recognize the comma as part of the number: the conversion stops and the rest of the string is cut, not rounded off.

8.8.15 Conversion from ASCII code to character and vice versa

ASCII is an abbreviation of American Standard Code for Information Interchange. This table contains standard code numbers which computers use for storing data. If a code contains 7 bits, 128 different combinations are possible; if there are 8 bits, 256 combinations are possible. The lowest codes, 0 to 31 represent control characters instead of printable signs.

The ASC() and CHR() functions respectively convert a character to an ASCII code and vice versa:

```
code = ASC(character)
character = CHR(number)
```

ASC() examples:

```
. ? ASC("A")
     65
. ? ASC("a")
     97
. ? ASC("1")
     49
```

CHR() examples:

```
. ? CHR(65)
A
. ? CHR(97)
a
```

Using the CHR() function, you are also able to generate
characters which do not occur on the keyboard, for instance, the so-called semi-graphical characters which
enable you to create frames.

Example:

```
. @5,0 SAY
  CHR(218)+REPLICATE(CHR(196),8)+CHR(191)
. @6,0 SAY CHR(179)+SPACE(8)+CHR(179)
. @7,0 SAY
  CHR(192)+REPLICATE(CHR(196),8)+CHR(217)
```

dBASE has a special command for creating a frame in
one go:

```
@ top left TO bottom right [border
  definition]
```

Unless otherwise specified, the border consists of a
single line. You may also specify the options DOUBLE
(for a double line) and PANEL for a thick line. In addition, you can also specify a chosen character between
inverted commas, or a character code using CHR(). A
simple box is made, in the example shown, using the
command:

```
. @ 9,0 TO 11,9
```

The following command produces a more frivolous result:

```
. @ 13,0 TO 15,9 CHR(3)
```

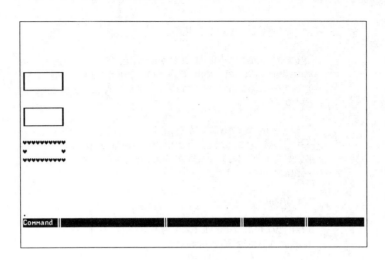

The CHR() function may also produce completely different results. Code 7 generates, for instance, a warning signal.

If the printer is switched on as the output device, you can use CHR() to transmit operating codes. The effect depends on the type of printer. Consult your printer manual. For Epson and other compatible printers, the following applies:

```
. SET PRINT ON
   * activates the printer
. ? CHR(27)+CHR(33)+CHR(1)
   * activates the Elite font
. ? CHR(27)+CHR(33)+CHR(49)    * Elite wide
. ? CHR(13)                     * line feed
. ? CHR(12)                     * new page
```

8.9   Functions for date fields

A date type field (D) always has a length of eight characters. dBASE has a number of specific functions for this type of data: DATE(), DAY(), MONTH(), YEAR(), DOW(), CDOW(), CMONTH() and the conversion functions CTOD() and DTOC().

If the functon value is of the N type, you can apply the function in a calculation. For instance: how many days have expired between date of ordering and the date of supply?

The system date, DATE()
The DATE() function requests the date from the computer. In this way, you can include the current date in a program.

Examples:

Imagine that today's date is 04/05/93 and you wish to know the date 35 days later.

```
. ? DATE()
04/05/93
. ? DATE() + 35
00/06/93
```

The date style depends on the SET DATE [TO] ... settings. In our case, that is 'British'. By means of the command SET MARK TO C_expression, you can define a character of your choice as the separator in a date. For example, you can choose C_expression = CHR(254).

```
. STORE DATE() TO today
. ? today
04/05/93
```

The day of the month, DAY()
The DAY() function displays the day from the current date.

Example:

```
. ? DAY(DATE())
       4
```

The day of the week, DOW() and CDOW()

The DOW() and CDOW() functions display respectively the number of the current day of the week and the name of the day.

Examples:

```
. ? DOW(DATE())
          3
. ? CDOW(DATE())
Tuesday
.. ? CDOW(DATE()+2)
Thursday
   * the day after tomorrow
```

The month, MONTH() and CMONTH()

The MONTH() and CMONTH() functions display respectively the number of the current month and the name of the month.

Examples:

```
. ? MONTH(DATE())
          4
. ? CMONTH(DATE())
May
   * the current month
. ? CMONTH(DATE()+60)
July
   * 60 days later
```

The system takes into account the varying lengths of the months. The newer versions of DOS also take leap years into account.

YEAR()

The YEAR() function displays the year from the current date.

Examples:

```
. ? YEAR(DATE())
     1993
```

```
. ? YEAR(DATE()+1000)
      1996
```

Conversion functions, CTOD() and DTOC()

In the dialogue between you and dBASE, you will be often required to convert data of the Date (D) type to data of the alphanumeric character (C) type, and vice versa.

```
CTOD()
   * character to date
DTOC()
   * date to character
```

The argument in the CTOD() function is of the C type: the input must be placed between brackets.

Examples:

```
. departure = "07/06/93"
07/06/93
. TYPE("departure")
C
. holidays = CTOD(departure)
07/06/93
. TYPE("holidays")
D
. ? holidays - DATE()
         34
   * thirty four days to go
```

In the following example, we shall not work with the system date, but with other random data of the type D.

```
. bth_date = CTOD("12/04/78")
12/04/78
. ? "My birthday is
  on"+LTRIM(STR(DAY(bthdate)))+
        "/"+LTRIM(STR(MONTH(bthdate)))
My birthday is on 12/4
   * congratulations Michael!
```

Displaying centuries in the date
The date can be displayed with or without centuries.
The latter is the default setting.

```
SET CENTURY on/OFF
```

Example:

```
. SET CENTURY ON
. USE address
. GO 5
ADDRESS: Record no.        5
. DISPLAY bth_date OFF
   * without record number
 BTH_DATE
 07/07/1907
. SET CENTURY OFF
. DISPLAY bth_date OFF
   * without record number
 BTH_DATE
07/07/07
```

8.10   Additional functions

In this section, we shall briefly discuss some of the other
more common functions provided by dBASE IV.

```
. ? os()
DOS 6.00
. ? diskspace()
   1406976
. ? version()
dBASE IV  2.0
. ? fkmax()
       28
. ? fklabel(18)
CTRL-F9
.
Command
```

(1) *? OS()*

The OS() function requests from the computer the name of the operating system. Some applications need this information in order to run properly.

(3) *? DISKSPACE()*

The DISKSPACE() function calculates the available disk space on the current disk. This function is convenient in a program which saves a file automatically or via a menu. Formulate, for instance, an error message if there is too little space:

```
IF DISKSPACE() < 25000 @ 23,0 SAY "Too
    little disk space."
```

(4) *? VERSION()*

The VERSION() function requests the dBASE version with which you are working. By means of this function, you can prevent an application jamming due to a version-oriented command.

(5) *? FKMAX()*

The FKMAX() function requests the number of function keys which you are able to configure yourself. Normally, these are the keys F2 to F10, Shift-F1 to Shift-F9 and Ctrl-F1 to Ctrl-F10. F1 always activates the Help function; you cannot alter this.

(6) *? FKLABEL(18)*

Requests the name of the function key which has been specified between the brackets. The first function key which you can configure yourself is F2; this receives the number 1.

You can regulate almost all the system settings via five menus in the SET full-screen editor (give the command SET). The configuration of the function keys is located in the *Keys* menu:

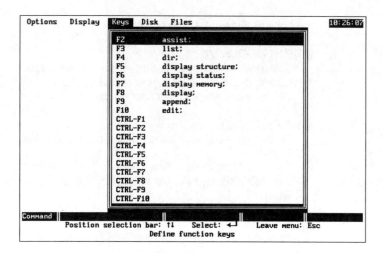

8.10.1 Functions for files

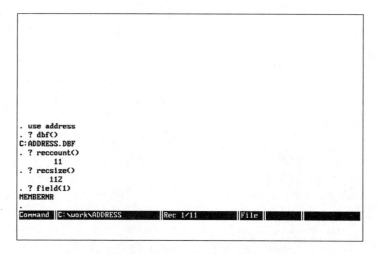

(1) *? DBF()*

The DBF() function requests which data file is opened. When in the command mode, this is displayed in the status line. There are also similar functions for index files: MDX() and NDX().

(2) *? RECCOUNT()*
This function counts *all* records in the current file, in-
cluding those marked for deletion if SET DELETION
ON is active, and also if a filter is active.

(3) *? RECSIZE()*
Calculates the size of a record by means of the field
lengths.
By multiplying the function values of RECCOUNT()
and RECSIZE(), the size of the file can be calculated.

(4) *? FIELD(1)*
Requests the name of the first field in the file.

9 Programming in dBASE IV

9.1 Terminology

dBASE works with two operating modes: the command mode and the program mode.

Command mode
In the command mode, the computer processes are influenced directly by means of dBASE and the operating system. The commands are entered one by one and with each dialogue with the computer you have to begin all over again. Previously entered commands can be recalled by means of the HISTORY buffer. We have worked in the command mode in all the previous chapters up until now.

Program mode
In the program mode, dBASE executes a series of commands which are stored in a *program*, which is a logical series of commands which together implement a task.

If the task has to be executed once again, you only have to activate the program. In programs, the same commands and functions are applicable as in the command mode. In addition, there are special operating commands which deal with branching and repetition in programs.

Program structure
A *linear* or *sequential* program works through the list of commands from beginning to end. This kind of program does not contain any branchpoints or loops. A linear series of commands is referred to as a *sequence*.

In most tasks, basic commands have to be repeated several times. In a program, that is called a loop structure. Calculating using a value which has been obtained in the previous part of the loop is called *iterating*.

In general, the way a program proceeds at a branch-point depends upon a condition. In dBASE it is not possible to to jump forwards or backwards to a random point in the program. There is no GOTO as in BASIC. However, in terms of overview and order, this is more of an advantage than a hindrance.

Generator

A generator is a utility program used in the construction of a program, a report, a form etc.

dBASE has generators for:

generator	activate in the command mode using CREATE/MODIFY ...	name in the Control Center
file structures	STRUCTURE	Data
view filter	QUERY/VIEW	Query
forms and templates	SCREEN	Forms
lists	REPORT	Reports
labels	LABEL	Labels
programs	APPLICATION	Applications

In a generator, you select an option by placing the cursor at the required position in a menu. The SCREEN, REPORT, LABEL and APPLICATION generators translate this into a list of commands which is stored as a program under a certain name.

In the following sections, we shall give examples of the application generator, the generator for input and output templates and the generator for lists.

The generator for labels resembles the other generators to such an extent that it is unnecessary to discuss it separately. The menus which appear when the command CREATE LABEL has been given are self-explanatory.

The nature of the application which you write using the generators is indicated by the name of these generators. Since the full dBASE IV command set and function set enable you to create much more than the specific generators do, we shall pay more attention to 'free' programming than to the generators in this section. The generators will be dealt with more extensively in the last three sections.

Word processing program
A dBASE program consists of ASCII characters without operating codes. Accordingly, you can write a dBASE program using any editor and any word processor which can store the text as pure ASCII text without formatting codes.

The internal word processor pops up everywhere in dBASE IV: in the SET command (see chapter 13), when writing memo fields etc. You can also activate the dBASE IV word processor separately in order to write a program:

```
MODIFY COMMAND file name
```

The file name consists of a maximum of eight characters plus an extension of three characters separated from the name by a point. The dBASE editor automatically uses the extension .PRG. If required, you may specify a different extension yourself, for instance, .DOC or .TXT.

In order to write a program with the name START.PRG, give the command:

```
. MODIFY COMMAND START
```

You can also define your own word processor as the standard editor. In the configuration file CONFIG.DB there is the command

```
TEDIT = editor
```

We have briefly mentioned this already in chapter 3 (see also section 13.2).

PUBLIC and PRIVATE variable types
Variables are not only distinguished in terms of storage location (file, memory) and type (numeric, logical), they are also subdivided according to availability.

In dBASE, a variable is referred to as being PUBLIC if the value is available in all parts of the system and in all programs and routines. It must also remain available when the module in which the first reference to the variable was made is closed.

A variable is PRIVATE if it is available only in the module in which it is used.

Variables in dBASE are always PRIVATE unless they have explicitly been specified as PUBLIC. PUBLIC variables are not automatically deleted from memory when a program is ended. We shall return to this topic in section 9.3.

9.2 Writing, saving and activating a program

9.2.1 Preparation

In the period in which you are busy becoming familiar with dBASE, it is certainly advisable to create the practice files on a diskette in drive A:. We shall presume that this is the case in the examples.

We shall write a program called START.PRG which should carry out the following tasks:

- activate drive A:,
- configure the function key combination by means of the command MODIFY COMMAND,
- clear the screen.

The function keys without Shift, Ctrl and Alt already have a default configuration which you can request by giving the command DISPLAY STATUS.

In chapter 13, you can find more commands which are suitable for inclusion in START.PRG.

9.2.2   Writing the program

Activate the dBASE IV word processor:

```
. MODIFY COMMAND START
```

A menu bar and a layout ruler with tabstops and a left margin appear on the screen. The type (Program) and the name of the current file are displayed on the status line. This part of the status line is not very reliable: this type indication is given with any random ASCII file and the file name is always shown without extension. This can lead to confusion if there are files which only differ in extension. The third box indicates the cursor position. The editor is normally in the insert mode (Ins).

Adopt the following lines:

```
* Program START.PRG
SET DEFAULT TO A:
SET FUNCTION CTRL-F1 TO "MODIFY COMMAND"
CLEAR
* End START.PRG
```

Lines which begin with an asterisk contain comment and explanation. They do not influence the execution of the program (but they do occupy disk capacity). Comment may also be placed behind a command.

If you add a semi-colon to the Ctrl-F1 configuration string, you do not need to confirm the command MODIFY COMMAND by pressing Enter. See the default configuration of F1 to F10.

9.2.3   Saving the program

There are various ways of saving a program:

■ by means of the key combinations: Ctrl-W and Ctrl-End,

■ by means of the menu options: *Layout, Save this program* and *Exit, Save changes and exit.*

If you switch to another file using the command *Layout, Modify a different program*, dBASE will ask via a dialog box if you wish to save the current file (assuming you have not already done this and the file has been modified).

From the editor, you can immediately activate the program which has just been written by giving the command *Exit, Run program.* You can also have dBASE IV check the program for faults first by applying *Exit, Debug program.* In the latter case, press Enter in the dialog box (Enter debug parameters:). See also subsection 9.2.7.

Press Enter to check the following line. Press Q to leave the debugger.

9.2.4   Activating the program

A dBASE program is activated using the DO command:

```
DO program name
```

Example:

```
. DO start
```

Subsequently, dBASE implements the commands in START.PRG one by one.

In the Control Center, the program is activated by highlighting it in the *Applications* panel and pressing Enter. (If the program is not displayed in the panel, move the cursor to the panel, then go to the catalog menu (Alt-C) and select the option *Add file to catalog*. The program will then be placed in the panel.) Press Enter twice to confirm your wish to run the program. dBASE IV translates the source file (.PRG) into a compiled version of the program (.DBO, object file). This is a version which contains the commands in a form which can be directly executed by the computer. This version can be executed more quickly, but it has the disadvantage that it is not legible and also cannot be altered using the editor. (Modifications are always made in the source file.) dBASE IV displays the progress of the compilation process (Compiling line...).

To start the program from MS-DOS, you can give the command:

```
C>dbase start
```

9.2.5   Printing the program

Text which has been stored on disk can be printed out using various commands (see also section 9.9).

Outwith dBASE
- leave dBASE using QUIT,
- transport the output to the printer using Ctrl-PrtSc,
- transport the file using TYPE name.ext,
- make the screen the default output device once more using Ctrl-PrtSc.

From dBASE
Within dBASE you can proceed as follows: either give a DOS command via the dBASE command RUN, or give a dBASE command:

```
RUN TYPE [d:]name.ext >PRN
TYPE [d:]name.ext TO PRINT
```

In the Control Center, the command is given using *Tools, DOS utilities, DOS, Perform DOS command* (or Alt-T, D, Alt-D, P).

Instead of giving commands in the command mode, you can also print the file from the editor. In the *Print* menu (Alt-P), you can find several options enabling you to influence the manner of printing:

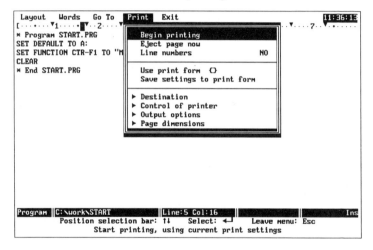

9.2.6   Modifying a program

In order to modify a program, you proceed in the same way as you would when writing a new program.

In the Control Center, highlight the required program in the *Applications* panel and press Enter. (If the program is not shown in the panel, place the cursor in the Applications panel and go to the *Catalog* menu using Alt-C. Select *Add file to catalog* and specify the required program. This is then placed in the *Applications* panel.) Select the *Modify application* option and press Enter (or only M).

Exercise

Extend the program with commands which, for instance, alter the screen features (SET COLOR TO ...).

9.2.7 The debugger

The dBASE debugger enables you to analyse your programs and track down errors and omissions. The debugger can be activated in four ways:

■ If you have given the SET TRAP ON command, the debugger will be activated automatically if an error occurs in the execution of a program.

■ If you press Esc during the execution of a program, the debugger will be activated automatically (this is only the case if you have previously given the SET TRAP ON command).

■ If you type DEBUG followed by the name of the program after the dot prompt, the program is loaded in the debugger.

■ When you have created a program, you can quit the editor by means of the *Exit, Debug program* option (see section 9.2.3).

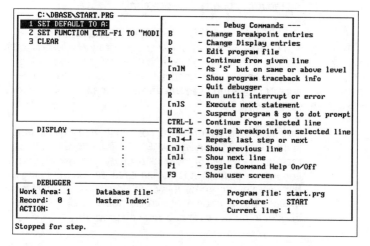

```
┌─ C:\DBASE\START.PRG ──────────────────────────────────────────────┐
│ 1 SET DEFAULT TO A:                    --- Debug Commands ---       │
│ 2 SET FUNCTION CTRL-F1 TO "MODI   B   - Change Breakpoint entries   │
│ 3 CLEAR                           D   - Change Display entries      │
│                                   E   - Edit program file          │
│                                   L   - Continue from given line   │
│                                   [n]N - As 'S' but on same or above level │
│                                   P   - Show program traceback info │
│                                   Q   - Quit debugger              │
│                                   R   - Run until interrupt or error │
│                                   [n]S - Execute next statement    │
│                                   U   - Suspend program & go to dot prompt │
│                                   CTRL-L - Continue from selected line │
│ ┌─ DISPLAY ──────────────────┐    CTRL-T - Toggle breakpoint on selected line │
│ │              :             │    [n]↵ - Repeat last step or next │
│ │              :             │    [n]↑ - Show previous line      │
│ │              :             │    [n]↓ - Show next line          │
│ │              :             │    F1  - Toggle Command Help On/Off │
│ └────────────────────────────┘    F9  - Show user screen         │
│ ┌─ DEBUGGER ─────────────────────────────────────────────────────┐ │
│ │ Work Area: 1    Database file:        Program file: start.prg   │ │
│ │ Record:   0     Master Index:         Procedure:    START       │ │
│ │ ACTION:                               Current line: 1           │ │
│ └─────────────────────────────────────────────────────────────────┘ │
│ Stopped for step.                                                  │
└────────────────────────────────────────────────────────────────────┘
```

The debugger screen is subdivided into a number of windows. At the right-hand side, there is a utility screen displaying a list of the debug commands. You can remove or activate this window by pressing F1.

The top window contains the program which you are going to debug. You will observe that each line has been allocated a number. There is always one line which has a different colour. That is the line showing your present position in the program. You can move through the program using the cursor keys or other key combinations (see the utility screen).

At the bottom of the screen, there is a window containing information such as the name of the program you are debugging, the current position in the program, which database is opened etc. The ACTION: prompt is shown in the lower left-hand corner. You can type your debug commands here.

You can place one or more expression in the DISPLAY window by means of the 'D' command. The debugger evaluates the expressions and displays the results in the right-hand side of the window. This enables you, for instance, to see which values a variable assumes during the runthrough of the program.

The BREAKPOINTS window is activated by the 'B' command. The debugger halts program execution when it encounters a breakpoint, which can be any logical expression. If a condition evaluates to true, the debugger stops the program and activates the debug window.

By means of an appropriate combination of expressions in the DISPLAY and BREAKPOINTS windows, most errors can be traced in the wink of an eye. However, practice makes perfect. It is advisable to try this out using a few simple programs in which you have deliberately 'concealed' a couple of errors, before using the debugger in more advanced working programs.

The other commands which are displayed in the utility window are self-explanatory.

One disadvantage of the debugger is that, if the program contains an error which discontinues the compilation of the program, you will not be able to activate the debugger. In cases like this, you will have to rely on the error message which is given during compilation.

9.3 Linear programs

In the most simple sort of programs, the commands are arranged in the same order of sequence as they are to be executed: when the program comes to the end of the list of commands, it has completed its task and the control returns to the command mode, the Control Center or the operating system (or the main program if the current program is a component or partial procedure of another program).

If you wish to implement the task once more, you will have to activate the program all over again. As mentioned above, these types of programs are called *linear* programs. The START.PRG program created in the previous section is an example of this.

We shall discuss a more extensive program in this section: LINDEMO.PRG, and by referring to this program we shall deal with the following topics:

■ specifying the dBASE work environment (SET commands),
■ programming input via the keyboard and output to the screen,
■ placing comment in the listing using * or &&,
■ displaying text while the program is being executed,
■ removing particular specifications of the work environment at the end of the program.

Exercise

A program which you are now about to create generates a numeric and an alphanumeric input field, and displays the specified values in the following way:

```
You have entered the number ...
The program has saved the name in capitals:
    ...
```

In the numeric field, the acceptable values lie between 400.00 and 799.00 and in the text field both small and capital letters are valid.

In the listing, comment is placed behind at least one asterisk.

In the command mode, begin by giving the command:

```
. MODIFY COMMAND LINDEMO.PRG
```

Proceed as follows on the new screen (omitting the description of the commands behind the asterisks):

```
* Test program LINDEMO.PRG *                              (1)
* Specifying the work environment:                        (2)
SET TALK OFF    && suppress interim results (system echo)
SET BELL OFF                                              (3)
SET ESCAPE OFF                                            (4)
SET CONFIRM ON                                            (5)


* First clear all
CLEAR ALL                                                 (6)
CLEAR                                                     (7)


* Declare field sorts, types and lengths                  (8)
PUBLIC numfield                                           (9)
numfield = 0                                             (10)
alphfield = SPACE(11)                                    (11)


* Input:                                                 (12)
@  5,10 SAY "Enter a number:"
```

```
@  5,50 GET numfield PICTURE "@Z 999.99";                    (13)
        RANGE 400.00,799.00
READ
@  7,10 SAY "Enter a name:"
@  7,50 GET alphfield PICTURE "@! AAAAAAAAAA"
READ

* Output:                                                    (14)
@ 10,10 SAY "You have entered the number "
@ 10,40 SAY numfield PICTURE "@B ########.##"
@ 12,10 SAY "The program has saved the name in capitals: "
@ 13,10 SAY alphfield
@20,10
WAIT                                                         (15)
* Reconstructing work environment                           (16)
SET TALK ON
SET BELL ON
SET ESCAPE ON
SET CONFIRM OFF

* End LINDEMO.PRG *
```

In the explanation of the SET commands, the default value is shown in capitals.

(1) You can include explanation and other documentation in a program using the comment sign * (or the NOTE command). These commands may *not* be placed after another command on the same line. Comment has no influence on the way in which the program is executed. Comment increases the legibility of the program. Generally, the program heading indicates who has written the program and when.

(2) The term 'work environment' refers to the settings used by dBASE when executing the program. The && command is the only one which may be placed on one line behind another command. SET TALK ON/off displays or suppresses the system echo (of assigned values, for instance).

(3) SET BELL ON/off enables or suppresses a warning signal in the case of invalid input or if the input is more lengthy than the field.

(4) SET ESCAPE ON/off makes it possible or impossible to discontinue a program using the Esc key.

(5) SET CONFIRM on/OFF makes it necessary or unnecessary to press Enter to confirm input (also in the case of a full field).

(6) Deletes variables (from previous programs) from memory, closes all other files.

(7) Clears the screen.

(8) Variables which are used in a program have to be declared first.

(9) PUBLIC <field name> makes the FIELD NAME field public (available everywhere). The contents remain available when the program is ended.

(10) numfield = 0 declares NUMFIELD as a numeric field.

(11) alphfield = SPACE(11) not only declares ALPHFIELD as an alphanumeric field, it also defines the length.

(12) These two groups of commands define the input at row 5, columns 11 and 51 for the numeric value, and at row 7, columns 11 and 51 for the alphanumeric value. (Remember that rows and columns are counted beginning at 0.)
The current input appears on the screen and may be altered there.
The @-SAY and the @-GET command may be combined to form one command: @ 5,10 SAY "Enter a number: " GET numfield ..., but then the input fields will not be placed under one another.

The @Z format function, together with the pattern "999.99" leads to numbers alone being valid and pre-zeroes not being shown.

(13) In contrast to the command mode, in the program mode a command may be spread over several rows if the rows end with a semi-colon.

In the second input command, the @! formatting function in combination with the "AAA..." pattern leads to letters alone being valid and these are automatically changed to capitals.

Both input commands are concluded separately with a READ command: it is not possible to move from one field to the other.

(14) The "@B" formatting function in combination with the "#########.##" pattern ensures that the number is displayed left-aligned with two decimal positions.

(15) If no WAIT command is given, the program continues immediately to the following command. Now this happens only when you press a random key.

(16) Removes the settings which are specific to this program.

9.3.1 Testing the program

Save the program according to one of the methods outlined above, and activate it in the program mode using *Run program* from the *Exit* menu or by giving the command DO lindemo in the command mode. The program generates the text:

```
Enter a number:
```

A little further in the same row, an input field containing five positions plus the decimal point is also created. You are interested in the virtues which contribute towards human progress such as love, hope and charity, so you enter the name 'Thatcher' in the name field. Although you only type one capital letter in the name, only capitals appear on the screen. Confirm the input with Enter. The program continues and waits until you press a random key to return to the level at which you activated the program:

```
    Enter a number:                    400.50

    Enter a name:                      THATCHER


    You have entered the number    400.50

    The program has saved the name in capitals:
    THATCHER




Press any key to continue...
Program                                                              Ins
```

Checking the field sorts

When the program has ended, you can check whether the PUBLIC variable NUMFIELD is still available in memory. Also try this out with the PRIVATE variable ALPHFIELD:

```
. ? numfield
        523
. ? alphfield
Variable not found: ALPHFIELD
   (in a dialog box)
```

Clear the NUMFIELD variable from memory using one of the following commands:

```
CLEAR ALL
CLEAR MEMORY
RELEASE numfield
```

Subsequently, the command for numfield will produce an error message.

The RELEASE command without further parameters clears all variables and makes the regained capacity available for use. This command can also be used within a program in order delete a PRIVATE variable; this is occasionally necessary due to shortage of memory capacity.

You can restrict the influence of the RELEASE command to the specified group of variables by means of the option ALL LIKE ... The option ALL EXCEPT ... deletes all variables except the specified group. In the examples, n* represents all variables whose name begins with the letter N.

Examples:

```
. RELEASE ALL LIKE n*
. RELEASE ALL EXCEPT n*
```

9.4   Repetitions in a program

9.4.1   Repetitions

Even if a program has to execute a routine several times in succession, you only need to write the relevant part of the program once. In dBASE you can repeat a part of a program as many times as is necessary, also depending on a condition if required:

```
DO WHILE condition
   commands
ENDDO
```

The number of times a loop is repeated depends on whether there is a condition or not and also on the position where the program carries out the test; in other words, at the beginning or at the end of the loop.

9.4.2   Loop with a start criterion

If the loop has a start criterion, the system checks in advance whether the condition has been satisfied: sometimes the loop is not implemented at all and the program continues with the next command.

dBASE has no special command for a loop with the condition at the end. A loop like this is always executed at least once, even if it turns out that the data do not satisfy the criterion.

If you are clever, you can use an extra condition to use a loop with a start criterion as a *loop with an end criterion*. If the extra criterion is satisfied at the beginning and the main criterion is or is not, depending on the circumstances, fulfilled at the end, the loop will be implemented at least once. This program construction takes place as follows:

```
condition_extra = .T.
   && CONDITION_EXTRA is TRUE
DO WHILE condition_extra
   ...commands...
   && execute task
   if main_condition = .F.
   && (due to the commands or

   && an external cause)
   then condition_extra = .F.
   && start condition invalid;

   && moves to the beginning and
ENDDO
continue ...
   && proceed from here onwards
```

In the main condition, all operators and functions which we discussed in section 5.7 are valid. The operating commands IF and DO CASE are so important that we shall return to them in detail later (in sections 9.5 and 9.6 respectively).

9.4.3 Loop with a counter

A loop with a counter is executed as often as is necessary to increase the number on the counter from the specified starting point to the specified end point. The counter is increased within the loop:

```
STORE starting value TO counter
   && COUNTER = starting value
DO WHILE counter < end value
   ...commands...
   && implement task
   counter = counter + 1
   && increase counter
ENDDO
continue ...
   && proceed from here
```

Example 1:

The program counts from 1 to 10 and increases a value by 500 with each passage, the starting point being 1000. The last value is shown on the screen.

```
* Program TLOOP1.PRG *
STORE 1 TO counter                        (1)
STORE 1000 TO sum                         (2)
DO WHILE counter <= 10                    (3)
   sum = sum + 500                        (4)
   counter = counter + 1                  (5)
ENDDO
CLEAR                                     (6)
@ 5,10 SAY sum                            (7)
* End    TLOOP1.PRG *
```

(1) Sets COUNTER at starting value 1.

(2) Sets SUM at starting value 1000.

(3) Runs the loop until the COUNTER memory variable reaches the value 10.

(4) Increases SUM by 500. The equals sign here (=) does not mean 'equal to' in this case; it represents an assignation: the value of SUM is the current value plus 500. It means 'becomes' in this usage.

(5) Increases COUNTER by 1.

(6) Clears the system echoes from the screen. Write a WAIT command on a separate line before this command if you wish to examine the interim results; if you are quick you can press the Pause key instead of specifying WAIT (proceed with a random key).

(7) Displays the current value of SUM on the screen. Immediately after this, the control returns to the point of departure: the command mode or the Control Center. In the former case, the screen will scroll a couple of lines until the prompt appears; in the latter, the final result will remain visible only for a moment.

Example 2:

The TLOOP program draws a frame which is constructed out of the graphic character CHR (177), around the words *Text input* containing spaces between the letters.

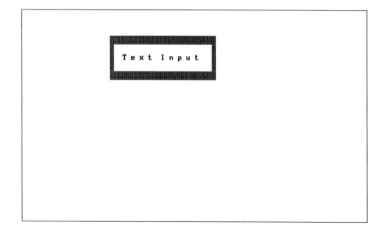

```
* Program TLOOP2.PRG *
SET TALK OFF                                    (1)
SET STATUS OFF
CLEAR ALL
CLEAR

STORE 3 TO row                                  (2)
STORE 20 TO column
DO WHILE column < 45
   @ row,column SAY CHR(177)
   STORE column + 1 TO column
ENDDO

STORE 4 TO row                                  (3)
DO WHILE row < 7
   @ row,20 SAY CHR(177)
   @ row,44 SAY CHR(177)
   row = row + 1
ENDDO

STORE 7 TO row                                  (4)
STORE 20 TO column
DO WHILE column < 45
   @ row,column SAY CHR(177)
   STORE column + 1 TO column
ENDDO

@ 5,23 SAY "T e x t   I n p u t"                (5)

WAIT " "

SET TALK ON                                     (6)
SET STATUS ON
* End TLOOP2.PRG *
```

(1) These commands define the work environment.

(2) Initializes the ROW memory variable with a value of
     3 and COLUMN with a value of 20.
     The loop draws the character with the ASCII value
     177 from the starting value 20 to the end value 44,
     thus making a total of 25 times. In dBASE versions

from III+ onwards, instead of this loop you can write:

```
@ 3,20 SAY REPLICATE(CHR(177),25)
```

The accumulating command can be abbreviated to COLUMN = COLUMN + 1 from dBASE III onwards (see also example 3).

(3) Assigns the starting value 4 to the ROW counter. As long as ROW is smaller than 7, the loop writes the character with the ASCII value 177 in columns 20 and 44, thus on rows 4, 5 and 6.

(4) As in (2), but now on row 7.

(5) Subsequently writes the text in the frame.

(6) Reconstructs the original work environment.

Example 3:

The program TLOOP3.PRG generates a bar using the character CHR (177) at a position and with a length which you subsequently specify in an input field behind the three questions:

```
On which row should the bar be placed?
In which column should the bar begin?
How long should the bar be?
```

The program listing is as follows:

```
* Program TLOOP3.PRG *
SET TALK OFF                                              (1)
CLEAR
CLEAR ALL
STORE 0 TO row
STORE 0 TO column
STORE 0 TO length

@ 1,05 SAY "On which row should the bar be placed? "     (2)
```

```
@ 1,60 GET row
@ 2,05 SAY "In which column should the bar begin? "
@ 2,60 GET column
@ 3,05 SAY "How long should the bar be? "
@ 3,60 GET length
READ

STORE column + length TO end                              (3)

DO WHILE column < end                                     (4)
   @ row,column SAY CHR(177)
   column = column + 1
ENDDO
* End TLOOP3.PRG *
```

(1) Alters the work environment.
     Declares the variables; this is necessary with respect to the @-GET commands.

(2) These commands define the input rows.

(3) Calculates the end position of the bar from the starting point (COLUMN) and specified length (LENGTH).

(4) Loop with a counter to draw the bar.

Now rewrite this command using the REPLICATE function.

Examine what happens if you draw the bar on row 22 using SET STATUS ON.

Exercise

Write the program TLOOP4.PRG which draws a frame just as TLOOP2.PRG, but now at a subsequently specified position relative to the top left-hand corner. Allow the width of the frame to depend on the amount of text in the input field. Calculate the length of the string using the LEN() function and use this value in the loop commands (keep in mind the spaces in front of and behind the text).

9.4.4   Perpetual loop with a stop condition

A perpetual loop is constructed by means of a condition which is always true: DO WHILE .T. The sign .T. (true) is stored in a system variable. Since the value does not change at any point in the loop, the loop is implemented endlessly.

The commands QUIT, RETURN, CANCEL and EXIT end a perpetual loop. Normally they are part of a conditional command using IF (more about this in section 9.5).

The structure of a perpetual loop is:

```
DO WHILE .T.
  && condition .T. is always TRUE
  ...commands...
  IF condition QUIT---->
  && if the condition is true, the loop
  && is discontinued and the program too
  ENDIF
ENDDO
```

The Discontinue commands have the following significance:

QUIT	return to the operating system
CANCEL	return to the dBASE command mode
RETURN	return to the level from which the program was activated
EXIT	move to the next command following ENDDO

9.4.5 Loop operation using the $ relational operator

The $ operator searches for a string in a previously specified string. The result is .T. if the search string is present. If not, the result is .F. and the loop is not executed.

Example:

By means of a loop, you wish to display a text which states how you can discontinue the current loop: 'Stop the loop by pressing 0, 1, 2 or 3'. As long as the specified number occurs in the string "456789" the program displays the statement. In order to have the program implement the loop at least once, we shall initialize the search string with "9".

The program listing is as follows:

```
* Program $LOOP.PRG *
n = "9"                                                      (1)
DO WHILE n$"456789"                                          (2)
    @ 5,10 SAY "Stop the loop by pressing 0, 1, 2 or 3"     (3)
    @ 6,10 GET n
    READ
ENDDO
* End $LOOP.PRG *
```

(1) Loads the alphanumeric character "9" in the memory variable N. The N text field has a length of 1 character. After one character, dBASE will produce a warning signal (unless SET TALK has been set to OFF), and the program automatically proceeds further.

(2) Implements the loop if N has one of the values 4, 5, 6, 7, 8 or 9.

(3) As soon as READ has loaded one of the characters 0, 1, 2 or 3 in N, the condition has become .F. and therefore the loop will no longer be carried out. The program will proceed further with the command following ENDDO, if any.

9.4.6   Operating the loop using the INKEY() function

The INKEY() function produces the key code of the key
pressed (an integer value). This makes it possible to
operate loops using keys which do not generate visible
characters, such as Del, Ins and the cursor keys.

key	INKEY()
cursor right	4
cursor left	19
cursor up	5
cursor down	24
Ins	22
Del	7
Home	26
End	2
PgUp	18
PgDn	3

This list is not complete by a long way. Consult the
dBASE manual under 'Commands and functions' for a
fuller explanation.

Example:

The program INKLOOP1.PRG displays the text 'Stop
by pressing the DEL key' until the KEY_CODE memory
variable has acquired the value 7 via the INKEY() function.

The program listing is as follows:

```
* Program INKLOOP1.PRG *
SET TALK OFF                                          (1)
CLEAR
key_code = 0                                          (2)
DO WHILE .NOT. key_code = 7                           (3)
   @ 5,10 SAY "Stop by pressing the DEL key"
   key_code = INKEY(10)                               (4)
ENDDO
CLEAR
```

```
* End INKLOOP1.PRG *
```

(1) Defines the work environment: block the system echo and clear the screen.

(2) Assigns the value 0 to the KEY_CODE memory variable. This does not satisfy the negatively formulated loop condition, so that the loop will be run at least once.

(3) The program remains in the loop until KEY_CODE receives the value 7 via INKEY().

(4) Assigns the key code of the key pressed to the KEY_CODE variable. The function argument is the number of seconds which dBASE IV waits before the following command is executed: that is the following runthrough of the loop. Thus, if there is no value, the program remains captive in the loop.

9.4.7   Nested loops

In some programs a loop occurs within another loop. This type of loop is called a *nested loop*. The inner loop must be concluded using the ENDDO command before the outer loop can be concluded.

Example:

The program INKLOOP2.PRG calculates the code of the key pressed and displays this, after confirmation, adjacent to the lettering on the key:

```
        Key pressed:              ASCII code:

                                      7

Stop by pressing Del
Confirm using Enter ...




INKLOOP2
```

The program contains two nested loops. The inner loop
is the input loop. The program remains in the loop as
long as i retains the value 0. As soon as you press a
key, i receives the value of the INKEY() function. Up
until that moment, a space is shown at the position 5,10.
This ensures that the input cursor remains at the appropriate place.

The outer loop displays the texts and the results. The
program waits at the end of each runthrough of the
outer loop. It only continues with the next runthrough
when you have pressed a key. This may be any key, but
it is a very simple program: it only continues faultlessly if
you press Enter.

When you have studied the program, you could try to
nest a second loop which precludes all other keys: replace the WAIT command with a new loop in which you
can request the Enter key code (13) using INKEY().

Similar to the INKLOOP1.PRG program, INK-
LOOP2.PRG can also be discontinued by pressing Del.

The program listing is as follows:

```
* Program INKLOOP2.PRG *
SET TALK OFF                                    (1)
SET ESCAPE OFF
CLEAR
i = 0                                           (2)
DO WHILE .NOT. i = 7                            (3)
   @ 2,10 SAY "Key pressed: "
   @ 2,40 SAY "ASCII code: "
   @ 8,0 SAY "Stop by pressing Del"
   i = 0                                        (4)
   DO WHILE i = 0                               (5)
      @ 5,10 SAY " "
      i = INKEY(10)
   ENDDO
   @ 5,10 SAY CHR(i)                            (6)
   @ 5,40 SAY ASC(CHR(i)) PICTURE "###"
   @ 8,0 SAY ""                                 (7)
   WAIT "Confirm using Enter ..." TO x          (8)
ENDDO
* End INKLOOP2.PRG *
```

(1) Alters the dBASE work environment. SET ESCAPE OFF prevents the program being ended by pressing Esc.

(2) Assigns the value 0 to the i memory variable just in case, for one reason or another, it had acquired a value which could influence the following loop.

(3) Runs through the outer loop as long as i does not have the value of Del, which is 7. We place the statement concerning the discontinuation of the program in column 0, in connection with the WAIT system statement at the end of the program.

(4) In the inner loop, i also receives the value 0 since the variable may have acquired a different value due to the previous runthrough.

(5) The inner loop is a delay loop: the program remains

in the loop until i receives a value other than 0 from INKEY(). The space at 5,10 clears the character defined in the previous outer loop (display loop). The cursor is then positioned at 5,11 for input. The ASCII code of the previous display loop is not deleted: the new value is written over it.

(6) Enters the character of the key pressed at 5,10. Writes the number of the ASCII code in a numeric field containing three positions, beginning at 5,40.

(7) Forcibly moves the cursor by means of an empty string to a more convenient position in connection with the system statement of the following command.

(8) Instead of the standard statement 'Press any key...' you can allocate your own message to the WAIT command. The TO x option leads to the character shown on the key being stored in an unused memory variable. If you do press Enter, no character will appear behind the points.

9.4.8   Loop for processes using a data file

In a program which processes sequential records, you cannot know in advance how many times the loop will have to be run. dBASE has a function which states whether or not the record pointer is located at the beginning or the end of the data file:

```
EOF()
```

A loop with the EOF() function generally has the following structure:

```
USE file
DO WHILE .NOT. EOF()
  ...commands...
  SKIP
ENDDO
```

When a file is opened, the record pointer is placed at number 1. Since a file almost always contains at least one record, the condition is fulfilled and the commands for processing the record are implemented.

The SKIP command places the pointer at the following record. This continues until the EOF() function acquires the value .T., that is, at the end of the file. Then the condition is no longer satisfied and the program leaves the loop.

Some commands automatically move on to the next record. In that case, SKIP is unnecessary.

It is possible to extend the question to the end of the file with a logical operator without additional parameters. However, for the effectiveness of a program it is better to apply this option along with a FOR condition (see EOFLOOP2.PRG).

Example 1:

(a) Display consecutively the names of the members in all records in the ADDRESS file.
(b) Display consecutively, for alteration purposes, the records of the women who belong to WHITE.

These program listings are as follows:

```
* Program EOFLOOP1.PRG *
* Display all names in the ADDRESS file *
SET TALK OFF                                    (1)
CLEAR ALL
USE address                                     (2)
DO WHILE .NOT. EOF()                            (3)
    DISPLAY name
    SKIP
ENDDO
SET TALK ON                                     (4)
RETURN                                          (5)
* End EOFLOOP1.PRG *
```

```
* Program EOFLOOP2.PRG *
* All records of the female members in
  WHITE *
SET TALK OFF
CLEAR ALL
USE address
DO WHILE .NOT. EOF()
   EDIT FOR white .AND. sex = "f"        (6)
ENDDO
SET TALK ON
RETURN
* End EOFLOOP2.PRG *
```

(1) Defines the work environment: close files and delete memory variables.

(2) Opens the ADDRESS file. The record pointer is located at number 1.

(3) The records are retrieved one by one (sequential) and the contents of the NAME field are displayed. The SKIP command moves the record pointer to the next record. When the last record has been reached, the pointer is located at the end of that record and that is also the end of the file: the internal variable for the EOF() function has then acquired the value .T.

(4) Restores the previous work environment.

(5) The RETURN command returns the control to the level from which the current program (the procedure, routine, module) was activated. In our example, this is the dBASE command mode (unless you have written the program using <create> in the *Applications* panel in the Control Center).

(6) The second example, by means of EDIT, retrieves only those records which satisfy the specified conditions. EDIT automatically places the record pointer at the next record after Enter in the last field: the SKIP command is superfluous.

Using the FIND and SEEK commands, you can look for values in the key field of indexed files. The record pointer then moves to the record where the search string has been encountered. If the command is unsuccessful, dBASE gives an error message; EOF() has then acquired the value.T.

Example 2:

Via the NAMEFILE.NDX index file, we shall search the address file for the record whose NAME field contains the search string.

The program then looks for the next search string until you press the End key.

```
* Program EOFLOOP3.PRG *
* Looking for a record with the specified name *
SET TALK OFF                                            (1)
CLEAR ALL
i = 0

DO WHILE .NOT. i = 7                                    (2)
   CLEAR
   @ 3,10 SAY "Stop by pressing Del, continue using any
   other key."

   search_name = SPACE(15)                              (3)
   @ 5,10 SAY "Which name are you looking for? "
     GET search_name
   READ

   USE address ORDER nameidx                            (4)
   SEEK search_name                                     (5)

   @ 08,10 SAY pctown                                   (6)
   @ 10,10 SAY "If the program displays no town,"       (7)
   @ 11,10 say "there is no record with the specified
   name."

   i = 0                                                (8)
   DO WHILE i = 0
```

```
      @ 3,61 SAY " "
       i = INKEY(10)
    ENDDO
 ENDDO
 SET TALK ON                                          (9)
 RETURN
 * End EOFLOOP3.PRG *
```

(1) Changes the dBASE work environment: closes files and deletes memory variables. The operating variable for the loop is initialized with 0.

(2) Just as in previous examples, you discontinue the loop by pressing Del (code 7).

(3) Declares a memory variable for the name you are seeking.
Requests input of the search string. Note: the string must consist of the first letters of the field (with SET EXACT ON it must be the complete literal field contents).

(4) Opens the ADDRESS file with the index NAMEINDX. The record pointer is located at the first record *in the index*: that is record number 3 of the main file. The system is now ready to begin the search.

(5) Searches for the specified name. If the name is absent, the record pointer is located at the end of the file. The system message 'Not found' is not displayed due to the command given at the beginning, SET TALK OFF.

(6) Displays the contents of the PCTOWN field if the record is found. If not, only a space is shown (the cursor moves to the next row).

(7) States that there is no record containing the specified name. (In the following section we shall discuss a better method of displaying a message in a situation like this: using the IF command.)

(8)   Delay loop for a key. When Del is pressed, the pro-
      gram leaves the outer loop and continues with the
      command after the ENDDO of this loop.

(9)   Restores the previous work environment and re-
      turns to the level from which the search program
      was activated.

In the Control Center, open the ADDRESS file in the usual way.
Select the NAMEIDX index from the ADDRESS.MDX index file
using the option *Order records by index* from the *Organize* menu.
The records are now listed according to name in the browse
screen.

Give the search command using *Go To, Index key search*. Type
the *first letters* of the name as the search string in the dialog box.
A couple of letters from the middle of a name will produce an error
message 'Not found'. Keep in mind the *Match capitalization* setting.

9.4.9   Loop operation using the clock

Using the TIME() function, we can construct a loop
which is operated by the current time.

Example:

The program TIMELOOP.PRG displays three different
times on row 1:

■ the time the program starts,
■ the time the program ends,
■ the current time.

The program adopts the first time from the system
clock. You must specify the stopping time yourself. The
program also adopts the current time in a loop from the
system clock.

```
* Program TIMELOOP.PRG *
SET TALK OFF                                            (1)
CLEAR
@ 1,0  SAY "Starting time"                              (2)
@ 1,14 SAY TIME()

STORE "00:00:00" TO stopping_time                       (3)
@ 1,26 SAY "Stopping time" GET stopping_time
READ

@ 1,53 SAY "Current time"                               (4)
DO WHILE stopping_time <> TIME()                        (5)
   @ 1,66 SAY TIME()
ENDDO
* End TIMELOOP.PRG *
```

(1) The work environment.

(2) Displays a text along with the system time at the moment the program executes the command.

(3) Declares the STOPPING TIME memory variable and loads the specified time in that variable.

(4) Displays a text.

(5) Each time the loop is run, the command compares the system time with the value specified in STOPPING TIME. In addition, the current time is displayed in the loop.

Exercise

Extend the TIMELOOP program to become an alarm clock. Add a loop to the end so that as soon as the stopping time has been reached, three characters CHR(219), CHR(32) and CHR(7) are displayed along with the message 'Coffee time!!' ten successive times on row 2.

Switch the acoustic warning signal on using SET BELL

ON and define the frequency and duration by means of SET BELL TO frequency,duration. The acceptable values for the frequency (tone) lie between 19 and 10,000 Herz. The duration ranges from 2 to 19 ticks (1 tick corresponds to approximately 0.055 seconds, 1 second is thus roughly 18.2 ticks).

9.5   Using IF at branchpoints

Types of branchpoints
Sometimes in a program, the nature and order of sequence of the commands are reliant on the circumstances. The decision structure in the case of branchpoints can be programmed in different ways.

The first structure is asymmetrical: the program is mainly linear, and only branches if a condition is fulfilled (IF construction).

In the second structure, the forking is equivalent: both branches have their own blocks of commands (IF-ELSE construction).

With multiple branching, the CASE command can be applied. This provides a particular set of commands for each of a series of specified circumstances.

9.5.1   Asymmetrical choice

```
IF condition
   ...commands...
ENDIF
```

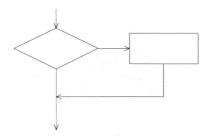

At the moment when the program reaches this structure, the system checks the CONDITION behind the IF
command. If the condition is true (.T.), the block between IF and ENDIF is executed. In the other case (.F.),
the program proceeds directly to the command after
ENDIF.

9.5.2   Equivalent choice

```
IF condition
    ...commands...
    ELSE
    ...commands...
ENDIF
```

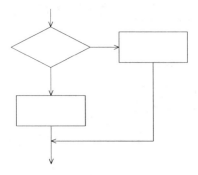

If the condition is true (.T.), the block behind IF is executed, otherwise the block behind ELSE is executed.
In both cases, the program subsequently proceeds with
the command after ENDIF.

9.5.3 Selecting by means of relational operators

In section 5.7, we dealt with the operators used to make comparisons in the context of creating filters. If the comparison is true, the condition has been fulfilled (for inclusion in the filter). In the following examples, the logical value of the comparison decides the choice of branch.

Examples:

We shall demonstrate the greater than (>) and the smaller than (<) operators in an asymmetrical and in an equivalent branching structure, using the programs IFDEM1.PRG and IFDEM2.PRG. Both programs compare the numeric memory variables A=10 and B=3. Since A is larger than B, the text 'A is larger than B' should be displayed on the screen. The second program contains an equivalent choice after the comparison 'A < B'. This is not true, so the ELSE command is executed (B is smaller than A).

The listings for these programs are as follows:

```
*Program IFDEM1.PRG *
SET TALK OFF                             (1)
CLEAR ALL
CLEAR
a = 10                                   (2)
b = 3
IF a > b                                 (3)
    @3,10 SAY "A is larger than B"
ENDIF
* End IFDEM1.PRG *

*Program IFDEM2.PRG *
SET TALK OFF                             (1)
CLEAR ALL
CLEAR
a = 10                                   (2)
b = 3
IF a < b                                 (4)
    @3,10 SAY "A is smaller than B"
```

```
    ELSE
    @3,10 SAY "B is smaller than A"
ENDIF
* End IFDEM2.PRG *
```

(1) Alters the work environment; closes files and clears the screen.

(2) Initializes the memory variables A and B with the specified values.

(3) The result of the comparison A>B is .T. (logically true). Therefore the text is displayed on the screen.

(4) The result of the comparison A<B is .F. (logically false). Therefore the program continues with the ELSE command and displays the text 'B is smaller than A' on the screen.

9.5.4 Choosing using logical operators

In an IF command condition, all logical operators are valid (see the description in section 5.11).

Examples:

The programs IFAND, IFOR and IFNOT demonstrate the IF command with a logical operator in the condition.

In the program IFAND, we shall initialize the memory variables A=3, B=5, C=3 and D=5. The condition tests whether A is equal to C and simultaneously whether B is equal to D. That is true so the text 'Matches' is shown on the screen.

In the program IFOR, we shall see that the 'Matches' text also appears if one of the statements linked by the OR operator is true.

The listings for these programs are:

```
* Program IFAND.PRG *
SET TALK OFF                          (1)
a = 3                                 (2)
b = 5
c = 3
d = 5
IF (a = c) .AND. (b = d)              (3)
    ? "Match"
    ELSE
    ? "Do not match"
ENDIF
* End IFAND.PRG *

* Program IFOR.PRG *
SET TALK OFF
a = 3
b = 5
c = 3
d = 5
IF (a = b) .OR. (b = d)               (4)
    ? "Match"
    ELSE
    ? "Do not match"
ENDIF
* End IFOR.PRG *

* Program IFNOT.PRG *
SET TALK OFF
a = 3
b = 5
c = 3
d = 5
IF .NOT. (a = b)                      (5)
    ? "Match"
    ELSE
    ? "Do not match"
ENDIF
* End IFNOT.PRG *
```

(1) Alters the work environment.

(2) Initializes the memory variables.

(3) Tests the condition. Both A=C and B=D are true; the condition is thus true (.T.). The 'Match' text is displayed.

(4) Although the first comparison A=B has the logical value .F., the condition is true in its entirety since the second comparison B=D has the logical value .T. The 'Match' text is also displayed here.

(5) The .NOT. operator examines the opposite of the comparison A=B. Since A<>B, the logical value of the condition is true. The program displays the 'Match' text.

9.5.5   Choosing using dBASE functions

dBASE provides a number of functions which can execute a test and produce a logical value which can be used with IF. The last two commands do not implement any checks, they are a supplement to the operation with loops.

ISALPHA()	tests whether the first character in a string is a letter
ISUPPER()	tests whether the first character in a string is a capital
ISLOWER()	tests whether the first character in a string is a small letter
FOUND()	states whether the search term occurs in the index file
DELETED()	tests whether the current record is marked for deletion
READKEY()	interprets the code of some operation keys
LOOP	skips the rest of the loop; returns to the beginning (DO WHILE)
EXIT	the program leaves the loop and proceeds after ENDDO

Example 1:

The program tests the NAME, SEX and RED fields according to various conditions and displays certain information if all conditions are fulfilled.

In the NAME field, the first character must be a letter. If not, the program immediately checks the next record. If it is a letter, the program checks whether this is a capital. If the answer is positive, the name is displayed in capital letters, otherwise the output field remains blank.

Subsequently, the program checks the (first) letter in the SEX field. If this is the letter m, the text 'Mister' appears. If this is the letter f, this is the text 'Ms.' In all other cases the output field remains blank.

The RED field is checked according to type and contents. A text is only displayed if it is a logical field. If the field is TRUE, the text 'room temperature' is displayed; if the field is FALSE, the text 'chilled' appears.

```
RAYLEIGH        Mister  room temperature
SKLODOWSKA      Ms.   chilled
BRAGG           Mister  chilled
RUTHERFORD      Mister  room temperature
TODD            Mister  room temperature
SANGER          Mister  chilled
HODGKIN         Ms.   room temperature
ROSS            Mister  room temperature
MACLEOD         Mister  chilled
MCCLINTOCK      Ms.   room temperature
DELEDDA         Ms.   chilled
Command  C:\work\ADDRESS        Rec EOF/11      File
```

The program listing is as follows:

```
* Program IFISTYPE.PRG *
SET TALK OFF                                    (1)
USE address
DO WHILE .NOT. EOF()                            (2)
   IF .NOT. ISALPHA(name)                       (3)
      SKIP
      LOOP
   ENDIF

   IF ISUPPER(name)                             (4)
      ? "   "
      ? UPPER(name)
   ENDIF

   IF ISLOWER(sex) .AND. sex = "m"              (5)
      ?? "   "
      ?? "Mister"
   ELSE
      IF sex = "f"
         ?? "   "
         ?? "Ms."
      ENDIF
   ENDIF

   IF (TYPE("red") = "L") .AND. red             (6)
      ?? "   "
      ?? "room temperature"
   ENDIF
   IF (TYPE("red") = "L") .AND. .NOT. red
      ?? "   "
      ?? "chilled"
   ENDIF
   SKIP
ENDDO
RETURN
* End IFISTYPE.PRG *
```

(1) Alters the work environment and opens the AD-
    DRESS file.

(2)   Runs the loop as long as the record pointer is not located at the end of the file (continue to the end of the file).

(3)   In the ADDRESS file, all names begin with a capital letter: all records are displayed. If the first character is a character other than a letter, the record is not displayed. Without SKIP, the record pointer would still be located at the same record after the LOOP command.

(4)   All names begin with a capital letter. The command ? " " displays two spaces and thus produces a blank line. The following output, again on a new line, consists of the name in capitals letters.

(5)   The test of the letters in the SEX field always produces a positive result, since we have entered these values in small letters.
      If the second condition finds the value f, the output continues further with two spaces on the same line, due to the double question mark **??**. Subsequently, the program displays the text 'Mister', or 'Ms.' in the case of the letter f.

(6)   If RED is a logical field with the contents .T., the member in the current record belongs to group 1. After two spaces, the program displays the description: 'room temperature'.
      The second text covers the other group: 'chilled'.

Exercise

Examine what happens when you have altered the first letter in a name to a small letter using BROWSE or EDIT. Solve this problem *in the program*.

Example 2:

The program ALTER.PRG looks for a record in the AD-

DRESS file with a name you specify. If the name occurs, the program gives the EDIT command. If the name is not found, the text 'No record found to edit' is displayed.

The program listing is as follows:

```
* Program ALTER.PRG *
SET TALK OFF                                    (1)
CLEAR
CLEAR ALL
USE address ORDER nameidx

sname = "                   "                    (2)
@ 18,10 SAY "Name? : " GET sname PICTURE
   "XXXXXXXXXXXXXXX"
READ

SEEK sname                                       (3)
IF .NOT. FOUND()                                 (4)
   CLEAR
   @ 20,10 SAY "No record found to edit"
ELSE
   EDIT
ENDIF
* End ALTER.PRG *
```

(1) Changes the work environment and opens the AD-DRESS.DBF file with the NAMEIDX index of the ADDRESS.MDX index file.

(2) Initializes the SNAME memory variable as a string of 15 spaces.
    Displays the text 'Name? :' as the prompt for input of the SNAME variable. The template accepts all characters.

(3) Searches for the record in which the contents of the NAME index field are identical to the SNAME variable.

(4) Asks whether the record is found. If so, the Edit module is activated along with this record. Repeated searching is possible via the *Go To* menu. If there is no such record, the program will state this. (Extend the program yourself for repeated searching in case the name does not exist in the file.)

Example 3:

The program DEL.PRG is aimed at deleting a specific record in the ADDRESS file. If the record does not exist there, it cannot be deleted of course. This should result in the message 'No record for deletion'. Otherwise, the record found is first marked for deletion. For security reasons, the program displays this record by means of the EDIT command. The word 'Del' is shown at the extreme right of the status line.

You register deletion marks using the *Mark record for deletion* option from the *Records* menu. This menu option switches to its opposite in the case of a record with a deletion mark: *Clear deletion mark*.

Finally, the program deletes the marked record(s) from the disk by means of the PACK command. This command copies the file without the marked records.

The program listing is as follows:

```
* Program DEL.PRG *
SET TALK OFF                                    (1)
CLEAR
CLEAR ALL
USE address ORDER nameidx

sname = "                    "                  (2)
@ 18,10 SAY "Name? : "
    GET sname PICTURE "XXXXXXXXXXXXXXX"
READ

SEEK sname                                      (3)
IF FOUND()
```

```
   DELETE
   EDIT FOR sname = name
ELSE                                           (4)
   CLEAR
   @ 20,10 SAY "No record for deletion"
   WAIT ""
ENDIF
CLEAR
PACK                                           (5)
* End WIS.PRG *
```

(1) As in example 2.

(2) Input as in example 2.

(3) Searches for the record in which the NAME field
     has the same contents as the SNAME memory
     variable, and marks the found record for deletion.

(4) Displays a message if there is no record with the
     specified name.

(5) Makes a compressed copy of the data file using
     PACK.

9.5.6 Discontinuing a loop with the choice Yes/No

Occasionally, a loop has to be ended, not due to circumstances caused by the data in a file or a counter in
a program, but owing to a decision made by the user.
We shall give a number of examples of ways of programming such situations.

Example 1:

The program YESNO1.PRG displays in succession all
records in the file by means of the EDIT command.

Normally, you leave EDIT using *Exit, Exit*, or Alt-E, E, or
using the key combination Ctrl-W or Ctrl-End. EDIT
then returns the control to the level from which the acti-

vation took place. We wish to discontinue the program prior to this and enable the user to alter the next record by means of a Y/N question if he/she wishes.

As long as dBASE is in the EDIT mode, you can move directly to the next or previous record by pressing respectively PgDn or PgUp.

The program listing is as follows:

```
* Program YESNO1.PRG *
SET TALK OFF                                    (1)
CLEAR ALL
USE address

DO WHILE .NOT. EOF()                            (2)
   EDIT
   @ 20,0 SAY " "                               (3)
   WAIT "Continue? (Y/N)" TO further            (4)
   IF UPPER(further) <> "Y"                     (5)
      RETURN
   ENDIF
   SKIP
ENDDO

SET TALK ON
RETURN
* End YESNO1.PRG *
```

(1) Changes the work environment, closes files and opens the ADDRESS file.

(2) Executes the loop to the end of the file. The EDIT command loads the current record in the template for alterations.

(3) Places the output cursor at the beginning of the 21st row.

(4) Discontinues the program, displays the specified text and saves the typed character in the FUR-THER memory variable. Since you have entered

your own text behind WAIT, this appears instead of the standard prompt (Press any key to continue...).

(5) Checks the contents of the FURTHER memory variable. If that is not the letter Y or y, the RETURN command returns the control to the level in operation prior to the YESNO.PRG. In other words, proceed with SKIP after Y or y.

Exercise

Write the program YESNO2.PRG in which the program accepts only the keys N and n, in order to discontinue a program. To do this, replace the commands for input and branching with the following sequence:

```
ACCEPT "Continue? (Y/N)" TO further
IF further$"Nn"
```

The IF command checks, by means of the $ operator, whether the contents of the FURTHER memory variable occur in the string 'Nn'. In that case, the program must stop with RETURN.

You can also formulate the condition as:

```
IF further = "N" .OR. further = "n"
```

Example 2:

We shall replace the operation of the loop which uses EOF() in the YESNO1.PRG with a condition which has a logical variable. The check using EOF() takes place in a separate loop. If a positive answer is given, the program is ended in an orderly way, otherwise the program continues with EDIT.

The program listing is as follows:

```
* Program YESNO3.PRG operating using DO
```

```
   WHILE .T. *
SET TALK OFF                                    (1)
CLEAR ALL
USE address
STORE .T. TO further2                           (2)
DO WHILE further2
    IF EOF()                                    (3)
       EXIT
    ENDIF
    EDIT
    @ 20,0 SAY " "
    ACCEPT "Continue? (Y/N)" TO further
    IF further$"Nn"
       STORE .F. TO further2                    (4)
    ENDIF
    SKIP
ENDDO
SET TALK ON
RETURN
* End YESNO3.PRG *
```

(1) Changes the work environment, closes files and opens the ADDRESS file.

(2) Initializes the FURTHER2 memory variable with the logical value .T.

(3) Leaves the loop when the record pointer is located at the end of the file. The program then continues with the first command after the current loop.

(4) Runs the loop until the FURTHER2 variable obtains the value .F. That is the case when the loop has registered the input N or n by means of the AC-CEPT command. Assignation of .F. to FURTHER2 ends the program by means of request rather than by lack of choice.

9.5.7   Discontinuing a loop after a page-oriented command

After having given a page-oriented command such as APPEND BROWSE, CREATE, EDIT, INSERT, MOD-IFY and READ, you can display which key was used last using the READKEY() function:

```
READKEY()
```

You can use the function value to influence the pro-gress of a program.

Example:

The program YESNO4.PRG retains how many times you have quit a record using Ctrl-W (save and exit). The program increases the NUMBER counter as soon as READKEY() receives the value 270. See the manual for additional READKEY() codes.

The program listing is as follows:

```
* Program YESNO4.PRG operated by $ *
SET TALK OFF                                (1)
CLEAR ALL
USE address
number = 0                                  (2)
further = "Yy"
DO WHILE .NOT. further$"Nn"                 (3)
   IF EOF()
      EXIT
   ENDIF
   EDIT
   IF READKEY() = 270                       (4)
      number = number + 1
   ENDIF
   @ 20,0 SAY " "
   ACCEPT "Continue? (Y/N)" TO further      (5)
   SKIP
ENDDO
CLEAR                                       (6)
```

```
@ 3,10 SAY "You have closed" +
  STR(number,3) + " records using Ctrl-W."
SET TALK ON
RETURN
* End YESNO4.PRG *
```

(1) Changes the work environment, closes files and opens the ADDRESS file.

(2) Deletes the previous value of the NUMBER memory variable. This variable serves to count the number of times that READKEY() has had the value 270 for Ctrl-W.
Initializes the FURTHER memory variable using "Yy". Any other definition is also acceptable except "Nn".

(3) Runs the loop until the FURTHER variable has a value other than N or n.

(4) This loop increases the NUMBER counter when READKEY() receives the value 270, thus, when you have pressed Ctrl-W.

(5) Asks whether you wish to continue Yes or No. Input of N or n means that at the beginning of the following runthrough (at the next record), the condition of the main loop is no longer fulfilled. The loop is then discontinued and the program proceeds further after ENDDO.

(6) Displays a text including the current value of NUMBER converted to a string. When Ctrl-W has been pressed twice, the display is:

```
You have closed   3 records using Ctrl-W.
```

Note: The program registers only the Ctrl-W key combination. *Alt-E, E* and *Alt-E, Enter* in EDIT do have the effect that the record is saved but READKEY() produces a different code for these actions.

9.6   Programs with multiple branchpoints

In many programs branching is necessary, providing multiple choice. Menus are an example of this. This can be realized with a series of nested IF commands, but the CASE command is much more elegant and orderly.

9.6.1   Nested IF commands

The structure outlined below provides a choice from four options:

```
IF condition1
...commands1...
ELSE
   IF condition2
   ...commands2...
   ELSE
      IF condition3
      ...commands3...
      ELSE
         IF condition4
         ...commands4...
         ENDIF
      ENDIF
   ENDIF
ENDIF
```

In this structure the conditions are tested consecutively. At each IF command, the program executes the commands if the condition is true, otherwise it moves on to the command after ELSE. It finds another IF command there and the series of commands is worked through in this way. As soon as a condition X is fulfilled, the program implements the corresponding block of X commands. Each level in the hierarchy of IF commands must be concluded using ENDIF. After a block of commands, the program proceeds after the ENDIF command from the current nested level.

> *Note:*   Commands between two ENDIF com-
>   mands belong to the higher of the two le-
>   vels in question.

Particularly when the command blocks are lengthy and
contain loops themselves, this way of working produces
a program which is difficult to read.

Example:

The program IFNEST.PRG first requests input for the
three numeric memory variables FIELD1, FIELD2 and
FIELD3. Subsequently, it displays several lines of text
which form a menu enabling a number of calculations.
The final menu option ends the program. The program
remains in the outer loop until you choose the last option.

```
Enter a value for A:  2

Enter a value for B:  3

Enter a value for C:  4

Select one of the numbers:

A + B + C              1
A - B                  2
A * B * C              3
A / B                  4
Stop                   9



The answer is:    9.00
Press Enter to continue
Select an option:
IFNEST
```

The program listing is as follows:

```
* Program IFNEST.PRG *
SET TALK OFF                                    (1)
choice = 0
CLEAR
?                                               (2)
```

```
INPUT "Enter a value for A:  " TO field1
?
INPUT "Enter a value for B:  " TO field2
?
INPUT "Enter a value for C:  " TO field3
?
? "Select one of the numbers:"
?
? "A + B + C                    1"               (3)
? "A - B                        2"
? "A * B * C                    3"
? "A / B                        4"
? "Stop                         9"
?

DO WHILE .T.                                     (4)
   INPUT "Select an option:           " TO
   choice                                        (5)
   @ 16,0 CLEAR                                  (6)
   IF choice = 1                                 (7)
   .   result = field1 + field2 + field3
   ELSE
      IF choice = 2
         result = field1 - field2
      ELSE
         IF choice = 3
            result = field1 * field2 *
   field3
         ELSE
            IF choice = 4
               result = field1 / field2
            ELSE
               IF choice = 9
                  CLEAR
                  RETURN
               ENDIF
            ENDIF
         ENDIF
      ENDIF
   ENDIF                                         (8)
   @ 19,00 SAY "The answer is: " +
   STR(result,7,2)
```

```
WAIT "Press Enter to continue"          (9)
ENDDO
* End IFNEST.PRG *
```

(1) Changes the work environment; clears the CHOICE menu variable and the screen.

(2) Displays a blank line and an output prompt alternately three times.
The INPUT command loads input in the memory variable via the keyboard. The menu is only displayed when the three numeric variables have received a value.

(3) The menu remains on the screen without scrolling in this program until the menu option 9 ends the program using RETURN.

(4) Beginning of the perpetual loop.

(5) The prompt for the value of the menu option CHOICE. Only the numbers 1, 2, 3, 4 and 9 are valid in this program. An invalid number sends the program directly to the output command. The RESULT variable then has no value. Other characters cause an error statement since the variable then automatically belongs to the alphanumeric type.

(6) Positions the cursor at 16,0 and clears the rest of the screen.

(7) Beginning of the interpretation of the chosen menu option.

(8) Displays the converted answer as a part of a string.

(9) Program pause. Another key than Enter is not invalid, but a visible character has the undesired effect of remaining visible on the screen behind the prompt.

9.6.2   Multiple branching using CASE

The combination of the operating commands DO CASE
and ENDCASE gives a much more orderly structure to
a program than a hierarchy of nested IF commands.

The general structure of the CASE command is:

```
DO CASE
   CASE condition1
         ...commands1...
   CASE condition2
         ...commands2...
   ...
   etcetera
   ...
   OTHERWISE
         ...commands...
ENDCASE
```

dBASE imposes no restrictions on the number of CASE
conditions and command blocks. The conditions are
evaluated in the order of sequence in which they are
registered in the program. The first value having the
value .T. leads to the corresponding command block
being executed. Then the program continues further
with the first command after ENDCASE. The other valid
cases, if any, remain untouched.

The CASE command makes it easy to write a program
with a menu. The examples below illustrate this.

Example 1:

The program CASEDEM1 will be created to allow you
to activate one of the programs YESNO1, YESNO3 or
YESNO4 according to your requirements. We have already dealt with these program earlier in this section.
They should be located on the same diskette or in the
same directory of the harddisk as CASEDEM1.

An external program is activated from a program by

means of the DO command:

```
DO program name [WITH parameter list]
```

We shall not yet use the WITH option in the example. We shall return to the topic of programming with modules and procedures in section 9.7.

To prevent the program returning to the command mode each time it has implemented a choice, we shall include the entire menu structure in a DO WHILE loop.

The program listing is as follows:

```
* Program CASEDEM1.PRG *
SET TALK OFF
DO WHILE .T.                                    (1)
   CLEAR
   choice = 0                                   (2)
   @ 03,10 SAY "CASE demo"                      (3)
   @ 04,10 SAY "========="
   @ 07,10 SAY "Program YESNO1    1"
   @ 09,10 SAY "Program YESNO3    2"
   @ 11,10 SAY "Program YESNO4    3"
   @ 15,10 SAY "Selection:"
   @ 15,30 GET choice PICTURE "9"               (4)
   READ
   DO CASE                                      (5)
      CASE choice = 1
         DO yesno1
         WAIT
      CASE choice = 2
         DO yesno3
         WAIT
      CASE choice = 3
         DO yesno4
         WAIT
      OTHERWISE                                 (6)
         RETURN
   ENDCASE
ENDDO
* End CASEDEM1.PRG *
```

(1) Beginning of the perpetual loop which is discontin-
     ued at (6) by a character other than specified in the
     menu.

(2) Initializes the CHOICE menu variable with the num-
     ber 0.

(3) Displays the menu texts.

(4) Input command for the CHOICE number of the se-
     lected menu option.

(5) If the contents of CHOICE conform to one of the
     tested cases, the program is executed which is ac-
     tivated by DO. The program then pauses until a
     random key is pressed, and it then continues with
     the command after ENDCASE: back to the begin-
     ning of the loop with ENDDO.

(6) If a key is pressed other than 1, 2 or 3, the program
     returns to the level prior to the activation (command
     mode, Control Center) by means of the command
     OTHERWISE RETURN.

     If you remove these instructions from the program,
     the program will remain perpetually in the main
     loop. You can then only return to the command
     mode using Esc in one of the activated programs.
     Instead of this, you can also define a menu option
     in order to end the program: CASE choice = 0 with
     RETURN as the command.

Example 2:

In extensive programs, a program structure with a loop
made up of CASE commands will not be enough. In
order to have a structure with submenus, nested CASE
loops will be necessary.

The program CASEDEM2 will be created to activate
one of the programs ALTER or DEL, as required. We
dealt with these programs earlier in this section. The

main loop of the program is a perpetual loop; the inner loop is controlled by the specified alphanumeric character in CHOICE (choice$"3456789") by means of the $ substring. The CHOICE variable is initialized with "9"; we can limit the number of valid characters for CHOICE by means of a template.

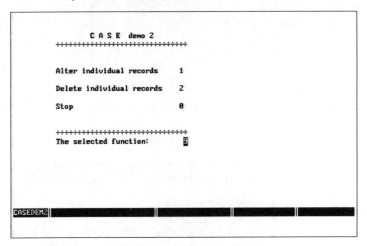

The program listing is as follows:

```
* Program CASEDEM2.PRG *
SET TALK OFF                                            (1)
CLEAR ALL
DO WHILE .T.                                            (2)
   CLEAR                                                (3)
   choice = "9"
   DO WHILE choice$"3456789"                            (4)
      @ 02,10 SAY "      C A S E  demo 2"               (5)
      @ 03,10 SAY "-----------------------------"
      @ 06,10 SAY "Alter individual records     1"
      @ 08,10 SAY "Delete individual records    2"
      @ 10,10 SAY "Stop                         0"
      @ 13,10 SAY "-----------------------------"
      @ 14,10 SAY "The selected function:"
      @ 14,40 GET choice PICTURE "9"                    (6)
      READ
```

```
      DO CASE                                          (7)
         CASE choice = "0"
            SET TALK ON
            RETURN
         CASE choice = "1"
            DO alter
            WAIT
         CASE choice = "2"
            DO del
            WAIT
      ENDCASE
      choice = "9"                                     (8)
      CLEAR
   ENDDO
ENDDO
* End CASEDEM2.PRG *
```

(1) Sets the work environment, deletes memory vari-
     ables and closes opened files. Add, if necessary:

     ■ other SET commands,
     ■ initializations of other variables,
     ■ a load command using RESTORE for variables
       which have been stored to a disk file using
       SAVE.

(2) Beginning of the perpetual outer loop. This loop is
     discontinued by RETURN after input of the number
     0.

(3) Clears the screen.
     Since the condition in the inner loop contains the
     CHOICE variable, this must already contain a value
     which occurs in the string of valid values in front of
     the DO WHILE loop, otherwise the program will not
     enter this loop. Use letters instead of numbers if the
     menu contains more than ten options.

(4) Beginning of the inner loop.

(5) Displays the menu texts. Instead of @-SAY, you
     can also display text using ?. In this case, include

leading spaces in the texts if you wish to have a margin. You can embellish the menu appearance using a frame or ornation and colours (SET COLOUR TO). You can make a program more compact by storing a block of @-SAY commands as an independent formatting program and activating it using the DO name.fmt command.

(6) Writes the specified character to the CHOICE variable. You can also do this using the commands ACCEPT, INPUT or using the INKEY() function.
The specified character has the following effect:

0:	ends the CASEDEM2 program.
1 or 2:	activates the program specified with the CASE command. When that program has ended, CASEDEM2 is continued.
One of the numbers in the string "3456789":	the CHOICE$"3456789" condition remains true and the program remains in the inner loop.
A random key:	the CHOICE$"3456789" condition is no longer true and the program leaves the inner loop. Since there has been no command to discontinue the main program, this continues with the assignation CHOICE=9 and returns with this value to back to the inner loop via the outer loop. The menu is again displayed on the screen.

(7) The selection options. Instead of RETURN, you can also use QUIT and CANCEL. See section 9.4 for the differences between these.

(8) Assigns a value which is valid for the execution of the inner loop to the CHOICE variable.
Clears the screen for a new start.

9.7 Programs with modules

Procedures

A program which is activated by another program is called a procedure (sometimes a routine or subroutine). The summoning program is called the main program. In the previous section, we have used the main program CASEDEM2 to handle the previously constructed programs ALTER and DEL as procedures by activating them using DO procedure name.

This kind of activation has to load the program in computer working memory first before the procedure can be executed. Loading often takes longer than the time required to execute the procedure. If a main program activates diverse procedures, the loading time can easily be more time-consuming than the calculation time for the main program as a whole.

9.7.1 Procedure files

In dBASE IV, you can gather a maximum of 1170 procedures in one procedure file. All these procedures are loaded in computer working memory in one go, and they remain available until you close the procedure file or switch off the computer. We presume that the RAM capacity is sufficient.

A procedure which is activated no longer needs to be loaded. This gains time.

A procedure file is written in the same way as a normal program is written in the dBASE word processor or in another editor or word processor. In the procedure file, each procedure is located between the commands PROCEDURE and RETURN.

```
PROCEDURE procedure name
    ...commands...
RETURN
```

A procedure file is loaded and closed from the main program using the commands:

```
SET PROCEDURE TO procedure file name
CLOSE PROCEDURE
```

Instead of giving the CLOSE command, you can also
give the command SET PROCEDURE TO, without
specifying a file name.

Within the main menu, a specific procedure is activated
in the normal way using DO procedure name.

```
DO procedure name
```

Example:

We shall change the CASEDEM2.PRG program into a
main program for address management functions with
the name ADMNGFUN.PRG. We shall fill the ADMG-
PROC.PRG procedure file with the ALTER.PRG and
DEL.PRG programs as procedures. If you have already
written these programs, it is very easy to make the
necessary alterations:

1 Open the program word processor using the command:

   ```
   MODIFY COMMAND admngfun
   ```

2 Load the text of the CASEDEM2 program in the
   empty work field using the menu option Alt-L, M
   (Modify a different program). Type the name
   CASEDEM2 in the dialog box behind the prompt
   'Enter a program to modify'. This program is now
   registered in the status line as the current file.

3 Change the comment lines and the appearance of
   the menu according to the listing given below.

4 Add the rows which refer to the opening and closing of the ADMGPROC procedure file.

5   Save the program under the proper name using Alt-L, S.

Go to work in the same way to create the procedure file.

The program listing is as follows:

```
* Program ADMNGFUN.PRG *
SET TALK OFF
CLEAR ALL
SET PROCEDURE TO admgproc                           (1)
DO WHILE .T.
   CLEAR
   choice = "9"
   DO WHILE choice$"3456789"
      @ 02,10 SAY "        C A S E   demo 2"
      @ 03,10 SAY "-----------------------------"
      @ 06,10 SAY "Alter individual records      1"
      @ 08,10 SAY "Delete individual records     2"
      @ 10,10 SAY "Stop                          0"
      @ 13,10 SAY "-----------------------------"
      @ 14,10 SAY "The selected function:"
      @ 14,40 GET choice PICTURE "9"
      READ
      DO CASE
         CASE choice = "0"
            SET TALK ON
            CLOSE PROCEDURE                          (2)
            RETURN
         CASE choice = "1"
            DO alter                                 (3)
            WAIT
         CASE choice = "2"
            DO del                                   (4)
            WAIT
      ENDCASE
      choice = "9"
      CLEAR
   ENDDO
ENDDO
* End ADMNGFUN.PRG *
```

The listing of the procedure file is as follows:

```
*** Procedure file ADMGPROC.PRG ***
* Procedure ALTER.PRG *
PROCEDURE alter                                              (5)
CLEAR
CLEAR ALL
USE address ORDER nameidx

sname = "                    "
@ 18,10 SAY "Name? : " GET sname PICTURE "XXXXXXXXXXXXXXX"
READ

SEEK sname
IF .NOT. FOUND()
   CLEAR
   @ 20,10 SAY "No record found to edit"
ELSE
   EDIT
ENDIF
* End procedure ALTER.PRG *

* ----------------- *

* Procedure DEL.PRG *
PROCEDURE del                                                (6)
CLEAR
CLEAR ALL
USE address ORDER nameidx

sname = "                    "
@ 18,10 SAY "Name? : " GET sname PICTURE "XXXXXXXXXXXXXXX"
READ

SEEK sname
IF FOUND()
   DELETE
   EDIT FOR sname = name
         ELSE
             CLEAR
             @ 20,10 SAY "No record for deletion"
         ENDIF
CLEAR
```

```
PACK
* End procedure DEL.PRG *
*** End procedure file ADMGPROC.PRG ***
```

(1) Opens the procedure file ADMGPROC.PRG.

(2) Closes the procedure file ADMGPROC.PRG.

(3) Activates the ALTER program which is located in
the procedure file.

(4) Activates the DEL program which is located in the
procedure file.

(5) and (6)   The order of sequences of the procedures
in the procedure file is not important. The
procedures always have the PROCE-
DURE command as the first command and
RETURN as the last.

9.7.2   Procedures with parameters

Instead of a procedure looking for and loading the data
itself, it is also possible to program the procedure in
such a way that it receives data as in the form of arguments when it is activated from the main program.
These data, the *parameters*, are placed behind the
WITH option in a DO command with a procedure name:

```
DO procedure name WITH parameter list
```

In the procedure, the parameters are defined by giving
the command PARAMETERS followed by a parameter
list:

```
PARAMETERS parameter list
```

The *names* of the variables in the two parameter lists do
not need to be identical, but the data do have to be in
the same *order of sequence*. In the procedure the
PARAMETERS command must always be the first
command.

Example:

We shall activate a procedure called PARADEM.PRG
from the main program DOWITH.PRG. During the activation, the date of birth of one of the wine-tasting club
members and the current system date is passed on to
the procedure. The procedure then calculates the age
of that member and returns this value to the main program. For this reason, the interface contains a return
parameter:

main program   WITH bth_date, DATE(), years

procedure   PARAMETERS bd, now, years

The BTH_DATE variable is a field from the ADDRESS
file; within the procedure, this value is used under the
name BD. The DATE() function requests the date in the
main program and transfers it to the procedure under
the name NOW. The difference between these data is
called YEARS in the procedure, and under this name
the age is passed on to the main program. Since we do
not know if the system clock was accurate when the
computer was started up, the program first asks the current date.

```
. do dowith


Current date is Thu 27/05/1993
Enter new date (dd-mm-yy):

   Rayleigh       01/01/42 27/05/93        51
   Sklodouska     02/02/67 27/05/93        26
   Bragg          03/03/62 27/05/93        31
   Rutherford     04/04/71 27/05/93        22
   Todd           07/07/07 27/05/93        86
   Sanger         05/05/18 27/05/93        75
   Hodgkin        10/10/10 27/05/93        83
   Ross           06/06/52 27/05/93        41
   Macloud        07/06/76 27/05/93        17
   McClintock     02/02/02 27/05/93        91
   Deledda        17/01/71 27/05/93        22
.
Command   C:\work\ADDRESS            Rec EOF/11      File
```

The main program listing is as follows:

```
* Main program DOWITH.PRG *
SET TALK OFF
SET HEADING OFF
RUN DATE                                            (1)
years = CTOD("         ")                           (2)
USE address
DO WHILE .NOT. EOF()
   DO A:\paramdem WITH bth_date, DATE(), years      (3)
   DISPLAY name, bth_date, DATE(), years OFF        (4)
   SKIP
ENDDO
* End main program DOWITH.PRG *


The PARADEM procedure listing is as follows:

* Procedure PARAMDEM.PRG *
PARAMETERS bd, now, years                           (5)
years = YEAR(now) - YEAR(bd)                        (6)
RETURN
* End procedure PARAMDEM.PRG *
```

The first time that you implement DOWITH.PRG, dBASE IV converts this to an object file with the extension .DBO. The .PRG source file is compiled.

(1) The RUN command executes a DOS program. The DOS program, DATE, requests a new value for the system date. In the case of computers with a clock powered by a battery, this command is superfluous; if you nevertheless include it in the list, you only have to press Enter to confirm the current value.

(2) Declares the YEARS memory variable with an initial value. Otherwise the DO command will give an error message that this value cannot be found.
It seems logical to reserve eight positions for the result of a calculation using converted date fields.
In the first runthrough of the loop, the YEARS variable has the length of the initialization value: a date

field which is created by the conversion of eight
spaces. dBASE IV normally reserves a field of ten
spaces for unformatted numeric output. In all subsequent cases, dBASE IV adjusts the type and
length of the loop to the current value of the YEARS
numeric variable. That is the age of the member in
the previous record given in the current format: a
total of ten numbers, a pre-sign, decimal point etc.
There are two solutions to this problem:

rough-and-ready: extend the initial value of
                  YEARS to ten spaces

more elegant: initialize YEARS with the num-
                  ber 00 and define an output
                  template with two numbers
                  (PICTURE "99") for YEARS.

(3) Activates the PARAMDEM procedure with parame-
    ters. Include the search path to the file in the com-
    mand, unless the file is located in the default
    directory. The first time you use the program,
    dBASE automatically regulates the compilation of
    the procedure file.

(4) Displays the contents of the specified variables.
    The OFF option suppresses the record numbers.

(5) The procedure parameter list. This is always the
    first command in the procedure.

(6) Calculates the difference between the year in the
    current date and that in the date of birth. The
    YEAR() function isolates the year in a date; the
    function value is numeric.
    The answer is not correct if the current month is
    prior to the month of birth (e.g. it is now May and
    the member was born in June). Write the following
    commands in the procedure after the calculation:

```
IF MONTH(now) < MONTH(bd)
   years = years - 1
ENDIF
```

9.7.3   Error procedure with the error number as parameter

It may occur that, using a program, you open a file which is already open. dBASE then displays an error message in a dialog box: 'File already open'. This message has the internal number 3 . Normally, you would have to discontinue the program, close the file in question and restart the program.

Using an error procedure, you can automize these actions within a program. Three commands are applied in this process. We shall illustrate these by means of an excerpt from a fictional program:

```
ON ERROR command
ERROR()
RETRY
```

The listing of the main program which caused the error is as follows:

```
* Program FMAIN.PRG *
ON ERROR DO err_proc                        (1)
USE file                                    (2)
...
* End FMAIN.PRG *
```

The error procedure contains a reaction to just one mistake:

```
* Procedure ERR_PROC.PRG *
IF ERROR() = 3                              (3)
   CLOSE DATABASES                          (4)
ENDIF
RETRY                                       (5)
* End procedure FPROC.PRG *
```

(1) The ON ERROR command only executes the command behind it if a dBASE syntactical error has occurred.

(2) Opens the file. If this should cause an error message, this is dealt with in the example program by the ERR_PROC procedure.

(3) Checks the value of the ERROR() function. If this is the number of the invalid attempt to open a file a second time, the loop is implemented.

(4) Closes *all* opened data files and the files belonging to these (index, memo and format files). Accordingly, this command also closes files which are not related to the error message.

(5) The RETRY command returns the control to the command in the main program which caused the blockage. This command is executed once more, but with closed files this time. In addition, RETRY resets the function value of ERROR() to 0.

9.8   Saving memory variables

Files containing variables
The values of variables which are not dependent on data in a file can be saved for use at a later date. dBASE has files with the extension .MEM (memory files) for this type of data.

9.8.1   Saving memory variables

The SAVE command saves all, or a specified part, of memory variables:

```
SAVE TO mem_file
     [ALL {LIKE | EXCEPT} template]
```

If the ALL LIKE or ALL EXCEPT options are not specified, the command writes the values of all memory variables to the file MEM_FILE.

The ALL LIKE option means that only those variables which conform to a specified pattern are saved.

The ALL EXCEPT option means that all variables are saved except those which conform to a specified pattern.

The wildcards ? and * are valid in the pattern.

Example:

Imagine that three variables receive a value:

```
. value  = 100
. number = 200
. name   = "string"
```

Transfer the survey of the system memory contents to a file by means of the command:

```
LIST MEMORY TO FILE mem.fil
```

The contents of the MEM.FIL (this is a random name) are identical to the list produced on the screen using LIST MEMORY.

Use the DISPLAY command if the list is too lengthy to fit on the screen:

```
        User Memory Variables

NAME      pub  C  "string"
NUMBER    pub  N        200  (200.000000000000000)
VALUE     pub  N        100  (100.000000000000000)

   3 out of 500 memvars defined (and 0 array elements)


        User MEMVAR/RTSYM Memory Usage

  2800 bytes used for 1 memvar blocks (max=10)
  1700 bytes used for 1 rtsym blocks (max=10)
     0 bytes used for 0 array element memvars
     6 bytes used for 1 memvar character strings

  4506 bytes total

        Print System Memory Variables

_BOX      pub  L  .T.
Press any key to continue...
Command
```

In memory, there are three PUBLIC variables, two of which are numeric (N) and one alphanumeric (C).

We shall save the variables in the VARSAVE.MEM file using the command:

```
SAVE TO varsave
```

In contrast to the display produced by the command LIST/DISPLAY MEMORY, the memory file only contains the variables which you initialized. The contents of the file are not directly legible: check these using the command MODIFY COMMAND varsave.mem.

Finally, we shall give three examples of patterns for the names of the memory variables.

```
SAVE ALL LIKE e* TO emem
```
Saves all variables of which the names begin with the letter E.

```
SAVE ALL LIKE ???r TO remem
```
Saves all variables of which the name consists of four letters, the last letter being an r.

```
SAVE ALL EXCEPT ??n* TO nmem
```
Saves all variables, except those of which the name has an n as the third letter.

9.8.2 Loading memory variables

The values of the variables which are stored in a .MEM file, can be loaded into memory using the RESTORE command.

```
RESTORE FROM mem_file [ADDITIVE]
```

The ADDITIVE option means that the variables which are to be loaded should not overwrite the current memory variables, but should be added.

Example:

Load the variables which we saved in the beginning of
this section in the VARSAVE.MEM file:

```
RESTORE FROM varsave
```

Display the contents of the memory using DISPLAY
MEMORY. The display is identical to that produced by
the same command in the previous part.

In the following example, we shall initialize the NEW
variable and request its value after we have loaded the
variables in the VARSAVE.MEM file. We shall do this
once with the ADDITIVE option and once without.

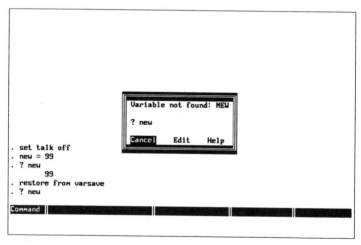

(1) Initializes a new memory variable.

(2) Requests the value of the variable.

(3) Loads the variables which were stored in the VAR-
SAVE.MEM file; they overwrite the current memory
variables.

(4) The NUMBER variable is no longer available and

the execution command causes an error message in a dialog box.

Repeat the series of commands, but now load the stored variables along with the ADDITIVE option. The execution command referring to NUMBER will not now cause an error message.

9.9 Commands and programs for printer output

In this section, we shall discuss all commands required to display data using the printer. In addition, we shall present a number of programs which enable you to shape data file display lists.

9.9.1 Printer protocol

It is often convenient, or even necessary, to see input and output not only on the screen but also in a more permanent form on paper. The SET PRINTER command activates or deactivates the printer. If the switch is set to ON, dBASE sends all output not only to the screen but also to the printer:

```
SET PRINTER ON/OFF
```

The command has no effect upon data which are entered or displayed by means of commands like APPEND, EDIT or BROWSE.

Reserved words in dBASE may be abbreviated to at least the first four letters. This command is generally shortened to SET PRINT. OFF is the default setting.

Instead of the typed command, you may also press the key combination Ctrl-P. Repeat this to deactivate the printer once more.

9.9.2   Protocol file

You can also save the input and output in the interactive (command) mode as text, in a protocol file. In this case also, the input and output in the page-oriented commands is not taken into account. Open a protocol file using the command SET ALTERNATE:

```
SET ALTERNATE TO protocol file name
```

Activate the defined protocol file using:

```
SET ALTERNATE ON/OFF
```

The protocol is written to the file with the specified name only when you have closed the protocol file. This can be done in two ways:

```
CLOSE ALTERNATE
SET ALTERNATE TO
```

9.9.3   Printer operation

The computer sends the data to the printer in the form of ASCII codes. The operating codes for the printer are also ASCII codes. If you know the decimal code of a control character for the printer, you can send this to the printer as an alphanumeric character in a string, using the conversion function:

```
CHR(code)
```

The decimal values of the ASCII codes lie between 0 and 255. Characters with codes between 32 and 126 represent the normal printable characters. Characters with codes between 0 and 31, and character number 127 are control characters. Control characters produce, for instance, a new line, a new page, a different font, larger or smaller print etc. on the printer.

Characters above 127 are not internationally standardized. The definition of these characters, thus, may differ according to the computer and the printer.

The examples shown below are valid for most printers. Consult the manual if the result turns out differently than described here.

Example 1:

This example is aimed at an Epson printer or a printer which is compatible with this norm. The printer first runs the paper through to a fresh sheet and then switches the printer to 72 lines per page with condensed print.

The listing for the program is as follows:

```
* Program PCONTRL.PRG *
SET PRINT ON                          (1)
? CHR(12)                             (2)
? CHR(13)                             (3)
? CHR(27)+CHR(67)+CHR(72)             (4)
? CHR(15)                             (5)
SET PRINT OFF                         (6)
* End PCONTRL.PRG *
```

(1) Activates the printer.

(2) Moves to the beginning of a new page (Form Feed).

(3) Moves to the beginning of the current line (Carriage Return) and to a new line (Line Feed).

(4) A combination of characters which begins with CHR(27) is called an escape sequence, because of the first character in the series.
The combination Esc, C, number defines the NUMBER of lines of text per page.

(5) Sets the printer to condensed print: 17 characters per inch (17 cpi).

(6) Sets the printer *off line*.

In the Control Center, you regulate the printer operation by first
opening either of the panels *Reports* or *Labels*. Then select *Print,
Control of Printer*.

Option	Significance
Text pitch	letter width
Quality print	print resolution
New page	new page before/after the report
Wait between pages	convenient if you use single sheet paper
Advance page using	select line feed or form feed
Starting control codes	enter printer control codes to alter style of print
Ending control codes	enter codes to turn off the print style

9.9.4 Displaying the contents of the screen on the printer

In dBASE, you can send the contents of the screen to
the printer. This demands two consecutive key combinations:

```
Shift-PrtSc
Ctrl-PrtSc
```

9.9.5 Output to the printer using the TO PRINT option

The LIST, DISPLAY, REPORT and LABEL commands
transfer the output to the printer by means of the option:

```
TO PRINT
```

The output does not then appear on the screen.

In the Control Center, many menus contain an option for transferring data to the printer.

9.9.6   Output to the printer using @-SAY

You can send formatted output from a program to the printer, to a file or to the screen by altering the default output device. Then give the command @ row,column SAY:

```
SET DEVICE TO PRINT
SET DEVICE TO FILE bestandsnaam
SET DEVICE TO SCREEN
```

In the Control Center, you can choose the data destination using *Reports* or *Labels* and then selecting *Print, Destination* (either with or without echo on the screen). The *Print* menu is not available in all panels.

Example programs which send records to the printer

In the Control Center, you can work out the examples shown below using the *Reports* panel. The survey generator works with the current data file, the current view filter or the current view file. The generator opens a screen providing seven menus and a work area which normally consists of five zones:

■ Header Band
■ Intro Band
■ Detail Band (data)
■ Summary Band
■ Footer Band

dBASE IV provides the possibility for a default layout of the report according to three models (via *Layout, Quick Layouts*):

Column layout	display the fields adjacent to one another, comparable to example 2;
Form layout	display of the record as a form (fields under each other);
Mailmerge layout	placing varying fields in a standard text (per record).

We refer you to section 9.11 for more extensive information concerning the survey generator.

Example 2:

In this example, we shall use the ADDRESS file with an index on the NAME field in addition to the CONTR and SEX fields:

```
INDEX ON sex+STR(contr,6,2)+name TO scnidx
```

From all records we wish to see on paper the contents of the following fields: MEMBERNR, NAME, FIRST_NAME, PCTOWN, C_STATUS, SEX, CONTR and RED.

The listing of the program is as follows:

```
* Program LISTPRN.PRG *
SET TALK OFF
CLEAR ALL                                              (1)
USE address INDEX scnidx
SET DEVICE TO PRINT                                    (2)
r = 0                                                  (3)
GO TOP                                                 (4)
DO WHILE .NOT. EOF()
   r = r + 1                                           (5)
   @ r,01 SAY membernr PICTURE "999"                   (6)
   @ r,05 SAY name PICTURE "XXXXXXXXXXXXXXX"
   @ r,21 SAY first_name PICTURE "XXXXXXXXXXXXXXX"
```

```
@ r,37 SAY pctown PICTURE "XXXXXXXXXXXXXXXXXXXXX"
@ r,58 SAY c_status PICTURE "A"
@ r,63 SAY sex PICTURE "A"
@ r,66 SAY contr PICTURE "@Z 999.99"
@ r,73 SAY red
   SKIP                                                           (7)
ENDDO
r = r + 1
@ r,0 SAY " "                                                     (8)
SET DEVICE TO SCREEN                                              (9)
SET TALK ON
RETURN
* End LISTPRN.PRG *
```

(1) Closes the opened files.

(2) Activates the printer for the output commands @ row,column SAY.

(3) The r variable places the output on a new row in a loop for each record. Prior to the loop, r is initialized with 0. The value increases by one at each run-through.

(4) The GO TOP and GO BOTTOM commands can also be used in an index file.

(5) Increases the r variable by 1 at the first output line. At the beginning of each runthrough of the loop, the output cursor is moved to the next line.

(6) The output commands.

(7) Places the record pointer at the following record (in the index file).

(8) Produces a blank line: this subsequent line feed ensures printing of the last record.

(9) Reconstructs the work environment.

In the survey generator, use the menu option *Fields, Add field* to place the required fields in the *Detail Band* at the current cursor position. Select one or more of the following possibilities in the survey:

■ a field from the data file,
■ use <create> to define an expression, a template etc. for a new calculated field,
■ a predefined field: current date and time, record number, page number,
■ a summary field for the current field (average, number of records etc.).

When you have designed the survey to your requirements, save the report file using the menu options *Layout, Save this report* (extension .FRG).

Now write a procedure file yourself, with the name RE-COUT, for the output commands of LISTPRN.PRG. This makes the output program more orderly.

Example 3:

Extend the output commands by adding a header above the list:

```
MEMBER Name First Name Town C_St MF Contr
   Red
```

Write the commands for this in the HEAD1.PRG procedure and extend LISTPRN later by activating this procedure (example 4).

The procedure listing is as follows:

```
* Procedure HEAD1.PRG *
r = 1                                    (1)
@ r,01 SAY "MEM"                         (2)
@ r,05 SAY "Name"
@ r,21 SAY "First Name"
```

```
@ r,37 SAY "Town"
@ r,58 SAY "C_St"
@ r,63 SAY "MF"
@ r,66 SAY "Contr"
@ r,73 SAY "Red"
r = r + 1                                    (3)
c = 1                                        (4)
DO WHILE c < 78                              (5)
   @ r,c SAY "_"
   c = c + 1
ENDDO
* End procedure HEAD1.PRG *
```

(1) Initializes the row number for the header with 1.

(2) Output commands.
     The positioning in columns can also be done rela-
     tively if you know the space between the columns.
     The PCOL() function displays the current position
     of the output cursor. For each subsequent output,
     the cursor is positioned in such a way that the col-
     umn heading is placed neatly above the field. The
     output commands are then as follows:

```
@ r,01          SAY "MEMBER"
@ r,PCOL() + 1  SAY "Name"
@ r,PCOL() + 11 SAY "First Name"
@ r,PCOL() + 7  SAY "Town"
@ r,PCOL() + 14 SAY "C_St"
@ r,PCOL() + 1  SAY "MF"
@ r,PCOL() + 1  SAY "Contr"
@ r,PCOL() + 2  SAY "Red"
```

In some columns the heading is longer than the
field, in some cases this is vice versa. It is sensible
to have the column numbers in the LISTPRN and
HEAD1.PRG output commands coincide by first
placing the headings and field lengths on paper.

In the survey generator, you can easily write the headings at the
required position in the *Header Band*.

(3) Increases the row counter by 1. Continue on row 2. Instead of increasing row number r in the output loop, you can also make use of the current row number in the PROW() function.

(4) Declares and initializes a column counter for the output loop in (5).

(5) The DO-WHILE loop produces underlining over a width of 72 screen positions. Printing using a loop like this is time-consuming. It can be done much more quickly using the command @ r,1 SAY "____...____". You may write this stripe as a full string, divided over two rows, if required, using the semi-colon (;). A more orderly manner is to give a command using the REPLICATE() function: @ r,1 SAY REPLICATE("_",72).

In the survey generator, type the underlining across the same width as the heading in the *Header Band*.

Example 4:

We shall round off the LISTPRN1 program which uses procedures to display the previously-mentioned data from the ADDRESS file under the header in HEAD1.

A new page
There is a special command to instruct the printer to continue on a new page:

```
EJECT
```

Note: Ensure that your printer is set to the proper page length, otherwise the output will begin at the wrong place on the new page.

In the example we wish the output to continue on a new page when:

■ the row counter is at 66,
■ the contents of the SEX field switches from "m" to "f",
■ the contents of the contribution field changes.

We shall formulate the first demand using a condition:

```
IF r > 66
    EJECT
ENDIF
```

In the case of an extensive address file, containing an output of two pages or more, r will have to begin counting again on a new page: r=r-66.

In the Control Center, the page length is defined by means of the menu option *Print, Page dimensions, Length of page*.

A change of field contents is evident from the difference between the previous and the current value. Accordingly, we declare two variables in which the current field contents are stored in order to compare them with the new value in the following loop: MF_OLD and CONTR_OLD. The values which the SEX and CONTR fields had in the previous record are stored here.

All conditions can be combined using the .OR. logical operator into one condition.

```
IF r > 66 .OR. sex <> mf_old .OR. contr <> contr_old
    EJECT
    r = r - 66
    DO head1
ENDIF
```

After all the modifications discussed above, the listing is now as follows:

```
* Program LISTPRN1.PRG *
SET TALK OFF
CLEAR ALL
```

```
USE address INDEX scnidx
SET DEVICE TO PRINT
r = 0
mf_old = sex                                                    (1)
contr_old = contr
DO head1                                                        (2)
GO 1
DO WHILE .NOT. EOF()
   IF r > 66 .OR. sex <> mf_old .OR. contr <> contr_old (3)
      EJECT
      r = r - 66
      DO head1
   ENDIF
   r = r + 1
   DO recout                                                    (4)
   mf_old = sex                                                 (5)
   contr_oud = contr
   SKIP
ENDDO
r = r + 1
@ r,0 SAY " "
SET DEVICE TO SCREEN
SET TALK ON
RETURN
* End LISTPRN1.PRG *
```

(1) Initializes the MF_OLD and CONTR_OLD variables with the contents of the SEX and CONTR fields (in the first record).

(2) Prints the heading with the underlining.

(3) Checks whether the condition for a new page has been fulfilled. If so, the EJECT command sends a control code to the printer. The new page begins with the header and the counter begins anew.

(4) The RECOUT procedure displays the various fields according to the output commands in LISTPRN (see example 2 in this section).

(5) In each runthrough of the main loop, the current

values of SEX and CONTR are stored in the help variables MF_OLD and CONTR_OLD in order to make a comparison with the values in the following record.

In the Control Center, the condition for a new page after a field change is created by adding a group zone for each feature. This is done using the menu option *Bands, Add a group band, Field value* while the cursor is located in the Intro band. Create group zones for the SEX and CONTR fields.

Example 5:

The following extension of LISTPRN1 consists of adding up the values in the CONTR field for each page, and showing the total of all contributions at the end of the report. For this, we shall declare two new memory variables for the interim results of the sum: INTERIM-SUM and TOTALSUM.

The listing for the program is as follows:

```
* Program LISTPRN2.PRG *
SET TALK OFF
CLEAR ALL
USE address INDEX scnidx
SET DEVICE TO PRINT
r = 0
interimsum = 0                                            (1)
totalsum = 0
mf_old = sex
contr_old = contr
DO head1
GO 1
DO WHILE .NOT. EOF()
   IF r > 66 .OR. sex <> mf_old .OR. contr <> contr_old
      IF sex <> mf_old .OR. contr <> contr_old          (2)
         r = r + 2
         @ r,67 SAY interimsum PICTURE "999.99"         (3)
         interimsum = 0
```

```
      ENDIF
      EJECT
      r = r - 66
      DO head1
   ENDIF
   r = r + 1
   DO recout
   interimsum = interimsum + contr
   (4)
   totalsum = totalsum + contr
   mf_old = sex
   contr_old = contr
   SKIP
ENDDO
r = r + 2
@ r,67 SAY interimsum PICTURE "999.99"                    (5)
r = r + 2
@ r,67 SAY totalsum PICTURE "999.99"
r = r + 1
@ r,0 SAY " "
SET DEVICE TO SCREEN
SET TALK ON
RETURN
* End LISTPRN2.PRG *
```

      (1) Initializes the two memory variables for adding up the contributions.

      (2) The contents of INTERIMSUM are printed at the bottom of the page, before the new page. This does not happen if the new page appears because the previous one is full (r = 66).
At the end of a group of records, INTERIMSUM receives the value 0 in order to be able to count the contributions of the following group.

      (3) Displays the value of INTERIMSUM according to a template. If you omit the formatting option, dBASE IV displays whole numbers without decimal zeroes: the column is no longer aligned. We shall reserve one position more for the summed values than in the CONTR field.

(4) These two commands calculate the interim results.

(5) At the end of the file, there is no switch of field contents: the INTERIMSUM for the last group must be calculated before the total sum.

Since the zones (group bands) which you created in the previous example have their own subtotal zone *Group x Intro Band*, you only need to define a sum field using *Fields, Add fields* when the cursor is at the appropriate position. Select *Sum* from the list of functions in the fourth column and define the new field by assigning a meaningful name, a description, the function (already specified), the field in which the summary is to be placed and the position in the report where the summary should come.

The formatting functions for the appearance of the field are shown under the line in the *Add field* submenu.

Example 6:

By means of a program we wish to make a selection from the records which is dependent upon the members swilling RED and those sipping WHITE. Any other members have been working for at least three years since completing their exams and have the 'gourmand' status. They belong to neither RED or WHITE. The directors belong, of course, to the gourmand group. Since there are no records in which the fields RED and WHITE both contain a logical NO, we will first change the RED field in the records of Mr Rutherford and Mr Todd into NO.

The selection on the input screen appears as follows:

```
Select a category:
          red               1
          white             2
          gourmand          3
```

The program selects the records using a filter.

```
SET FILTER TO red
SET FILTER TO white
SET FILTER TO (.NOT. red) .AND. (.NOT. white)
```

The listing for the program is as follows:

```
* Program SELECT1.PRG *
SET TALK OFF
SET DEVICE TO SCREEN
CLEAR ALL
r = 0
cat = 0                                                    (1)
CLEAR
@ 3,20 SAY "Select a category:"                            (2)
@ 5,20 SAY "red                  1"
@ 6,20 SAY "white                2"
@ 7,20 SAY "gourmand             3"
@ 8,20 SAY "Your choice: "
@ 8,37 GET cat PICTURE "9" RANGE 1,3
READ
USE address
DO CASE                                                    (3)
   CASE cat = 1
      SET FILTER TO red
   CASE cat = 2
      SET FILTER TO white
   CASE cat = 3
      SET FILTER TO (.NOT. red) .AND. (.NOT. white)
ENDCASE
GO TOP
SET DEVICE TO PRINT
DO head1
DO WHILE .NOT. EOF()                                       (4)
   r = r + 1
   DO recout
   SKIP
ENDDO
r = r + 1
@ r,0 SAY " "
SET DEVICE TO SCREEN
SET TALK ON
RETURN
```

```
* End SELECT1.PRG *
```

(1) Initializes the CAT memory variable for the category selection.

(2) The output commands for the input template with a choice for the selection from the membership file.

(3) Branch to the filter of the selected option.

(4) Ouput of the selected records to the printer.

In the Control Center, a survey of the selection is made, not by using the source file itself, but by using view filter in the Queries panel. We have already made a view filter in chapter 5 for the members who live in Cambridge.

Highlight <create> and make view filters according to the three definitions used above. Type the selection condition in the *Condition box*.

Make the survey using the report file which you programmed in the previous example.

Using the application generator you can create a program to display processes via a self-made menu (see section 9.10).

Example 7:

The SELECT2 program will make a selection based on three criteria: the category, the civil status and the sex. This only requires extending the variables in the filter conditions:

```
SET FILTER TO red .AND. sex = LOWER(sx)
                  .AND. c_status =
   LOWER(cs)
```

The SX variable contains the specified letter for the sex, and CS contains the letter for the civil status (married, single, divorced).

The listing for the program is as follows:

```
* Program SELECT2.PRG *
SET TALK OFF
SET DEVICE TO SCREEN
CLEAR ALL
r = 0
cat = 1
sx = SPACE(1)                                               (1)
cs = SPACE(1)
CLEAR
@ 3,20 SAY "Select a category:"                             (2)
@ 5,20 SAY "red              1"
@ 6,20 SAY "white            2"
@ 7,20 SAY "gourmand         3"
@ 8,20 SAY "Your choice: "
@ 8,37 GET cat PICTURE "9" RANGE 1,3
READ
@ 10,10 SAY "Male or female? (m or f)"
@ 10,50 GET sx PICTURE "A"
READ
@ 12,10 SAY "Which civil status? (s, m or d)"
@ 12,50 GET cs PICTURE "A"
READ
USE address
DO CASE                                                     (3)
   CASE cat = 1
      SET FILTER TO red .AND. sex = LOWER(sx) ;
                          .AND. c_status = LOWER(cs)
   CASE cat = 2
      SET FILTER TO white .AND. sex = LOWER(sx) ;
                          .AND. c_status = LOWER(cs)
   CASE cat = 3
      SET FILTER TO (.NOT. red) .AND. (.NOT. white) ;
                    .AND. sex = LOWER(sx) ;
                    .AND. C_status = LOWER(cs)
ENDCASE
GO TOP
SET DEVICE TO PRINT
DO head1
```

```
DO WHILE .NOT. EOF()                                           (4)
    r = r + 1
    DO recout
    SKIP
ENDDO
r = r + 1
@ r,0 SAY " "
SET DEVICE TO SCREEN
SET TALK ON
RETURN
* End SELECT2.PRG *
```

(1) Initializes the memory variables for the specified selection letters.

(2) The output commands for the input template for the selection criteria.

(3) Branch for the chosen criteria. The LOWER() function converts the input to small letters since the SEX and C_STATUS fields contain small letters.

(4) Output commands for the selected records.

Example 8:

The SELECT3 program is to filter the records between two specified membership numbers. To do this, first make an index on the MEMBERNR field:

```
INDEX ON membernr TAG mnridx
```

In the Browse and Edit screens, this can be done using the option *Organize, Create new index*.

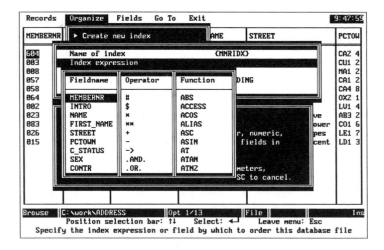

Now sort the file according to the new index:

    SET ORDER TO TAG mnridx

In the Browse and Edit screens, this can be done using the menu option *Organize, Order records by index*. Select the required tag from the list. The index expression is located next to the highlighted tag name as a reminder.

The program listing is as follows:

```
* Program SELECT3.PRG *
SET TALK OFF
SET DEVICE TO SCREEN
CLEAR ALL
r = 0
snr = SPACE(3)                                                          (1)
enr = SPACE(3)
CLEAR
@ 3,10 SAY "Enter the numbers"                                          (2)
@ 8,10 SAY "Start at member number: "
@ 8,50 GET snr PICTURE "999"
READ
@ 10,10 SAY "End at member number: "
```

```
@ 10,50 GET enr PICTURE "999"
READ
USE address ORDER mnridx
SET FILTER TO (membernr = snr .OR. membernr > snr);       (3)
            .AND. (membernr = enr .OR. membernr < enr)
GO TOP
SET DEVICE TO PRINT
DO head1
DO WHILE .NOT. EOF()
   r = r + 1
   DO recout
   SKIP
        ENDDO
        r = r + 1
        @ r,0 SAY " "
        SET DEVICE TO SCREEN
        SET TALK ON
        RETURN
        * End SELECT3.PRG *
```

(1) Initializes the memory variables containing the spe-
     cified member numbers. The records which lie be-
     tween these numbers are to be sent to the printer.
     SNR is the starting number, ENR the end number.

(2) The output commands for the input template.

(3) The filter condition is: only those records are dis-
     played in which the MEMBERNR field contains a
     value equal to or greater than SNR and equal to or
     smaller than ENR.

9.10   Writing programs using the
         application generator

Introduction
An application generator is a program which constructs
another program according to specified features.

In dBASE IV, the application generator is activated in

the command mode using:

```
CREATE APPLICATION name
```

In the Control Center, activate <create> in the *Applications* panel. When the dialog box appears on the screen, press A for the option *Applications Generator* (or press Cursor Right, Enter). The other option in this box, *dBASE program*, loads the text editor which you can use to write a program entirely according to your own requirements and style.

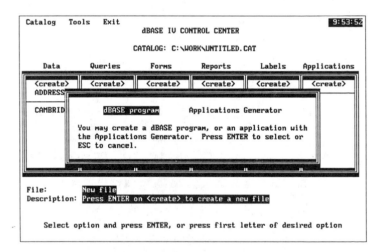

Example 1:

We wish to create a program which you can use to perform the following tasks using the address file:

■ add new records,
■ modify existing records,
■ physically remove deleted records,
■ examine and edit records,
■ adapt the file indices to changed circumstances.

The application generator creates a program behind the scenes using the familiar commands APPEND, EDIT, PACK and BROWSE. You hardly need to do anything at all. We shall describe the program development in terms of the screens which appear successively.

Stage 1
After specification of the command 'CREATE APPLICATION AM1', a series of questions appears on the screen. Their significance is outlined in the bottom line.

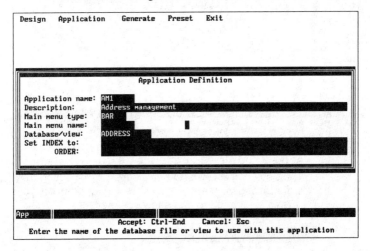

Stage 2
Answer the questions using the data in the figure. Accept BAR as the main menu type. The database is, of course, ADDRESS.DBF; the ADDRESS.MDX multiple index file is used there automatically, so that you do not need to enter anything on the two lines referring to the index. When the data have been specified, press Ctrl-End.

Stage 3
The application generator design screen is now displayed with a window which you can use as a title window. The text in the window may be replaced by your own text, or for instance, the text in the example shown

below. You can use all the common word processing keys (such as Del or Ins) in this window. You can delete a whole line of original text using Ctrl-Y.

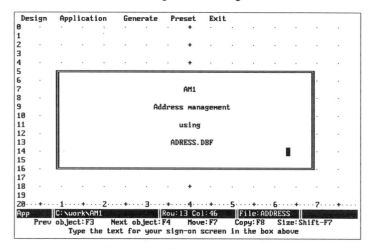

Stage 4

Then select the *Generate quick application* option from the *Application* menu. A window will appear on your screen similar to the one shown below.

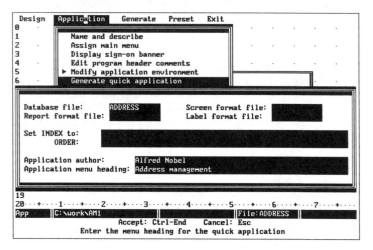

The database file is already specified. You now only need to specify your name and a heading for this program. Press Ctrl-End to close the window and confirm the control question with Yes. Then the miracle occurs: dBASE IV creates an application of a couple of hundered lines without errors, in the wink of an eye.

When dBASE IV has completed the compilation, it returns to the level from which the application generator was activated (the dot prompt or the Control Center). You can now activate the application from the dot prompt using

```
DO AM1
```

In the Control Center, highlight the name in the *Applications* panel and press Enter.

Stage 5
We shall now examine the program text which the generator has produced. To do this, we shall load it in the dBASE editor using the command:

```
. MODIFY COMMAND af1
```

The listing shown below is the program which has been created by the generator. Owing to the usage of a number of procedures and a program function, it remains orderly, even if it has a length of almost four hundred lines.

If you were to write the program yourself, you would probably lose more time in tracking down all the mistakes than in writing the program. This indicates the virtue and the capability of the application generator: it performs this task without problem or error.

It is remarkable that almost the half of the program consists of commands to construct the screen in exactly the proper way. The real work is done in the ACTION procedure.

```
*************************************************************************
* Program......: C:AM1
* Author.......: Alfred Nobel
* Date.........: 5-28-93
* Notice.......: Type information here or greetings to your users.
* Generated by.: dBASE IV version 2.0
* Description..: Address management

* Notes........:
*************************************************************************

SET CONSOLE OFF
IF TYPE("gn_apgen") = "U"  && We were not called from another APGEN
   program
   CLEAR ALL
   CLEAR WINDOW
   CLOSE DATABASE
   gn_apgen = 1
ELSE
   gn_apgen = gn_apgen + 1
   PRIVATE gc_bell, gc_carry, gc_clock, gc_century, gc_confirm,
   gc_deli,;
          gc_escape, gc_safety, gc_status, gc_score, gc_talk,
   gc_color,;
          gc_proc
ENDIF

*-- Window for pause message box (ON ERROR)
DEFINE WINDOW Pause FROM 15,00 TO 19,79 DOUBLE
ON ERROR DO PAUSE WITH [Error occurred on line ]+LTRIM(STR(LINE())) +[
   of procedure ]+Program()
ON KEY LABEL F1 DO quickhlp

*-- Store initial SETs to variables
gc_bell   =SET("BELL")
gc_carry  =SET("CARRY")
gc_clock  =SET("CLOCK")
gc_century=SET("CENTURY")
gc_confirm=SET("CONFIRM")
gc_cursor =SET("CURSOR")
gc_deli   =SET("DELIMITERS")
gc_escape =SET("ESCAPE")
```

```
gc_proc    =SET("PROCEDURE")
gc_safety  =SET("SAFETY")
gc_status  =SET("STATUS")
gc_score   =SET("SCOREBOARD")
gc_talk    =SET("TALK")

SET CLOCK OFF
CLEAR
SET CONSOLE ON

*-- Sets for application
SET BELL ON
SET CARRY OFF
SET CENTURY OFF
SET CONFIRM OFF
SET CURSOR OFF
SET DELIMITERS TO ""
SET DELIMITER OFF
SET ESCAPE ON
SET SAFETY ON
SET SCOREBOARD OFF
SET STATUS OFF
SET TALK OFF

*-- Set global variables
gn_barv  = 0                && Initialize bar value variable
gn_error = 0                && Variable to store error() number
gn_send  = 0                && Return variable from popup
gc_brdr  = "2"              && Border style for menu box - See
    Procedure
lc_heading = "Address management" && Menu heading string

gl_color = ISCOLOR()
gc_scope = ""
SET ESCAPE ON
SET STATUS ON


USE ADDRESS

*-- Define the main popup menu for Quickapp
SET BORDER TO DOUBLE
```

```
DEFINE POPUP quick FROM 7,27
DEFINE BAR 1 OF quick PROMPT " Add Information" MESSAGE "Add records
    to database ADDRESS"
DEFINE BAR 2 OF quick PROMPT " Change Information" MESSAGE "Edit
    records in database ADDRESS"
DEFINE BAR 3 OF quick PROMPT " Browse Information" MESSAGE "Browse
    database ADDRESS"
DEFINE BAR 4 OF quick PROMPT " Discard Marked Records " MESSAGE "Purge
    deleted records in database ADDRESS"
DEFINE BAR 5 OF quick PROMPT " Exit From Am1" MESSAGE "Exit program to
    dBASE"
ON SELECTION POPUP quick DO Action WITH BAR()


*-- Window to cover work surface during edit, append, etc.
DEFINE WINDOW work FROM 0,0 TO 21,79 NONE

*-- Window for area below menu heading & for running reports/labels in
DEFINE WINDOW desktop FROM 4,0 TO 21,79 NONE

DEFINE WINDOW printemp FROM 10,25 TO 15,56

*-- Display heading centered on the screen.
DO menubox WITH lc_heading

*-- Show the menu so we don't get a flash if the user hits arrow keys
    or ESC
SHOW POPUP quick
SAVE SCREEN TO quick
*-- Display Quickapp menu centered on the screen.
DO WHILE gn_barv <> 5 && Prevent user from exiting with arrow keys or
    ESC
  ACTIVATE POPUP quick
ENDDO


* Restore SET environment the best we can
SET BELL &gc_bell.
SET CARRY &gc_carry.
SET CLOCK TO
SET CLOCK &gc_clock.
SET CENTURY &gc_century.
SET CONFIRM &gc_confirm.
```

```
SET CURSOR &gc_cursor.
SET DELIMITERS &gc_deli.
SET ESCAPE &gc_escape.
SET FORMAT TO
SET PROCEDURE TO (gc_proc)
SET STATUS &gc_status.
SET SAFETY &gc_safety.
SET SCORE  &gc_score.
SET TALK   &gc_talk.


IF gn_apgen = 1 && We were not called from another APGEN program
   CLEAR WINDOW
   CLEAR POPUP
   CLEAR ALL
   CLOSE DATABASE
ELSE
   RELEASE WINDOWS work, desktop
   RELEASE SCREEN quick
   RELEASE POPUP quick
   gn_apgen = gn_apgen - 1
ENDIF
ON ERROR
ON KEY LABEL F1
RETURN
* EOP: C:AM1.prg


***************************************************************************
* Procedures...: C:AM1.Prc
* Author.......: Alfred Nobel
* Date.........: 5-28-93
* Notice.......: Type information here or greetings to your users.
* Generated by.: dBASE IV version 2.0
* Description..: Address management


* Notes........:
***************************************************************************


*-- Here is a sample procedure file to show the power of procedures.
*-- This example - Menubox displays a menu heading box with a centered
   heading.
PROCEDURE MenuBox
PARAMETER lc_m_name
```

```
*-- Parameter lc_m_name - is the title variable for the menu
   PRIVATE cInfo, cBox
   cInfo = ColorChk( "I" )
   cBox = ColorChk( "B" )

   SET CLOCK OFF
   @ 1,0 FILL TO 2,79 COLOR &cInfo
   DO CASE
     CASE gc_brdr = "0"
       @ 1,0 CLEAR TO 3,79
     CASE gc_brdr = "1"
       @ 1,0 TO 3,79
     CASE gc_brdr = "2"
       @ 1,0 TO 3,79 DOUBLE COLOR &cBox
   ENDCASE
   SET CLOCK TO 2,68
   @ 2,1 SAY SUBSTR(CDOW(DATE()),1,3)+'. '+DTOC(DATE())+' '  COLOR
   &cInfo
   @ 2,41 - (LEN(lc_m_name)/2) SAY lc_m_name  COLOR &cInfo
RETURN
*-- EOP: MenuBox



FUNCTION ColorChk
PARAMETERS pc_WhichCo
*-----------------------------------------------------------------------
* DESCRIPTION
*    _ColorChk() returns a string representing one of eight
*    possible color attribute values.
*-----------------------------------------------------------------------

   PRIVATE lc_colattr, lc_whichco, ln_count, ln_stop_at, lc_attrib

   lc_whichco = UPPER(LEFT(pc_whichco,1))
   lc_attrib  = SET("ATTRIBUTE")

   IF lc_whichco $ "MTBIF"
     lc_colattr = SUBSTR(lc_attrib, AT("&", lc_attrib) + 2)
   ELSE
     lc_colattr = LEFT(lc_attrib, AT("&", lc_attrib) - 2)
   ENDIF
```

```
  DO CASE
    CASE lc_whichco = "F"
      ln_stop_at = 4
    CASE lc_whichco = "I"
      ln_stop_at = 3
    CASE lc_whichco $ "BP"
      ln_stop_at = 2
    CASE lc_whichco $ "TH"
      ln_stop_at = 1
    OTHERWISE
      ln_stop_at = 0
  ENDCASE

  ln_count = 1

  DO WHILE m->ln_count <= m->ln_stop_at
    lc_colattr = SUBSTR(m->lc_colattr, AT(",", m->lc_colattr) + 1)
    ln_count = m->ln_count + 1
  ENDDO

RETURN IIF("," $ lc_colattr, ;
            LEFT(lc_colattr, AT(",", lc_colattr) - 1), ;
            lc_colattr ;
          )
*-- EOF: ColorChk( pc_WhichCo )


PROCEDURE get_sele
*-- Get the user selection & store BAR into variable
gn_send = BAR()   && Variable for print testing
DEACTIVATE POPUP
RETURN

PROCEDURE Action
PARAMETERS bar
*-- Get the user selection & store BAR into variable
gn_barv = bar
lc_toprnt=''
SET MESSAGE TO
IF LTRIM( STR( gn_barv)) $ "123"
   SET CURSOR ON
ENDIF
```

```
DO CASE
   CASE gn_barv = 1
      *-- Add information
      SET MESSAGE TO 'Appending records to file ADDRESS'
      APPEND
   CASE gn_barv = 2
      *-- Change information
      SET MESSAGE TO 'Editing file ADDRESS'
      EDIT
   CASE gn_barv = 3
      *-- Browse information
      SET MESSAGE TO 'Browsing file ADDRESS'
      BROWSE
   CASE gn_barv = 4
      *-- Remove information (Pack file address)
      ACTIVATE WINDOW desktop
      @ 2,0 SAY "Packing database ADDRESS to REMOVE records marked for
   deletion..."
      @ 3,0
      SET TALK ON
      PACK
      GO TOP
      ?
      WAIT
      SET TALK OFF
      DEACTIVATE WINDOW desktop
   CASE gn_barv = 5
      DEACTIVATE POPUP
ENDCASE
SET MESSAGE TO
SET CURSOR OFF
RESTORE SCREEN FROM quick
RETURN


PROCEDURE Pause
PARAMETER pc_msg
*----------------------------------------------------------------------
* Procedure to display a message or errors in a window
* Parameters : pc_msg = message line
*----------------------------------------------------------------------
   PRIVATE lc_msg, lCursor
```

```
IF TYPE("lc_message")="U"
   gn_error=ERROR()
ENDIF
lc_msg = pc_msg
lc_option='0'

ACTIVATE WINDOW Pause
IF gn_error > 0
   IF TYPE("lc_message")="U"
     @ 0,1 SAY LEFT( [An error has occurred !! - Error message:
  ]+MESSAGE() , 76 )
   ELSE
     @ 0,1 SAY LEFT( [Error # ]+lc_message , 76 )
   ENDIF
ENDIF

@ 1,1 SAY LEFT( lc_msg, 76 )
lCursor = SET( "CURSOR" ) = "ON"
SET CURSOR OFF
WAIT " Press any key to continue..."
IF lCursor
   SET CURSOR ON
ENDIF

DEACTIVATE WINDOW Pause

RETURN
*-- EOP: Pause WITH pc_msg


PROCEDURE quickhlp
*--  If you want to include help for a quickapp uncomment the lines
   below and
*--  put your help @ say's into the case statements
*ACTIVATE WINDOW desktop
*CLEAR
DO CASE
   CASE BAR() = 1
   CASE BAR() = 2
   CASE BAR() = 3
   CASE BAR() = 4
   CASE BAR() = 5
```

```
ENDCASE
*WAIT
*DEACTIVATE WINDOW desktop
RETURN


*-- EOF: C:AM1.prg
```

Example 2:

The AM1 Quick Application is a complete, though simple program. We shall now write a second program under the name AM2 which appears rather differently and restricts the user a bit more:

■ The user may only alter those records in which "s" or "d" is registered in the C_STATUS field. Only the NAME and C_STATUS fields may be altered. The menu option is: 'C_Status'.
■ In the BROWSE screen, the user may only alter the NAME, FIRST_NAME, STREET and PCTOWN fields. The other data are not displayed. The menu option is: 'Address data'.
■ By means of a menu option 'Female members', the user can display a list of the NAME, FIRST_NAME and SEX fields of all female members.

We shall again construct the program step by step:

Stage 1
First give the command CREATE APPLICATION AM2. Define the application in the first screen in the same way as in AM1, but now add 'version 2' in the Description line. Type MAIN in the 'Main menu name' line. Press Ctrl-End in order to save the definition. In the following description screen, clearly indicate that this program only enables you to make limited alterations to the ADDRESS.DBF (for instance, 'User-oriented management of the ADDRESS.DBF file').

Stage 2

Now the actual development of the objects (modules, components) of the program begins. Select the *Horizontal bar menu* option from the *Design* menu. Select <create> in the options box and specify the name MAIN. Press Ctrl-End: on row 2, a box appears across the entire width of the screen. Enter the menu names as follows:

- press F5,
- type: Modify,
- press F5.

Type two spaces and repeat the procedure to specify the menu name 'Stop'.

Stage 3

In stage 2, you have produced a menu bar at the top of the screen. Now a menu should be linked to the menu name 'Modify'. Accordingly, select the *Attach pull-down menus* option from the *Menu* menu.

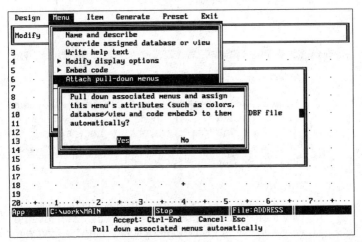

This ensures the menu will open when you select its name in the program shortly. In the same *Menu* menu, now select *Save current menu*. The data in the menu bar are saved.

In order to create the *Modify* menu, select *Pop-up menu* from the *Design* menu. Select <create> in the options box which subsequently appears. The menu name is MODIFY. The empty menu window is then opened. Type the menu options under one another. It is not necessary to use F5 to open and close a field as is the case with a bar menu.

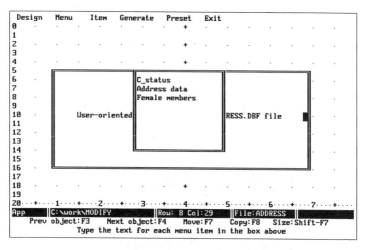

Select *Save current menu* once more from the *Menu* menu. The menu display on the screen is now complete in principle. In order to prevent the program being becoming too extensive, we shall not link any menu options to the *Stop* menu at present.

Stage 4

In this stage, the procedures which are implemented via the menus are defined. First display the main menu on the work surface (the screen) again using the *Horizontal bar menu* option from the *Design* menu and then MAIN in the options box. Highlight the menu name *Modify*. Then open the *Item* menu and select *Change action* followed by *Open a menu*. Specify the type of menu (press the spacebar until POP-UP appears) and the menu name: MODIFY.

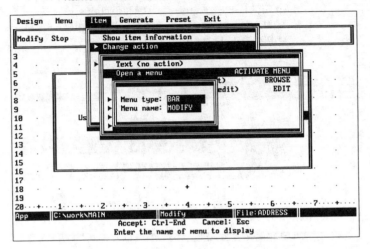

Press Ctrl-End to save the specifications. You do not need to execute this process for the *Stop* menu, since no pull-down menu is linked to it. Save the menu bar again using the *Save current menu* from the *Menu* menu.

Stage 5
Go to work in the same way in order to link processes to the *Modify* menu options:

- open the *Design* menu,
- select *Pop-up menu*,
- select *MODIFY*,
- open *Item* (the status line shows that C_status is still marked),
- select *Change action*,
- select *Edit form*.

The marking is moved by means of the Tab key in the subsequent window.

- mark the *Mode* field,

- press the spacebar to set the menu option to EDIT,
- at FIELDS, enter: c_status,
- at FILTER: c_status = "s" .OR. c_status = "d",
- change all other yes/no options to NO (press the spacebar) except *Allow record EDIT?*,
- press Ctrl-End.

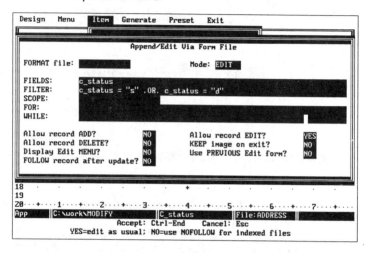

When you press Ctrl-End, the window is closed. Press PgDn to mark the next menu option of your menu. This is only shown on the status line. Define the *Address data* menu option in the same way by choosing *Item, Change action, Browse.* The figure below shows the relevant data. Save the data using Ctrl-End.

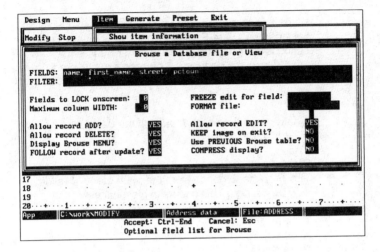

Press PgDn again to define the last menu option, *Female members.*

- select *Change action,*
- select *Display or print,*
- select *Display/list,*
- define the item as shown below.

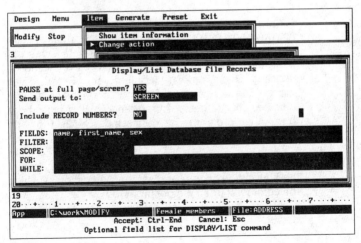

When specifying the field names, you can use the list of
field names (Shift-F1): highlight the required fields in
succession, pressing Enter to confirm the choice each
time. Close the options list by pressing Ctrl-End. Save
the definition of this menu option by pressing Ctrl-End
again.

Finally, save the entire *Modify* menu using *Menu, Save
current menu*.

Stage 6
The *Stop* menu option from the main menu should now
also be defined. This occurs in a similar way:

■ open *Design*,
■ select *Horizontal bar menu*,
■ select *MAIN*,
■ mark the *Stop* menu option,
■ open *Item*,
■ select *Change action*,
■ select *Quit*,
■ press Enter twice to confirm the specification,
■ open *Menu*,
■ select *Save current menu* and *Clear work surface*.

Stage 7
You have now defined everything, but the whole is not a
program yet. This still has to be generated. Open the
Generate menu and check the MENU.GEN setting by
selecting *Select template* (confirm using Enter). Then
choose *Begin generating*. The counter on the status line
indicates the number of program lines. In fact, more
than one program is generated: AM2.APP and
AM2.PRG.

Select *Exit, Save all changes and exit* in order to quit
the application generator. Test the application by giving
the command (from the dot prompt):

```
DO AM2
```

Before the application is activated, it is first compiled.

This means that it is translated into computer language. This occurs each time you alter something in the source code. If everything has gone smoothly, no error messages will appear.

When you are testing the program, you will observe that it is still irritatingly primitive. For instance, when you have requested the Browse screen containing address data, there are no indications how to quit this browse screen again (Esc or Ctrl-End).

When AM1 was applied, it was evident that a large part of the program only deals with the display of data. This is also the case here: we have restricted ourselves to the more general outlines. You should enter the details yourself, assisted by the application generator.

9.10.1   The DEFINE commands

In the program created by the application generator, you may have noticed some commands which we have not yet discussed: the DEFINE commands. We shall deal briefly with these commands here.

If you wish to create menus which are specially geared to your own requirements, you can use the define commands to specify the menu options.

DEFINE BAR

The DEFINE BAR command defines a single option in a pop-up menu.

Syntax:
DEFINE BAR line number OF popup name PROMPT character expression [MESSAGE character expression][SKIP [FOR condition]]

DEFINE BOX

The DEFINE BOX command defines a box to be printed
around lines of text.
Syntax:
DEFINE BOX FROM print column TO print column
HEIGHT numeric expression [AT LINE print
line][SINGLE/DOUBLE/border definition string]

DEFINE MENU

DEFINE MENU is used together with DEFINE PAD
(see below) to define a menu.

Syntax:
DEFINE MENU menu name [MESSAGE character ex-
pression]

DEFINE PAD

The DEFINE PAD command is used to define a single
pad in a bar menu. If you want to define more than one
pad in a menu, repeat the command with the same
menu name until all the pads are defined.

Syntax:
DEFINE PAD pad name OF menu name PROMPT
character expression [AT row, column][MESSAGE
character expression]

DEFINE POPUP

A pop-up menu is a screen window containing special
fields, messages and a border. The DEFINE POPUP
command defines a pop-up window's name, location,
border, prompts and message line.

Syntax:
DEFINE POPUP name FROM row1, column1 [TO

row2, column2][PROMPT FIELD field name/PROMPT
FILES [LIKE skeleton]/PROMPT STRUCTURE][MES-
SAGE character expression]

DEFINE WINDOW

Using DEFINE WINDOW you can define windows, bor-
ders and screen colours for windows.

Syntax:
DEFINE WINDOW name FROM row1, column1 TO
row2, column2 [DOUBLE/PANEL/NONE/border definition string][COLOR [standard][,enhanced][,frame]]

9.11   Creating reports using the report generator

You can create reports containing database information
using the report generator. The report structure is automatically stored in a program file with the extension
.FRM (the legible source file has the extension .FRG).
You can use this file for the display of data on the
screen or via the printer.

In addition to data from the database, reports may contain titles and column listings, and also totals and subtotals from numeric fields. The output may be arranged to
depend on certain conditions, for example: display all
members who pay a contribution of eight pounds.

Activating the report generator
The report generator is activated using the following
command:

```
CREATE REPORT report name
```

In order to alter an existing report, give the following
command:

```
MODIFY REPORT report name
```

In the Control Center, a new report is made by placing the cursor on <create> in the *Reports* panel and pressing Enter. An existing file can be modified by placing the cursor on the name of the file and then pressing Enter.

The main menu of the report generator provides the following options:

Layout	Select the sort of report (Quick layouts - Column, Form, Mailmerge), the layout (Box, Line), linking a database or view.
Fields	Add, Remove, Modify fields in the report.
Bands	Select the indexed fields for which the totals and subtotals should be calculated; print options for groups of records.
Words	Display options for the report text, such as centring, bold, underlining.
Go To	This option provides functions to move to a certain row or field in lengthy reports.
Print	Print options for the entire report.
Exit	Save or discontinue.

Example:

In a report, the male and female members who pay eight pounds contribution are to be displayed in two groups. In each group, the subtotal of the contribution is to be calculated and the total contribution is to be shown at the end of the report. The surname, the first name, the sex and the contribution should be shown for each of these members. The report should appear as follows:

01/06/93

```
                    LIST OF MEMBERS
                 female and male members
              who pay £8.00 contribution

NAME                FIRST_NAME      SEX   CONTR
Hodgkin             Dorothy         f       8.00
McClintock          Barbara         f       8.00
Sklodowska          Marya           f       8.00
**Subtotal**                               24.00


NAME                FIRST_NAME      SEX   CONTR
Bragg               William         m       8.00
Macloud             John            m       8.00
Rayleigh            John            m       8.00
Ross                Ronald          m       8.00
Rutherford          Ernest          m       8.00
Todd                Alexander       m       8.00
**Subtotal**                               48.00

***Total***                                72.00
```

For this example, the address file must be indexed on the fields SEX, CONTR and NAME under the name SCNIDX. This indexing is necessary for the calculation of subtotals and totals.

We shall describe the creation of the report step by step.

Stage 1: creating the index file
```
. USE address
. INDEX ON sex+STR(contr,6,2)+name TAG
  scnidx for contr = 8.00
```

Stage 2: opening the file and activating the report generator
```
. USE address ORDER scnidx
. CREATE REPORT adlist
```

Stage 3: specifying the format using the Layout menu

Open the *Layout* menu and select *Quick layouts*. Then choose *Column layout*. This enables you to create a report in which the record fields are placed adjacent to one another in columns, comparable to the layout of the Browse screen.

Form layout places the fields in the report in the same layout as the Edit screen, and *Mailmerge layout* enables you to use the report data in form letters which are to be sent to several people.

When you have chosen *Column layout*, the structure of the ADDRESS data file is shown in the design screen. A report is always divided into five *bands*, each having its own function. In the final report, bands which are superfluous can be discarded.

```
 Layout   Fields   Bands   Words   Go To   Print   Exit          11:56:26
 [ · · · · • · ▼ · 1 · · · · • ▼ · · · 2 · · · ▼ • · · · · 3 · ▼ · · • · · · · ▼ · · · · · • ▼ · 5 · · · · ▼ · · 6 · · · ▼ • · · · 7 · ▼ · · • · · · ·
 Page       Header   Band─────────────────────────────────────────────────

 Page No. 999
 DD/MM/YY

 MEMBERNR  INTRO       NAME              FIRST_NAME       STREET            PC
 Report    Intro    Band──────────────────────────────────────────────────
 Detail             Band───────────────────────────────────────────────────
 XXXXXXXX  XXXXXXXXXX  XXXXXXXXXXXXXX  XXXXXXXXXXXXXX  XXXXXXXXXXXXXXXXXXXX  XX
 Report    Summary Band──────────────────────────────────────────────────
 Page      Footer  Band─────────────────────────────────────────────────




 Report  ║C:\work\ADLIST          ║║Line:0 Col:0    ║║File:Address ║        Ins
              Add field:F5   Select:F6   Move:F7   Copy:F8   Size:Shift-F7
```

Stage 4: specifying the page width

The ruler is located directly above the first band. This is the first thing we need. The default line width is 253 characters, which of course does not fit on to normal paper.

Select *Words, Modify ruler* in order to activate the ruler. The cursor is located on the square bracket ([) which symbolizes the left margin. Using the Cursor Right key, move the cursor to position 50 and press the other square bracket key (]) to define the right margin. Press Enter to confirm the command.

Stage 5: the Header Band
dBASE IV places several predefined fields in the header band: the page number, the date and the field names. The header is displayed at the top of each page of the report.

This report is so small that it fits on to one page. Accordingly, we shall suppress the page number. Use Cursor Down to move the cursor to the row containing the Page No. field and press Ctrl-Y to delete the entire row. Use Cursor Up to move the cursor to the first row of the header band and press Ctrl-Y once more in order to delete the unnecessary blank row.

Using Ctrl-Y, you can delete all rows in a band one by one, except the last row. This must be done using *Words, Remove line*, when you have placed the cursor on the appropriate row.

Stage 6: the Intro Band
The Intro Band is used to place a title at the top of the first page of the report. In addition, you may also give a concise description in the Intro Band of the contents of the report. If the insert mode is active, add a new line by pressing Enter.

In the design screen of the figure shown, the Intro Band is closed: there is no empty line displayed under the heading. A closed band means that it will not be included in the report, even if data are shown there.

Position the cursor on the heading of the Intro Band and press Enter to open it. Then move the cursor to the empty line of the Intro Band using Cursor Down and type 'LIST OF MEMBERS'. Choose *Words, Position,*

Center in order to centre the title. Press Enter four times
to add new lines, and type the rest of the report title.
Centre this text in the same way.

Stage 7: selecting the report fields
We shall only use four fields for the report in four columns. The other fields should be removed, and the four
fields should be placed next to one another at the
proper positions. Accordingly, the field templates in the
Detail Band and the corresponding field names in the
Header Band should be removed.

To remove a field, proceed as follows:

■ switch off the insert mode; check bottom right-hand
  corner,
■ place the cursor on the field template in the detail
  band; this is now highlighted,
■ press the Del key, the field template disappears,
■ place the cursor on the first character of the field
  name in the header band,
■ press F6: Select,
■ highlight the field name using Cursor right,
■ press the Del key, the field name disappears.

Remove the fields MEMBERNR, INTRO, STREET,
PCTOWN, C_STATUS, BTH_DATE, RED, WHITE and
NOTE in this way. The field names and field templates
from BTH-DATE onwards can be removed in one go if
you use F6 to select the last section of the line before
pressing Del.

Stage 8: moving report fields
If you were to print the report in its present form, two
lines would be used for each selected record. You can
check this by means of *Print, View report on screen.*
The problem of the title and fields names being in the
wrong order is solved in the following step.

Move a field name as follows:

■ place the cursor on the field name,

- press F6: Select,
- select the entire field name using Cursor Right, conclude by pressing Enter,
- move the cursor to the new position on the line,
- press F7: Move,
- press Enter.

Since a field name and a field template are generally not equal in length, it is advisable to move the field template directly after moving the field name. You are then able to see just where the next column can begin. A field template is automatically wholly marked as soon as the cursor is placed on a part of it. Press F6 and then Enter to make and conclude the selection.

Also move the field 99999.99 in the Summary Band. We shall discuss this later.

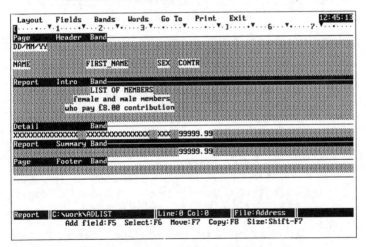

Stage 9: grouping records

In order to group records, the Detail Band has to be divided into group bands. In our present example, there are two groups, created on the basis of the SEX field. Place the cursor on the heading of the Intro Band and choose *Bands, Add a group band*. Press Enter to con-

struct a Group Band based on a *Field value* and select
SEX from the options list.

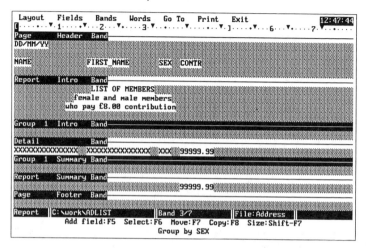

In the design screen, a Group Intro Band and a Group
Summary Band are added on either side of the Detail
Band. The Intro Band is an appropriate place for the
field names. Select the field names from the Header
Band and move them to the Intro Band of Group 1.

Stage 10: adding up subtotals
A subtotal of the group members' contribution should be
placed in the Group 1 Summary Band. Place the cursor
on the first line of this band, at position 39. This is the
first position of the CONTR column. Press F5: Add field
and select SUM in the SUMMARY column.

Specify a name for the field in the subsequent dialog
box, for instance 'subtotal'. Then specify the *Field to
summarize on*: CONTR. Finally alter the size of the
Template to suit the CONTR field. Press Ctrl-End to include the field in the design. Type the text '**Subtotal**'
at the beginning of the line and add a blank line to make
the layout more orderly.

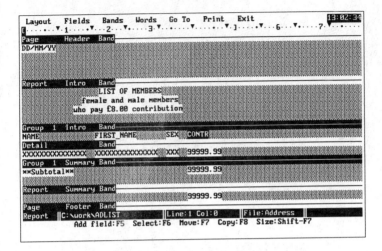

Stage 11: adding up a total
We have already moved the field for the total to position 39 of the Summary Band. All we have to do now is type the text '***Total***' at the first position of the line.

The report is complete. Select *Print, View report on screen* to get a preview of how it will look. See section 9.9 for a description of the print options.

Stage 12: saving the report
Select *Layout, Save this report* to save this design interim. It is advisable to do this each time you have finished off a part of the report which does not contain any mistakes. If you then become embroiled in fields and bands where confusion reigns, quit the report generator using *Exit, Abandon changes and exit*, and request the faultless version by giving the command from the dot prompt:

```
MODIFY REPORT adlist
```

When the report is completed, select *Exit, Save changes and exit* in order to return to the dot prompt.

9.11.1   Modifying a report

You can easily modify an existing report using the report generator. Activate the report using the command

```
MODIFY REPORT report name
```

You can then add Group Bands (see stages 7 and 8), or remove them (place the cursor on the Group Band header and select *Bands, Remove group*). You may also add or remove fields (see stage 8) or adjust the sizes etc.

9.12   Creating forms using the form generator

dBASE provides standard forms for entering, altering and appending data. In the Edit screen, all fields of a record are placed under one another. In the Browse screen, the fields are placed adjacent to one another. The forms are used in conjunction with the commands APPEND and EDIT and they contain all fields in the data file.

If you are not content with the standard forms, you can design your own forms or create them using the form generator. A form created using the generator is stored legibly as a SCREEN file with the extension .SCR and as a format file with the extension .FMT.

Activating the form generator
Activate the form generator using the following command:

```
. CREATE SCREEN form name
```

You can alter a form which already exists using:

```
. MODIFY SCREEN form name
```

Example:

We wish to make a form with the name ADFORM for our address file:

```
. USE address
. CREATE SCREEN adform
```

In the Control Center, you create a new form by placing the cursor on <create> in the *Forms* panel and pressing Enter. To modify an existing form, highlight the name of the form and press Enter.

The main form generator menu now appears showing the following options:

Layout	Select *Quick layout* in order to display the record structure of the edit screen. This menu allows you to draw lines and to save the form or to link it to another database file.
Fields	For adding, removing or modifying fields.
Words	This menu allows you to design text and to place it at the required position on the screen.
Go To	To move to the required field
Exit	Save or cancel.

When the form generator has been activated, the *Quick layout* option of the *Layout* menu is marked. Although you can place all field names and templates in the template manually, it is much more convenient to proceed from the basic layout. Thus, press Enter.

The record structure of the ADDRESS database file now appears on the screen in the same layout as the edit screen. In our present example, only the MEMBERNR, NAME, FIRST_NAME, STREET, PCTOWN, CONTR, RED and NOTE fields are required. We shall remove the other fields.

This can be done in two ways. Depending on the cursor
position, you can use the menu option *Fields, Remove
field* to display the options box. Select a name and
press Enter. The template disappears. Remove the field
name placing the cursor on the first character and press
Del as often as is necessary. You can also remove the
template by placing the cursor on it and pressing Del.

When you have removed the superfluous fields, the
screen should appear as follows:

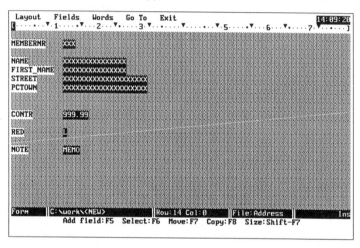

The field types are coded using symbols:

symbol	field type
X	character field
9	numeric field
L	logical field
MEMO	memo field

The number of symbols in the field indicates the maximum field length. The position of the decimal point indicates the number of decimals in numeric fields.

Using F2, you can examine the result at any moment

during the designing. Press Shift-F2 to return to the design screen. Here, you are able to adjust the fields by means of the usual keys:

F5: Add field
Insert a new field.

F6: Select
Select a field. Extend the selection by pressing Cursor Right, and conclude the selection by pressing Enter.

F7: Move
Move a field.

F8: Copy
Copy a field to another position in the design.

Shift-F7: Size
Adjusting the size of a field using the cursor keys.

The first three function keys have been dealt with extensively in the previous section. Other functions for designing the form can be found in the menus:

Layout, Box and *Layout, Line*
In order to draw lines and boxes on the screen, dBASE uses the same positions which are also used for text and numbers. Thus, if you wish to underline a field name, first add an empty line under the field name.

A box is made by selecting the option, placing the cursor at the top left-hand corner of the box, pressing Enter, moving the cursor to the bottom right-hand corner of the box and pressing Enter again.

Words,Display
Adjusting the screen colours.

Words, Position
Centring or aligning the text either right or left.

Saving the form

Leave the design screen using *Exit, Save changes and exit*. The following command enables you to check if the form really has been saved (add a drive letter and path if you are not working from the harddisk):

```
. RUN DIR adform.*
```

As a result of the * wildcard, both the data from the SCREEN and the FORMAT file are displayed. The SCREEN file (ADFORM.SCR) contains the data for the creation or the modification of the FORMAT file (AD-FORM.FMT). The program which generated the form using @SAY and GET commands is located in the FORMAT file.

In order to modify this program, give the following command:

```
. MODIFY SCREEN adform
```

In the Control Center, place the cursor on the name ADFORM in the *Forms* panel, press Enter and select *Modify layout*

You can now make alterations to the program.

Using the form

You can now use the form which you have just created for the APPEND, EDIT, CHANGE, INSERT and READ commands, by giving the following command:

```
. SET FORMAT TO form name
```

When you have finished, deactivate the form using one of these commands:

```
. CLOSE FORMAT
. SET FORMAT TO
```

Example:

You wish to add new data to the address file by means
of the self-made ADFORM.FMT form:

```
. USE address
   * open the address file
. SET FORMAT TO adform
   * activate the form
. APPEND
   * start up the add program
. CLOSE FORMAT
   * close down the form
```

Adopting form data in a text file

In the *Words* menu, you can select the options
Write/read text file and then *Write selection to file*. This
option writes the contents of the design screen in an
ASCII text file. Specify a name for the file, without an ex-
tension. The file automatically receives the extension
.TXT.

A text file created in this way can be loaded and edited
by any editor or word processor. The file contains information concerning the row and column positions of
each field, the structure of the field and the fields in the
form.

10   Working with several files

10.1   A sample system for contribution administration

In all the program examples which we have dealt with up until now, we have worked with a single database file. However, it is one of the characteristic features of a relational database that it is able to combine data from several files in a meaningful way. dBASE too provides a number of special commands for this function. In order to illustrate working with several files, we have designed a sample system.

The exercise program which we shall use in this chapter is to be applied to record the contributions of an association or club. We shall use the ADDRESS file as the point of departure, as in previous chapters. We shall also create a second file, CONTRIBA, to store the contribution data.

The sample system consists of the main program, CONTRAD.PRG (contribution administration) and the programs CONTRIB.PRG (contribution) and CONTRPAY.PRG (contribution payments). The main program, CONTRAD.PRG, displays a menu on the screen from which the user can choose one of five functions by means of number keys.

The illustration below displays the options menu of the main program, CONTRAD.PRG. The five menu options correspond to the execution of five subroutines. Three of these are components of the main program. We have made separate programs for the others: CONTRIB and CONTRPAY. All components are summoned from the main program.

```
CONTRIBUTION ADMINISTRATION
---------------------------------------------------

Write invoices                             1

Book payments                              2

Delete paid invoices                       3

Examine list of members per page           4

Exit                                       0

Selection:                                 9
---------------------------------------------------
If the required record does not exist in
the file, you will return to this menu.
```

The scheme below clarifies the structure of the sample system:

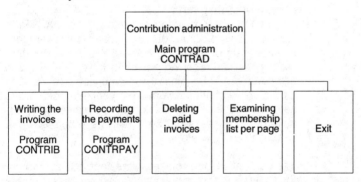

The various sections of the package perform the following:

Writing the invoices

Menu option 1 activates the CONTRIB program which enters data in the CONTRIBA file. We shall discuss the structure of this file shortly. This file contains a registration of all unpaid contributions, and shows also the membership number, the contribution month, the invoice date and the payments to date of those members who are behind in their payments. We shall assume that the payments should be made monthly. Therefore, each month a record with the due contribution should be written in the file for each member.

We could, of course, enter the required data each month, but that is rather laborious. Accordingly, it is more sensible to have the data for the CONTRIBA file automatically generated by the CONTRIB program. This program has the following tasks:

- adopting the membership numbers and contributions of all members from the ADDRESS file,
- asking the user to enter the contribution month once, for all contribution records,
- taking the computer system date as the invoice date,
- numbering the contribution records consecutively.

Registering payments
The second menu option activates the CONTRPAY program. This program displays the address and contribution data of all members on the screen. The user can register the received payments here. The received payments are set against the contribution due. As long as the entire contribution has not yet been paid, a due sum is indicated. Contribution which exceeds the requirements appears on the screen as a negative due sum (with a minus sign).

The calculation takes place via the contribution number: the CONTRIB program assigns a (consecutive) number to each contribution record. The user specifies the contribution number when entering the payments. The data of the member with the corresponding number then appear on the screen. The incoming payment can now be handled.

The calculation of payments could also be regulated by means of the names of the members, perhaps even more efficiently. However, we have opted for a system

using numbers, since this is the most widely-used
method in practice.

Deleting paid invoices
The third menu option serves to delete all contribution
records in the CONTRIBA file, in which the due contribution has been paid in full. All records which still contain due sums are transported to the following month's
contribution.

Examining the membership list per page
The fourth menu option enables the user to display a list
of all members with contributions due. Each item contains data from two different files: the name of the member from the ADDRESS file on the one hand, and the
contribution number, the contribution month and the
outstanding payment from CONTRIBA on the other.

Exit
This option ends the program.

10.2   Collecting data for the CONTRIBA
file using CONTRIB

The CONTRIB program adds the contribution records
for the current contribution month to the CONTRIBA file
by means of the data in the ADDRESS file. Records
with unpaid contributions from previous months may
also be located in the CONTRIBA file. For this reason,
new data are appended to the existing data.

The CONTRIBA file
The number of contribution records to be processed depends on the number of members whose data are
stored in the ADDRESS file. Accordingly, a link must be
made between the ADDRESS file and the CONTRIBA
file. This occurs via the MEMBERNR and CONTR fields
which are identical in both files.

The complete structure of the CONTRIBA file is shown

below. You can create this file using the command
CREATE contriba.

field	field name	field type	length	decimals
1	CONTNR	numeric	5	
2	MEMBERNR	character	3	
3	CMONTH	numeric	2	
4	DATE	date	8	
5	CONTR	numeric	8	2
6	PAYMENT1	numeric	8	2
7	PAY_DAT1	date	8	
8	PAYMENT2	numeric	8	2
9	PAY_DAT2	date	8	
10	DUE	numeric	8	2

The fields have the following significance:

CONTNR
: This field contains the automatically assigned contribution number which is used in the processing of the payments. The ultimate value which is saved in this field is stored as the MCONTNR memory variable in the MCONTNR.MEM memory file before the CONTRIB program is ended. At the beginning of the following session, the contents of this variable are read again from the file, and form the basis of the subsequent CONTRNR value.

MEMBERNR
: The membership number is taken from the field of the same name in the ADDRESS file, using APPEND.

CMONTH
: The contribution month. This information is the basis of the new calculations. The user must specify the contribution month as a number between 1 and 12 each time the CONTRIB program is activated.

DATE   The invoice date. This corresponds to the system date on the day that the CONTRIB program is run.

CONTR   The contribution from the ADDRESS file.

PAYMENT1/2   Payments and the dates of pay-
and   ments. The data are further pro-
PAY_DAT1/2   cessed by the CONTRPAY program.

DUE   Contribution which has not yet been paid. This is the difference between the total contribution to be paid and the amount already remitted.

After each CONTRIB session, the CONTRIBA file is indexed according to membership number under the name MNRCDAT. You have to do this yourself the very first time.

The CONTRIB program

The CONTRIB program adds the records containing the contribution invoices for the new month to the CONTRIBA file. The records are numbered consecutively. The number of the first added record is one greater than the number of the last record from the previous program session. This number is read into the MCONTNR memory variable from the MCONTNR.MEM file at the beginning of the program.

There is no built-in control over several sessions within one month in the program. If the program is activated more than once for the same month, the same records are added several times to the end of CONTRIBA. However, you can easily program this type of control yourself. The specified month should be compared to the month in the previous session. If the two months are identical, the program is discontinued.

The CONTRIB program is as follows:

```
* CONTRIB.PRG program *
SET SAFETY OFF                                              (1)
SET TALK OFF
CLEAR ALL                                                   (2)
RESTORE FROM mcontnr                                        (3)
mcontnr = mcontnr + 1                                       (4)

USE contriba                                                (5)

pntr = 0                                                    (6)
GO BOTTOM
STORE RECNO() TO pntr
IF pntr > 1
   pntr = pntr + 1
  ELSE
   pntr = 1
ENDIF

CLEAR                                                       (7)
mdat = 00                                                   (8)
@ 05,10 SAY "Contribution month:"
@ 05,40 GET mdat picture "99" RANGE 1,12
READ

APPEND FROM ADDRESS                                         (9)
GO pntr

DO WHILE .NOT. EOF()                                        (10)
   REPLACE contnr WITH mcontnr
   REPLACE date WITH DATE()                                 (11)
   REPLACE cmonth WITH mdat
   REPLACE due WITH contr - (payment1 + payment2)           (12)
   mcontnr = mcontnr + 1
   SKIP
ENDDO

SAVE TO mcontr                                              (13)
INDEX ON membernr TO mnrcdat

RETURN
* end CONTRIB.PRG *
```

(1) SET SAFETY OFF ensures that the new value of the MCONTNR variable from the MCONTNR.MEM file may be written over the previous contents of this variable without a safeguard question.

(2) All files are closed and all variables deleted.

(3) The value of the MCONTNR variable is read from the MCONTNR.MEM file and made available to the program. The contribution number of the last record in the CONTRIBA file is stored each time in the MCONTNR variable. The subsequent contribution number must be one greater than the last number. Accordingly, this variable is increased in the next row: mcontnr = mcontnr + 1.

In the loop at (10), the value of MCONTNR is allocated to the CONTNR file variable by means of REPLACE contnr WITH mcontnr. Subsequently, MCONTNR is increased by one again: mcontnr = mcontnr + 1.

At (13), the ultimate value which has been stored in MCONTNR is saved in MCONTNR.MEM by means of SAVE TO mcontnr. In order to be able to use the program system, you must ensure that there is a file available with the name MCONTNR.MEM containing the starting value 0, prior to the first activation of the system. This is done using the following two options:

```
. STORE 0 TO mcontnr
. SAVE TO mcontnr
```

See also section 10.5.

(4) The last saved contribution number is increased by one.

(5) The CONTRIBA file is opened.

(6) The PNTR memory variable is created for the record number of the first record which is to be added using APPEND. This record pointer is necessary

for the correct processing of the new records which
are to be included. There are two possible situations: either CONTRIBA contains no records, or
CONTRIBA still contains one or more records from
previous months. In the former case, the first new
record must receive the number 1. In the latter
case, the record number of the first new record
must be one greater than the number of the last old
record.

To begin with, PNTR is defined as a numeric variable with the value 0. Then the internal dBASE
pointer placed at the last record in the file using GO
BOTTOM. Subsequently, the new position is
adopted in PNTR using STORE RECNO() TO pntr.
If there are no records in the file as yet, GO BOT-
TOM will produce record number 1. The same
value is thus also located in the PNTR variable. In
this case, PNTR should retain the value 1. If, on the
other hand, there are records in the file already,
PNTR must be increased by one. These two cases
are distinguished from one another by an IF test.

Prior to new data being adopted into the records in
the loop at (10), the record pointer is placed on the
first new record using GO pntr.

(7) The screen is cleared.

(8) The input of the contribution month in MDAT. This
     variable has to be defined in advance, since a GET
     command is used for the input. The parameter PIC-
     TURE "99" ensures that only numbers can be en-
     tered. RANGE 1,12 accepts only numbers between
     1 and 12.
     In the loop at (10), the specified month value is
     adopted into the CMONTH field using the com-
     mand REPLACE cmonth WITH mdat.

(9) For each member, a record with the invoice is
     added to the contribution file at the beginning of a
     new contribution month. Thus, the number of rec-
     ords added to CONTRIBA is equal to the number of
     members in ADDRESS. Only data in fields which

are identical in both files are adopted. Thus, this refers only to the MEMBERNR and CONTR fields.
The remaining CONTRIBA fields are still empty.

To prevent empty records in ADDRESS being
adopted into CONTRIBA, you can delete the empty
records in ADDRESS using:

```
. DELETE FOR membernr = "     "
. PACK
```

(10) In this DO-WHILE loop, the CONTNR, DATE,
CMONTH and DUE fields are assigned the appropriate values.

(11) The DATE field receives the current system date
from the computer as its value.

(12) Payments received are deducted from the contribution due, shown in the CONTR field. Any remaining
sum is registered in the DUE field.

(13) The last contribution number is saved in the
MCONTNR.MEM file. Subsequently, the CONTRI-
BA file is again indexed on the MEMBERNR key
field under the name MNRCDAT. This is necessary
since new records have been added to the file.

10.3   Access to several files

The contribution administration system must process
the ADDRESS and CONTRIBA data files simultaneously. For this, it is necessary that both these files be
loaded into computer memory at the same time. dBASE
allows you to reserve so-called *work areas* (special
parts of memory) for certain files and to open these files
there. These work areas are fenced off from one another: data from a certain area cannot be written over
data from another area. If you wish to work with the data
in a particular file, you must first address the corresponding work area. By means of special commands,
you can work simultaneously with two files in separate
areas.

Selecting the work areas
The following command enables you to select a work area in order to open a file there or to work with a file which has been previously opened in that area:

```
SELECT area
```

dBASE manages a separate record pointer for each area; this pointer can be manipulated totally independently of other record pointers.

A maximum of 40 work areas can be reserved. dBASE uses the numbers 1 to 40, the letters A to J or a work area name to designate there.

Example:

The ADDRESS and CONTRIBA indexed files must be opened in two separate work areas:

```
. SELECT 1          && or SELECT A
. USE address ORDER memnridx
. SELECT 2          && or SELECT B
. USE contriba ORDER mnrcdat
```

The first command selects work area 1 or A. The indexed address file is then opened. The second SELECT command selects work area 2 or B. The indexed contribution file is opened there. Work area 2 remains active for further processing since this was the last SELECT command.

The ALIAS option
The ALIAS option enables you to specify an alias for a file when you open it:

```
USE file name ORDER index name ALIAS alias
   name
```

Example:

Both indexed files in the previous examples should be

accessible via shorter names: ADR (address) and CTR (contriba).

```
. SELECT 1
. USE address ORDER memnridx ALIAS adr
. SELECT 2
. USE contriba ORDER mnrcdat ALIAS ctr
```

This not only saves typework, it helps prevent mistakes. It is now possible to select a work area by means of the designated alias name. If you wish to select the contribution file work area subsequent to the above commands, you can now do this by specifying either SELECT 2 or SELECT B, or SELECT ctr. The last command is more clear than the others.

We shall encounter more applications which make use of aliases a little later in this book.

The SEL.PRG program
We wish to use the ADDRESS and CONTRIBA indexed files in various examples. Therefore, it would be convenient if you were to place the above field example commands in a small program. Create this program using MODIFY COMMAND sel.prg. The SEL.PRG program is as follows:

```
* SEL.PRG program *
CLEAR ALL
SELECT 1
USE address ORDER memnridx ALIAS adr
SELECT 2
USE contriba ORDER mnrcdat ALIAS ctr
* end SEL.PRG program *
```

You do not need to type these commands once again if you have alrady done so above. You can automatically adopt the file and field definitions which are currently in memory into a VIEW file. Give the following command:

```
. CREATE VIEW FROM ENVIRONMENT
```

dBASE asks for a name for the VIEW file. Specify the name VIEWDEMO for instance. When you have confirmed the name by pressing Enter, dBASE creates the VIEWDEMO.VUE file. This file contains the same commands as SEL.PRG. You can activate the VIEW file later by means of the command SET VIEW TO viewdemo.

It is also possible to create the VIEW file in dialogue form. To do this, give the command:

```
. CREATE VIEW viewdemo
```

A menu will now appear in which you can mark files and fields using the cursor, in order to adopt them into the VIEW file. This corresponds to the process which we have dealt with in previous chapters.

Examining the effect of SELECT
In order to see the effects of the SELECT commands in the SEL.PRG program, activate this program using:

```
. DO SEL
```

If you have created a VIEW file, the command is as follows:

```
. SET VIEW TO VIEWDEMO
```

Enter the commands shown below and examine the results.

To begin with, request all records from the files in both work areas:

```
. SELECT 1
. LIST membernr,name,contr OFF
. SELECT 2
. LIST membernr,contnr,date,contr,due OFF
```

Now display certain records:

```
. SELECT 2
. FIND 003
. DISPLAY membernr,contnr

. SELECT 1
. FIND 083
. DISPLAY membernr,name

. SELECT 2
. DISPLAY membernr,contnr
```

The second DISPLAY membernr, contnr should produce the same output as the first. Nothing has changed
in the meantime in work area 2.

Displaying the current status
If you no longer know exactly which files are open in
which area, you can acquire a list of the current system
status by specifying:

```
DISPLAY STATUS
```

A list of the work areas and the opened data, index and
memo files appears on the screen. You can also see
which database is active at that moment.

10.4   Linking records from two files

You can create a logical link between two files which
share a common key field. Both files must be opened in
separate work areas and the work area of the first file
should be active. Apart from an exception which we
shall describe below, the second file must also be indexed on the key field and the key field may only occur
once. The second file is addressed by means of an
alias. You can only make one link from each work area
to another work area.

The following command creates the link:

```
SET RELATION TO key field INTO aliasnaam
```

The link is disconnected using:

```
SET RELATION TO
```

The process is as follows: imagine you have opened an address file in work area 1 and selected the record in which the number 003 is located in the MEMBERNR key field. In work area 2, the CONTRIBA file has been opened; this also contains the MEMBERNR key field. If you now create a link between these two files, dBASE will automatically search for a record with the value 003 in the MEMBERNR field. If this record cannot be found, the record pointer is placed at the end of the file.

Exception: Instead of using a key field, you can also link records which have the same record number to each other. In this case, however, the second file may not be indexed. The command is then as follows:

```
SET RELATION TO RECNO() INTO alias name
```

Note: If you specify a numeric key, dBASE presumes that the files are to be linked by means of the record numbers.

Example:

Open the ADDRESS and CONTRIBA files as in the DO sel examples mentioned above. Then link the records of the two files to one another using the command:

```
. SET RELATION TO membernr INTO adr
```

After the commands in SEL.PRG, work area 2 is still active, since this was the last area activated. The MEMBERNR field is the common key field of the files. Thus, a link can be made from work area 2 to the ADDRESS file in work area 1, via this key field.

If, from the currently activated work area, you wish to address fields in a file in another work area, you can do this by typing the second file alias and the signs -> in front of the field names.

Example:

In the non-active work area 1, the address file is opened under the alias ADR. Now you wish to display the contents of the NAME field in this file. Therefore, give the following command:

```
. LIST adr->name
```

You can now display a list of membership numbers and contributions from the CONTRIBA file and the corresponding names from ADDRESS:

```
. LIST membernr,adr->name,contr
```

You can also give the following command using the letter of the work area instead of the name of the file:

```
. LIST membernr,A->name,contr
```

The field names of the file in the active work area are displayed on the screen without additional information. The fields in the non-active ADDRESS file are provided with the alias and the signs ->.

You can also display the data from certain records, for instance:

```
. DISPLAY adr->name,membernr,contr FOR
  membernr="064"
```

This command displays data from both files concerning the member with number 064.

```
. GO 5
. DISPLAY adr->name,membernr,contr
```

This command displays data from record number 5.

```
. DISPLAY A->name,membernr,contr FOR
  A->name="Todd"
```

This command displays data from both files concerning
the member called Todd according to the NAME field in
the ADDRESS file. The ADDRESS file is designated
here by the work area letter A.

Creating a VIEW file
The links which have been made using the SEL.PRG
program and the SET RELATION commands can be
automatically stored in a VIEW file. To do this, give the
following command:

```
. CREATE VIEW FROM ENVIRONMENT
```

Specify the name VIEWDEM1, for example. The VIEW
file now created by dBASE can be activated at any time
by the command:

```
. SET VIEW TO VIEWDEM1
```

Clearing a previous SET RELATION command
You can cancel the effect of a previous SET RELATION
command by means of:

```
. SET RELATION TO
```

After this command, the ADDRESS file is no longer
linked to the CONTRIBA file. You can check this by giving the following command once more:

```
. DISPLAY adr->name,membernr,contr FOR
  membernr="083"
```

Because the link no longer exists, the ADR->NAME column now remains empty.

Link to a file without a unique key
The ADDRESS file which we have used as the second
file up until now, contains a unique key. In contrast, the
same membership number may occur several times in

the CONTRIBA file. If a link is made to a file like this, only the data in the first record found during a search are displayed. Successive data with the same key are thus inaccessible.

If you examine the CONTRIBA file, you will find that two monthly contributions are due in the case of some members. Thus, the MEMBERNR key field contains the same value for different records and accordingly is not unique. If you now make a link from the ADDRESS file to CONTRIBA, only the first of two records with an identical member number is shown each time.

Try this out using the following commands:

```
. DO SEL                                              (1)
. LIST membernr,contnr,payment1,payment2,due          (2)
. SELECT 1                                            (3)
. SET RELATION TO membernr INTO ctr                   (4)
. LIST membernr,ctr->contnr,contr,ctr->due            (5)
```

(1) Opens both files.

(2) Displays a list of file data. In the MEMBERNR column, you will see the records with double membership numbers.

(3) Selects work area 1.

(4) Creates a link with the contribution file (alias CTR) via the non-unique MEMBERNR key field.

(5) In the list which now appears on the screen, only the first of a group of records with the same number is shown. Thus, less records are shown than actually exist in the CONTRIBA file.

10.5   Entering and booking contributions using CONTRPAY

The CONTRPAY program has the job of processing incoming payments and balancing them against the contributions due. This program is activated by the main program along with a contribution number. We shall describe the main program in the following section.

The processing template

The CONTRPAY program places a processing template on the screen for each member. The following figure shows the template for the member Bragg:

```
C o n t r i b u t i o n   P a y m e n t Month:   3
-------------------------------------------------

Member Number:        015
Name:                 Bragg               ,William

Contribution number:   3    Contribution:      8.00
Due:                        8.00
Payment1 amounted to        0.00 Payment:   ▮▮▮▮▮▮
```

The template contains the membership number, the name and first name from the ADDRESS file and the contribution month, the invoice and the sum due from the CONTRIBA file. There are no previous payments registered for this member. Accordingly, '0.00' is located behind 'Payment1'. The program awaits input of a payment. The cursor is positioned behind 'Payment'.

If the user had entered a payment for this month, this would be shown as Payment1 and there would be a second line on the screen showing:

```
Payment2 amounted to          0.00      Payment:
```

The user can now enter a sum at the current cursor position. The payments entered are balanced against the sums due. The new due payment is shown behind 'Due'. If too much has been paid, this is shown as a negative value.

The CONTRPAY.PRG program appears as follows:

```
* CONTRPAY program *
CLEAR
@ 03,10 SAY "C o n t r i b u t i o n   P a y m e n t s"
@ 03,50 SAY "Month:"
@ 03,58 SAY  cmonth
@ 05,10 SAY "------------------------------------------"
@ 08,10 SAY "Member Number:"
@ 08,30 SAY  adr->membernr
@ 10,10 SAY "Name:"
@ 10,30 SAY  adr->name
@ 10,50 SAY ","
@ 10,51 SAY  adr->first_name
@ 13,10 SAY "Contribution number:"
@ 13,30 SAY  contnr
@ 13,40 SAY "Contribution:"
@ 13,54 SAY  contr
@ 15,10 SAY "Due:"
@ 15,31 SAY  due
@ 17,10 SAY "Payment1 amounted to"
@ 17,33 SAY  payment1
@ 17,42 SAY "Payment:"

IF payment1 = 0                                          (1)
   @ 17,55 GET payment1 PICTURE "@Z 999.99"
   READ
ENDIF

@ 19,10 SAY "Payment2 amounted to"                       (2)
@ 19,31 SAY  payment2
@ 19,42 SAY "Payment:"
```

```
@ 19,55 GET payment1 PICTURE "@Z 999.99"
READ

REPLACE due WITH contr - (payment1 + payment2)            (3)
@ 15,31 SAY due
@ 20,0                                                    (4)
WAIT
RETURN
* end CONTRPAY program *
```

(1) Input for PAYMENT1 will only be requested if no first payment has been registered as yet.

(2) If no PAYMENT2 needs to be entered, the user only needs to press the Enter key.

(3) Calculates and displays any remaining sum (is shown as a negative sum if too much has been paid).

(4) The command @ 20,0 positions the cursor in row 20, preceding the WAIT command.

10.6   Contribution administration using CONTRAD

We are now ready to approach the main program for the contribution management, CONTRAD. This program operates the entire system. It contains the menu commands for the menu dealt with in section 10.1, the starting commands for the CONTRIB.PRG and CONTRPAY.PRG programs and a couple of small subroutines for the processing of the menu options 1, 4 and 0.

The main program essentially consists of two nested loops (compare section 9.3). The four menu options can be chosen by means of the keys 1 to 4. The program can be ended using 0. This returns you to the dBASE prompt.

The listing of the CONTRAD main program is as follows:

```
* CONTRAD program *
DO WHILE .T.
   SET TALK OFF
   SET STATUS OFF
   SET SCOREBOARD OFF
   CLEAR
   selection = "9"

   DO WHILE selection$"56789"
      @ 03,10 SAY "CONTRIBUTION ADMINISTRATION"
      @ 04,10 SAY "-------------------------------------------"
      @ 07,10 SAY "Write invoices                         1"
      @ 09,10 SAY "Book payments                          2"
      @ 11,10 SAY "Delete paid invoices                   3"
      @ 13,10 SAY "Examine list of members per page       4"
      @ 15,10 SAY "Exit                                   0"
      @ 17,10 SAY "Selection:"
      @ 17,53 GET selection PICTURE "9"
      @ 19,10 SAY "-------------------------------------------"
      @ 20,10 SAY "If the required record does not exist in"
      @ 21,10 SAY "the file, you will return to this menu."
      READ
      DO CASE
         CASE selection = "0"
            SET TALK ON
            SET STATUS ON
            SET SCOREBOARD ON
            RETURN
         CASE selection = "1"
            DO contrib
         CASE selection = "2"
            CLEAR
            CLEAR ALL
            DO sel
            SET RELATION TO membernr INTO adr
            mcontnr = 0
            @ 15,10 SAY "Contribution number:"
            @ 15,52 GET mcontnr PICTURE "@Z 99999"
            READ
```

```
            LOCATE FOR contnr = mcontnr
            IF FOUND()
               DO contrpay
            ENDIF
         CASE selection = "3"
            CLEAR ALL
            DO sel
            SELECT 2
            DELETE ALL FOR due = 0
            PACK
         CASE selection = "4"
            CLEAR
            CLEAR ALL
            DO sel
            SET RELATION TO membernr INTO adr
            DISPLAY ALL membernr,adr->name,contnr,cmonth,due
            WAIT
      ENDCASE
      selection = "9"
      CLEAR
   ENDDO
ENDDO
* end CONTRAD.PRG program *
```

What the program does depends on the user. The selection is stored in the SELECTION variable (CASE
construction):

■ If the user enters selection 0, the system echo is activated again and the loop is exited via RETURN.
■ If the user enters selection 1, the CONTRPAY.PRG
program activates CONTRIB.PRG. This program
adds a new contribution record to the CONTRI-
BA.DBF file for each member in the ADDRESS file.
■ If the user enters selection 2, the screen is cleared, all
opened files are closed, the ADDRESS and CON-
TRIBA files are opened by the SEL.PRG program in
work areas 1 and 2, and the link is made between
these two files via the member number. Subsequently, the program asks you to specify the contribution number for which a payment has to be book-
ed. The number is stored in the MCONTNR variable.

Using the command LOCATE FOR contnr = mcontnr, the relevant record is sought in the CON-TRIBA file. If a corresponding record is found, the CONTRPAY.PRG program is activated using DO contrpay.

■ If the user enters selection 3, the same files are opened as in selection 2. Then work area 2 is activated and all records in which the value 0 is located in the DUE field are cleared.

■ If the user enters selection 4, the same files are opened as in selection 2 and a link is made via the member number. Then a list is displayed which has been sorted according to member number with all records from CONTRIBA, supplemented by the NAME field from the ADDRESS file.

10.6.1 Use of the contribution administration system

Preparations
Before you are able to put the contribution administration system to use, you must execute two preparatory actions:

(1) The MCONTNR.MEM variables file must be created. Define an MCONTNR variable with the value 0 and save it on disk:

```
. STORE 0 TO mcontnr
. SAVE TO mcontnr
```

(2) All empty records should be deleted from the AD-DRESS file:

```
. USE address
. DELETE FOR membernr = "    "
. PACK
```

Example 1:

Start the program using DO contrad. Select option 1 from the menu: 'Write invoices' and enter a 3 for March,

for example, when the program asks you to specify a
month. When the CONTRIB program has created the
records for the contribution invoices, the menu appears
once again.

You can now activate option 4 in order to gain a list of
the contents of the CONTRIBA file. The record number
and the contribution number are registered for each
member. (These two numbers are identical at the very
first activation of the contribution administration system.) The number 3 is shown throughout the CMONTH
column, and the DUE column indicates the contribution
which the corresponding member still has to pay:

RecNr	MEMBERNR	ADD->NAME	CONTNR	CMONTH	DUE
8	002	Ross	8	3	8.00
2	003	Sklodowska	2	3	8.00
1	004	Rayleigh	1	3	8.00
4	008	Rutherford	4	3	8.00
3	015	Bragg	3	3	8.00
9	023	Macloud	9	3	8.00
11	026	Deledda	11	3	5.63
5	057	Todd	5	3	8.00
6	058	Sanger	6	3	5.63
7	064	Hodgkin	7	3	8.00
10	083	McClintock	10	3	8.00

Example 2:

You can return to the menu by pressing a random key.
Now select option 2: 'Book payments'. Enter the number 3 behind the 'Contribution number:' prompt in order
to book a payment of 8.00 by Bragg (member number
015). As soon as the program has found the corresponding contribution record, the CONTRPAY.PRG
program is activated. This program displays the input
template on the screen (see also section 10.5). You can
now enter the sum of 8.00 at the cursor position. The
screen displays an immediate processing of this sum.

Now enter the sums for the contribution numbers 1, 5, 7

and 8. Rutherford (contribution number 4) pays a first instalment of 4.00. Subsequently, activate option 4 again. The file should look like this:

RecNr	MEMBERNR	ADR->NAME	CONTNR	CMONTH	DUE
8	002	Ross	8	3	0.00
2	003	Sklodowska	2	3	8.00
1	004	Rayleigh	1	3	0.00
4	008	Rutherford	4	3	4.00
3	015	Bragg	3	3	0.00
9	023	Macloud	9	3	8.00
11	026	Deledda	11	3	5.63
5	057	Todd	5	3	0.00
6	058	Sanger	6	3	5.63
7	064	Hodgkin	7	3	0.00
10	083	McClintock	10	3	8.00

Example 3:

Now select option 3, 'Delete paid invoices'. The records for which the complete due sum has been paid, are removed. By subsquently activating option 4, you can check that the CONTRIBA file indeed only contains records in which the value in the DUE field is not equal to 0:

RecNr	MEMBERNR	ADR->NAME	CONTNR	CMONTH	DUE
2	003	Sklodowska	2	3	8.00
4	008	Rutherford	4	3	4.00
9	023	Macloud	9	3	8.00
11	026	Deledda	11	3	5.63
6	057	Sanger	6	3	5.63
10	083	McClintock	10	3	8.00

Example 4:

You now wish to write out invoices for the month of April. Select option 1 and specify 4 for the month. The invoice records for the month of April will now be added

to the CONTRIBA file. You can display the current state
of the file by selecting option 4:

```
Record#  Membernr adr->name    contnr cmonth    due
     14  002     Ross            20     4      8.00
      1  003     Sklodouska       2     3      8.00
      8  003     Sklodouska      14     4      8.00
      7  004     Rayleigh        13     4      8.00
      2  008     Rutherford       4     3      4.00
     10  008     Rutherford      16     4      8.00
      9  015     Bragg           15     4      8.00
      4  023     Macloud          9     3      8.00
     15  023     Macloud         21     4      8.00
      6  026     Deledda         11     3      5.63
     17  026     Deledda         23     4      5.63
     11  057     Todd            17     4      8.00
      3  058     Sanger           6     3      5.63
     12  058     Sanger          18     4      5.63
     13  064     Hodgkin         19     4      8.00
      5  083     McClintock      10     3      8.00
     16  083     McClintock      22     4      8.00
Press any key to continue...
```

In addition to the old records, 2, 4, 6, 9, 10 and 11,
eleven new records have been added, with the contribution numbers 12 to 23.

10.7   Creating a new file from two existing files

We now wish to create a file with the name CONDUE.
In this, for each member, the MEMBERNR and NAME
fields from the ADDRESS file and the CONTNR and
DUE fields from the CONTRIBA should be adopted.
Then the contents should be shown on the screen. The
following data should appear:

```
. use condue
. list
Record#   MEMBERNR CONTNR NAME              DUE
      1   002        20 Ross              8.00
      2   003         2 Sklodouska        8.00
      3   003        14 Sklodouska        8.00
      4   004        13 Rayleigh          8.00
      5   008         4 Rutherford        4.00
      6   008        16 Rutherford        8.00
      7   015        15 Bragg             8.00
      8   023         9 Macloud           8.00
      9   023        21 Macloud           8.00
     10   026        11 Deledda           5.63
     11   026        23 Deledda           5.63
     12   057        17 Todd              8.00
     13   058         6 Sanger            5.63
     14   058        18 Sanger            5.63
     15   064        19 Hodgkin           8.00
     16   083        10 McClintock        8.00
     17   083        22 McClintock        8.00
.
Command  C:\work\CONDUE          Rec EOF/17      File
```

Using the following command, you can create a new file using the data in two existing files:

```
JOIN WITH alias TO new file
  FOR condition FIELDS field list
```

By means of this command, a file which was previously activated by SELECT is combined with the specified alias file to form a new file. If you wish to save the new file on another drive or in another directory, you will have to add the appropriate information to the file name.

A condition may look like this, for instance:

```
FOR membernr = CTR->membernr
```

Records will only be adopted if the condition is fulfilled.

Behind FIELDS, you should enter a list of fields which are to be placed in the new file. You can indicate the difference between the two files by means of the alias and the -> signs. If you do not specify a FIELDS section in the command, all fields from both files will be adopted. If the maximum number of 128 fields is exceeded, dBASE will not create the new file.

Creating the CONDUE file
Open the ADDRESS and CONTRIBA files using the
SEL.PRG program discussed in section 10.3 and acti-
vate work area 1:

```
. DO sel
. SELECT 1
```

Now give the following JOIN command:

```
. JOIN WITH ctr TO condue FOR membernr = ctr->membernr
    FIELDS membernr,ctr->contnr,name,ctr->due
```

dBASE sets the record pointer on the first record of the
ADDRESS file and compares the MEMBERNR key with
the field of the same name in all records of the CON-
TRIBA file. If a record having the same number is found
in CONTRIBA, the fields specified in the command are
copied from both files to the new CONDUE file. Subsequently, dBASE places the record pointer on the second record in ADDRESS and conducts the same check.
This process is repeated until all records in the AD-
DRESS file have been examined.

Now the CONDUE file has been created. After giving
the following commands, a list of members will appear
on the screen as at the beginning of this section:

```
. USE condue
. LIST
```

10.8   Placing sums in a new file

You can have balances calculated from the contents of
numeric fields in a sorted or indexed file, and the results
can be placed in a new file. This may be a convenient
method of gaining more insight into a great deal of data.

Examine the list of the CONDUE file once more:

```
. use condue
. list
Record#    MEMBERNR CONTNR NAME              DUE
        1  002         20 Ross              8.00
        2  003          2 Sklodouska        8.00
        3  003         14 Sklodouska        8.00
        4  004         13 Rayleigh          8.00
        5  008          4 Rutherford        4.00
        6  008         16 Rutherford        8.00
        7  015         15 Bragg             8.00
        8  023          9 Macloud           8.00
        9  023         21 Macloud           8.00
       10  026         11 Deledda           5.63
       11  026         23 Deledda           5.63
       12  057         17 Todd              8.00
       13  058          6 Sanger            5.63
       14  058         18 Sanger            5.63
       15  064         19 Hodgkin           8.00
       16  083         10 McClintock        8.00
       17  083         22 McClintock        8.00


Command  C:\work\CONDUE                Rec EOF/17        File
```

As you see, various records are repeated. You wish to create a new CONSUM file in which each name only occurs once, along with sum of the values in the DUE fields. The result of this should appear as follows:

```
. list
Record#    MEMBERNR NAME              DUE
        1  002       Ross              8.00
        2  003       Sklodouska       16.00
        3  004       Rayleigh          8.00
        4  008       Rutherford       12.00
        5  015       Bragg             8.00
        6  023       Macloud          16.00
        7  026       Deledda          11.26
        8  057       Todd              8.00
        9  058       Sanger           11.26
       10  064       Hodgkin           8.00
       11  083       McClintock       16.00


Command  C:\work\CONSUM               Rec EOF/11        File
```

Each member only appears once in the CONSUM file. The DUE field now contains the sums of all payments due.

This compression is executed using the TOTAL command. More information concerning this command is given in section 8.7. The syntax is as follows:

```
TOTAL ON key_field TO destination_file
        [FIELDS field_list]
        [FOR/WHILE condition]
```

Example:

The CONSUM file shown above is produced in this way:

```
. USE condue                                    (1)
. TOTAL ON membernr TO tmp FIELDS due           (2)
. USE tmp                                       (3)
. COPY TO consum FIELDS membernr,name,due       (4)
. USE                                           (5)
. DELETE FILE tmp.dbf
. USE consum                                    (6)
. LIST                                          (7)
```

(1) The CONDUE file is opened. This file has already been sorted on the MEMBERNR field. If this had not been done, the file would either have to be sorted or indexed before activating the TOTAL command.

(2) The sums for the DUE numeric field are calculated for all records with the same key field. The fields are copied to the new CONSUM file along with the sums in the DUE field. dBASE displays the number of records processed (17) and the number copied (11).

(3) A temporary file, TMP, is opened to store the sums.

(4) Copies the contents of TMP to a new file, CONSUM, with the exception of the CONTNR field.

(5) Closes and deletes the temporary file.

(6) Opens the new CONSUM file.

(7) Display the eleven records in this file (see above).

10.9 Updating a main file using a mutation file

If you are working with data which alter regularly, it is advisable not to make these alterations directly in the main file, for safety reasons. Modify these data via a utility file, check them and then adjust the main file.

Example:

Via the CONTNR key field, you wish to update the PAYMENT1, PAYMENT2, and DUE fields in the main CONTRIBA file with the payments in the UPDAT utility file. The UPDAT file consists of the CONTNR, PAYMENT1 and PAYMENT2 fields.

The following command serves to update a main file with data from a so-called mutation file:

```
UPDATE ON key_field FROM mutation_file
  REPLACE main_file field1 WITH mutation_file field1,
    [..., main_file fieldn WITH mutation_file fieldn]
  [RANDOM]
```

The files should be sorted or indexed on the key field. The key field must have the same name in both files. The key field must be unique in main file. The mutation file may be designated by its alias.

The REPLACE routine regulates the substitution of fields in the main file by fields in the mutation file. The fields in the mutation file are indicated by the file alias and the pre-signs ->. Each main field is linked to a mutation field by means of a separate WITH clause. Mathematical expressions may also be specified instead of mutation fields.

The RANDOM option should be specified if the main file

is not sorted or indexed in ascending order.

Creating the UPDAT mutation file

In order to illustrate how this command works, we shall
require the UPDAT mutation file. Copy the structure of
the CONTRIBA file as follows:

```
. USE contriba
. COPY STRUCTURE TO updat FIELDS
  contnr,payment1,payment2
```

Then copy the data from the CONTRIBA file to the new
file:

```
. USE updat
. APPEND FROM contriba
```

dBASE displays that 17 records have been added. Now
index the mutation file under the name CONIDX:

```
. INDEX ON contnr TAG conidx
```

All records with unpaid contributions are now located in
the UPDAT file. However, the PAYMENT1 and PAY-
MENT2 fields still contain the value 0 (except for PAY-
MENT1 in the second record). In order to assign them
significant values, enter the following data:

```
. USE updat ORDER conidx
. EDIT FOR CONTNR = 2    (press Enter, and specify) 8.00
. EDIT FOR CONTNR = 6                               5.63
. EDIT FOR CONTNR = 17                              8.00
. EDIT FOR CONTNR = 13                              8.00
```

The following data should now be located in the UPDAT
file:

```
. list
Record#  CONTNR PAYMENT1 PAYMENT2
      1       2    8.00
      2       4    4.00
      3       6    5.63
      4       9
      5      10
      6      11
      7      13    8.00
      8      14
      9      15
     10      16
     11      17    8.00
     12      18
     13      19
     14      20
     15      21
     16      22
     17      23
.
Command  C:\work\UPDAT          Rec EOF/17      File
```

Indexing the main file

The main file must also be indexed on the CONTNR
key field. Give the following commands:

```
. USE contriba
. INDEX ON contnr TAG conidx
```

Updating the CONTRIBA main file

First open the CONTRIBA and UPDAT indexed files:

```
. CLEAR ALL
. SELECT 1
. USE contriba ORDER conidx ALIAS ctr
. SELECT 2
. USE updat ORDER conidx ALIAS upd
```

Activate the CONTRIBA file in work area 1:

```
. SELECT 1
```

Now give the update command:

```
. UPDATE ON contnr FROM upd REPLACE
      payment1 WITH upd->payment1,
```

```
        payment2 WITH upd->payment2,
        due WITH
   contr-(upd->payment1+upd->payment2)
```

The substitution process is set in motion. The contents of the PAYMENT1 and PAYMENT2 fields in the CONTRIBA file are replaced by the fields of the same name from the UPDAT mutation field. The value in the DUE field of the CONTRIBA file is reduced by the sum of the PAYMENT1 and PAYMENT2 fields from the UPDAT file.

Display the modified contents of CONTRIBA on the screen as follows:

```
. SELECT 1
. LIST contnr,membernr,contr,payment1,
  payment2,due
```

The following data should appear on the screen:

```
. sele 1
. list contnr,membernr,contr,payment1,payment2,due
Record#   contnr membernr    contr payment1 payment2     due
   1         2 003        8.00     8.00     0.00     0.00
   2         4 008        8.00     4.00     0.00     4.00
   3         6 058        5.63     5.63     0.00     0.00
   4         9 023        8.00     0.00     0.00     8.00
   5        10 083        8.00     0.00     0.00     8.00
   6        11 026        5.63     0.00     0.00     5.63
   7        13 004        8.00     8.00     0.00     0.00
   8        14 003        8.00     0.00     0.00     8.00
   9        15 015        8.00     0.00     0.00     8.00
  10        16 008        8.00     0.00     0.00     8.00
  11        17 057        8.00     8.00     0.00     0.00
  12        18 058        5.63     0.00     0.00     5.63
  13        19 064        8.00     0.00     0.00     8.00
  14        20 002        8.00     0.00     0.00     8.00
  15        21 023        8.00     0.00     0.00     8.00
  16        22 083        8.00     0.00     0.00     8.00
  17        23 026        5.63     0.00     0.00     5.63

Command  C:\work\CONTRIBA        Rec EOF/17        File
```

The UPDATDEM program

In the program described below, the time of the previous update of the files is displayed on the screen before the execution of the UPDATE command. dBASE provides the LUPDATE() function to perform this. This function shows the date of the previous update of an opened database, for example:

```
. USE address
. ? LUPDATE()
10/05/1993
```

The function reads the file date of the ADDRESS.DBF file on disk and displays this in the form of a date field.

The date of the previous modification may be an important piece of information. In certain situations an unexpected date may give reason to discontinue a program. The date display is followed by a yes/no question in the UPDATE.PRG program:

```
* UPDATDEM.PRG program *
CLEAR ALL                                               (1)
SELECT 1
USE contriba ORDER conidx ALIAS ctr
SELECT 2
USE updat ORDER conidx ALIAS upd

SELECT 1
STORE LUPDATE() TO datctr                               (2)
SELECT 2
STORE LUPDATE() TO datupd

further = "?"                                           (3)
CLEAR
@ 3,5 SAY "Previous CONTRIBA update:"
@ 3,45 SAY DTOC(datctr)                                 (4)
@ 4,5 SAY "Mutation file created on:"
@ 4,45 SAY DTOC(datupd)
@ 6,5 SAY "Continue? (Y/N)"
@ 6,45 GET further PICTURE "X"
READ
IF further$"Nn"
   RETURN
ENDIF
```

```
SELECT 1                                              (5)
UPDATE ON contnr FROM upd ;
REPLACE payment1 WITH upd->payment1, ;
        payment2 WITH upd->payment2, ;
        due WITH contr-(upd->payment1+upd->payment2)
* end UPDATDEM.PRG program *
```

(1) The two files are opened in different work areas.

(2) The date of the previous modifications to the CON-
TRIBA file is assigned to the DATCTR variable,
and that of UPDAT to the DATUPD memory variable. Accordingly, both data can be displayed later
without having to switch work areas.

(3) The FURTHER variable for the yes/no question is
initialized.

(4) The update data are shown as a character field.

(5) Work area 1 is activated for the UPDATE command. Pay special attention to commas and semi-
colons: the commas are part of the command, the
semi-colons allow you to divide the command into
several rows, making it more orderly and legible.

10.10 Linking records from three files

The SET RELATION command enables you to link only
two files. However, linking several work areas makes it
possible to connect more than two files to each other. In
the following example, we wish to link the fields from the
ADDRESS, CONSUM and DEPT files via the MEM-
BERNR key field.

The ADDRESS file is the sample file which we have
used for many other examples in this book already. The
CONSUM file was created in section 10.7. We require
the DEPT file as the third file. This file is to consist of the
MEMBERNR (field type: character, length: 3) and the
DEP (field type: character, length: 1) fields. Create this

file and enter the following data:

RecNr	MEMBERNR	DEP
1	004	R
2	003	W
3	015	W
4	008	R
5	057	R
6	058	W
7	064	R
8	002	R
9	023	W
10	083	R
11	026	W

Index the CONSUM and DEPT files on the MEM-BERNR key field as follows:

```
. USE consum
. INDEX ON membernr TAG mnrsum
. USE dept
. INDEX ON membernr TAG mnrdep
```

Type out the following short program and save it as SEL2.PRG:

```
* SEL2.PRG program *
CLEAR ALL
SELECT 1                                      (1)
USE address ORDER memnridx ALIAS adr
SELECT 2
USE consum ORDER mnrsum ALIAS con
SELECT 3
USE dept ORDER mnrdep ALIAS dep

SELECT 2
SET RELATION TO membernr INTO adr             (2)
SELECT 3
SET RELATION TO membernr INTO con             (3)
* end SEL2.PRG program *
```

(1) The ADDRESS, CONSUM and DEPT indexed files are opened under aliases.

(2) The CONSUM indexed file in work area 2 is linked to the ADDRESS indexed file in work area 1.

(3) The DEPT indexed file in work area 3 is linked to the CONSUM indexed file in work area 2.

When this program has been activated and executed using DO sel2, the DEPT file is active since the last SE-LECT command activated work area 3. Just to be certain, we shall place a SELECT command in front of each example, even if this is not really necessary.

Example 1:

The following command displays fields from three different files - the MEMBERNR field from the DEPT file, the NAME field from the ADDRESS file and the DUE field from the CONSUM file:

```
. SELECT 3
. LIST membernr,adr->name,con->due
```

Example 2:

We wish to display the same fields as in example 1, but now only for member number 057:

```
. SELECT 3
. FIND 057
. DISPLAY membernr,adr->name,con->due
```

Example 3:

We wish to display the same fields as in the previous examples, but now under certain conditions:

```
. SELECT 3
. DISPLAY membernr,adr->name,con->due
     FOR add->name = "Todd"
```

```
. DISPLAY membernr,adr->name,con->due
    FOR dep = "W" .AND. add->sex = "f"
```

Caution: It is essential that these commands are entered from the work area in which the links
were made. In the examples above, that is
work area 3 with the DEPT file. If, for instance, work area 1 is activated, complete
data from the ADDRESS file cannot be displayed. The data from the CONSUM and
DEPT files are missing.

11 Converting files to a different file format

Because most application programs use their own file format which is not interchangeable with the format of other programs, generally files from one program cannot be directly used by other programs. For this reason, each advanced application program provides facilities for the import and export of files. In this terminology, 'importing' means that a file from another program is converted to a format which can be used by the current program. 'Exporting' means that one's own file is converted to a format which can be used by another program.

dBASE data files consist of a header and the file data. The header contains information concerning the dBASE version, the date of the last update, the number of records, the number of bytes used by the header itself, the number of bytes per record and a complete field description of the data file. Other programs cannot cope with this header. Accordingly, when exporting, it has to be removed and replaced by other data, if necessary. Vice versa, when importing, dBASE has to construct a header when data are read in.

11.1 Importing and exporting files in dBASE

dBASE has commands enabling you to import and export files. Here the COPY and APPEND commands are applied along with a type option at the end:

```
COPY TO other_file [FIELDS field_list]
  [FOR/WHILE condition] [type]

APPEND FROM other_file
  [FOR condition] [type]
```

Prior to a file being imported using APPEND FROM, the structure of the dBASE file to be created has to be defined by means of the command CREATE file_name.

You can apply the following options for TYPE at the end of a COPY or APPEND command. Each option corresponds to a certain file format:

SDF
This abbreviation represents the general file exchange format - System Data Format. This is a format with a fixed record length without field limit signs. Each record is concluded by CR/LF (Carriage Return/Line Feed). We shall refer to this format in the future as 'ASCII files with a fixed record length'.

DELIMITED This is also a general file exchange format. However, the records have a variable length and separators are used to divide the fields from one another. Normally, these are commas and inverted commas, but these may be altered by means of the WITH option. Just as in the case of the SDF format, the records end with CR/LF. We shall refer to this format in the future as 'ASCII files with a variable record length'.

SYLK
The Multiplan format.

DIF
The VisiCalc format.

WKS
The Lotus 1-2-3 format.

Apart from these formats, dBASE IV 2.0 also supports the DBASEII, DBMEMO3, FW2 and RPD formats.

Note:
In addition to COPY and APPEND, dBASE also provides the IMPORT and EXPORT commands, which enable you to convert files from or to a number of special file formats (including the Framework format and the old dBASE II format).

Converting a dBASE file to an ASCII file with a fixed record length

The following command enables you to convert a dBASE file to an ASCII file with a fixed record length:

```
COPY TO other_file SDF
```

SDF files can easily be further processed using most programming languages and some word processors.

Example 1:

We wish to copy the MEMBERNR, NAME, FIRST_NAME, STREET and PCTOWN fields in the ADDRESS file to an ASCII file with a fixed record length. The new file is to be called SDFADD. If you do not specify an extension, the file automatically receives the extension .TXT:

```
. SELECT 1
. USE address
. COPY TO sdfadd FIELDS membernr,name,
     first_name,street,pctown SDF
```

Caution: The COPY command **must** be specified on **one** line.

You can examine the contents of the file using the following command:

```
. MODIFY COMMAND sdfadd.txt
```

```
 Layout   Words   Go To   Print   Exit
[......▼1.....▼..2....▼....3..▼.....4▼......▼5.....▼.6....▼...7..▼.....
004Rayleigh      John        18 Argon Avenue     CA2 4WS Cambridge
003Sklodouska    Marya       34 Radium Rd        CU1 2MC Currie
015Bragg         William     42 Crystal Crescent LD1 3WH Leeds
008Rutherford    Ernest      37 Charge Court      MA1 2HE Manchester
057Todd          Alexander   1 Vitamin View      CA1 2BB Cambridge
058Sanger        Frederick   3 Insulin Isle      CA4 8NB Cambridge
064Hodgkin       Dorothy     9 Pepsin Park       OX2 1XR Oxford
002Ross          Ronald      17 Malaria Mews     LV1 4IN Liverpool
023Macloud       John        35 Diabetes Drive   AB3 2CT Aberdeen
083McClintock    Barbara     Translocation Tower CO1 6DN Cornell
026Deledda       Grazia      36 Sardinia Slopes  LE1 7IT Lands End




 Program  C:\work\SDFADD          Line:1 Col:1                        Ins
```

Converting a dBASE file to an ASCII file with a variable record length

The DELIMITED option is used to convert a dBASE file to an ASCII file with a variable record length:

```
COPY TO other_file DELIMITED
```

The DELIMITED option ensures that the spaces at the end of the text fields are removed, that all text fields are placed between inverted commas and that commas are placed between the consecutive fields. Files such as these can be used for the mail merge function in some word processing programs.

Example 2:

We shall create a text file with inverted commas and commas as separators:

```
. USE address
. COPY TO mailadd.dat FIELDS
  name,first_name,street,
    pctown,contr,sex DELIMITED
```

Examine the result using:

```
. MODIFY COMMAND mailadd.dat
```

```
 Layout   Words   Go To   Print   Exit
▐····•····▼1····•··▼··2····▼····3··▼·•····4▼····•·▼5····•·▼··6····▼····7··▼·•····
"Rayleigh","John","18 Argon Avenue","CA2 4WS Cambridge",8.00,"m"
"Sklodouska","Marya","34 Radium Rd","CU1 2MC Currie",8.00,"f"
"Bragg","William","42 Crystal Crescent","LD1 3WH Leeds",8.00,"m"
"Rutherford","Ernest","37 Charge Court","MA1 2HE Manchester",8.00,"m"
"Todd","Alexander","1 Uitamin View","CA1 2BB Cambridge",8.00,"m"
"Sanger","Frederick","3 Insulin Isle","CA4 8NB Cambridge",5.63,"m"
"Hodgkin","Dorothy","9 Pepsin Park","OX2 1XR Oxford",8.00,"f"
"Ross","Ronald","17 Malaria Mews","LU1 4IN Liverpool",8.00,"m"
"Macloud","John","35 Diabetes Drive","AB3 2CT Aberdeen",8.00,"m"
"McClintock","Barbara","Translocation Tower","CO1 6DN Cornell",8.00,"f"
"Deledda","Grazia","36 Sardinia Slopes","LE1 7IT Lands End",5.63,"f"




Program ▐C:\work\MAILADD      ▐▌Line:1 Col:1  ▐▌        ▐▌            Ins
```

Converting a dBASE file to an ASCII file with a variable record length and with spaces as field separators

If you do not wish to include commas and inverted commas in the text file, use the DELIMITED option along with the additional option WITH BLANK:

```
COPY TO other_file DELIMITED WITH BLANK
```

Example 3:

We shall create a text file containing member number, name and first name, using spaces as separators:

```
. USE address
. COPY TO spacadd.dat FIELDS
  membernr,name,first_name
      DELIMITED WITH BLANK
. MODIFY COMMAND spacadr.dat
```

The result is a text file in which the fields specified in the command are displayed next to one another only separated by a space:

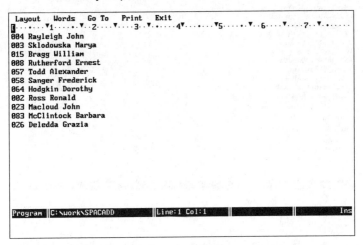

Converting a dBASE file to an ASCII file with a variable record length and with field separators of one's own choice

If, in addition to a comma, an extra field separator is to be placed in the text file (e.g. a colon), this sign must be explicitly specified behind WITH. The general syntax of this form of the COPY command is as follows:

```
COPY TO other_file DELIMITED WITH sign
```

Example 4:

We shall create a text file with a variable record length and with the colon as an extra separator:

```
. USE address
. COPY TO doubadd.dat FIELDS name,first_name
    DELIMITED WITH :
. MODIFY COMMAND doubadd.dat
```

The result is:

```
 Layout   Words   Go To   Print   Exit
[····•····▼1····•··▼··2····▼····3··▼··•····4▼······•··▼5·····•··▼··6····▼····7··▼··•·····
:Rayleigh:,:John:
:Sklodowska:,:Marya:
:Bragg:,:William:
:Rutherford:,:Ernest:
:Todd:,:Alexander:
:Sanger:,:Frederick:
:Hodgkin:,:Dorothy:
:Ross:,:Ronald:
:Macloud:,:John:
:McClintock:,:Barbara:
:Deledda:,:Grazia:




Program  C:\work\DOUBADD          Line:1 Col:1                          Ins
```

Converting a dBASE file to a file for Multiplan, Visi-Calc or Lotus 1-2-3

You can easily convert the information in a dBASE data file to the format suitable for one of the Multiplan, Visi-Calc or Lotus 1-2-3 spreadsheet programs. You are then able to further process the data, to execute calculations, or create graphs and diagrams based on numeric fields etc. The general syntax is as folows:

```
COPY TO other_file SYLK/DIF/WKS
```

Example 5:

We wish to perform a calculation in Lotus 1-2-3 using the contribution payments from the ADDRESS file. To do this, we shall copy this field along with the member number and name to a Lotus worksheet with the name CONTRIBU:

```
. USE address
. COPY TO contribu FIELDS
```

```
membernr,name,contr WKS
```

Now quit dBASE, start up Lotus 1-2-3 and load the file. You can now process it further using the Lotus 1-2-3 functions.

You can export dBASE data to Multiplan (option SYLK) and VisiCalc (option DIF) in the same way.

Converting an ASCII file with a fixed record length to a dBASE file

In order to convert an ASCII file with a fixed record length to a dBASE file, use the following command:

```
APPEND FROM other_file SDF
```

Example 6:

We wish to import the data from the SDFADD.TXT ASCII text file which has a fixed record length, into a dBASE file. To do this, we must first define the structure of the dBASE file:

```
. CREATE addsdf
```

Import only the NAME and FIRST_NAME fields into the dBASE file. Define these fields as follows:

	field name	field type	width	dec
1	NAME	character	15	
2	FIRST_NAME	character	15	

Answer N to the question 'Input data records now?'. Subsequently open the (empty) file and import the data from the SDFADD.TXT text file:

```
. USE addsdf
. APPEND FROM sdfadd.txt SDF
```

Now display the contents of the new file on the screen using LIST:

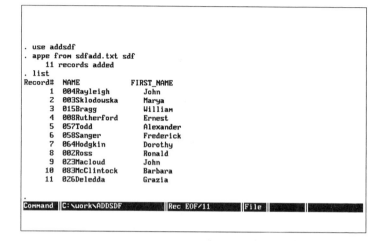

```
. use addsdf
. appe from sdfadd.txt sdf
    11 records added
. list
Record#  NAME            FIRST_NAME
      1  004Rayleigh       John
      2  003Sklodouska     Marya
      3  015Bragg          William
      4  008Rutherford     Ernest
      5  057Todd           Alexander
      6  058Sanger         Frederick
      7  064Hodgkin        Dorothy
      8  002Ross           Ronald
      9  023Macloud        John
     10  083McClintock     Barbara
     11  026Deledda        Grazia
.
```

| Command | C:\work\ADDSDF | Rec EOF/11 | File |

As you see, dBASE has taken the original member number from the SDFADD.TXT file to be a part of the NAME field. Therefore, you can draw the following conclusion:

Rule: If you only require a part of the fields in a file in another format, first import all the fields and then remove the superfluous fields within dBASE.

Converting an ASCII file with a variable length to a dBASE file

To convert an ASCII file with a variable record length to a dBASE file, give the following command:

```
APPEND FROM other_file DELIMITED
```

Example 7:

You wish to import all fields from the MAILADD.DAT file into the ADDMAIL.DBF file. The dBASE file structure has to be defined first, just as in the previous example. We shall do this, not by defining the entire structure once again, but by copying the relevant part from the ADDRESS file:

```
. USE address
. COPY STRUCTURE TO addmail FIELDS
  name,first_name,
    street,pctown,contr,sex
```

You can now import the data. You are only interested in the data concerning members who pay 8.00:

```
. USE addmail
. APPEND FROM mailadd.dat FOR contr=8.00
  DELIMITED
```

Importing data from a Multiplan, VisiCalc or Lotus 1-2-3 file

You can easily import data from a file having a Multiplan, VisiCalc or Lotus 1-2-3 spreadsheet program file format. The general syntax is as follows:

```
APPEND FROM other_file SYLK/DIF/WKS
```

Example 8:

You wish to import data from the CONTRIBU Lotus worksheet. Begin by defining the structure of the dBASE file with the name ADDLOTUS:

```
. CREATE addlotus
```

Define the MEMBERNR, NAME and CONTR fields.

Then import the data using:

```
. APPEND FROM contribu WKS
```

You can import data from Multiplan (option SYLK) and VisiCalc (option DIF) in the same way.

If the first record contains a series of column-listed data from the spreadsheet, it is advisable to remove this in advance using a word processor or an editor. You can also delete the unwanted record later in dBASE using:

```
. GO 1
. DELETE
. PACK
```

Importing and exporting files in dBASE 361

12   Installing dBASE

Before installing dBASE, you must make copies of all
original diskettes using the DOS program DISKCOPY.
Work only with these copies. If you have two identical
diskdrives (two drives with the same physical formats
and the same storage capacity), you can do this using
the following command:

```
DISKCOPY a: b:
```

Always insert the original diskette in drive A: and the
diskette on which the copy is to be made in drive B:.

If you have two dissimilar drives (with different physical
formats) or one diskdrive and a harddisk, make the
copies in one drive using the command:

```
DISKCOPY a: a:
```

or:

```
DISKCOPY b: b:
```

In this case, DOS will ask you several times to switch
diskettes. This depends on the available memory capacity. Pay close attention when the *SOURCE diskette*
and the *TARGET diskette* (destination diskette) are requested.

Subsequently use the INSTALL installation program. If,
for instance, you are going to install from drive A:, give
the following consecutive commands:

```
A:
INSTALL
```

Follow the instructions on the screen closely. If you are
not familiar with the 'Cache' facility, do not have dBASE
install cache. You are probably already using
SMARTDRV.SYS from DOS or WINDOWS. Both make

the dBASE cache superfluous. If required, you can install the cache later by means of the *Reconfigure* menu
from DBSETUP.

In order to be able to work with dBASE, your computer
must have 640 Kb RAM memory, of which 450 KB must
be available for dBASE during working. dBASE IV only
works from the harddisk upon which 4.5 Mb free capacity is required for installation.

During installation, you can indicate that dBASE should
make the necessary adjustments in CONFIG.SYS automatically. If you wish, you can also do this yourself
using an editor or a word processor which is able to
work with pure ASCII files (without layout information).

13   Configuring dBASE

13.1   Setting the parameters for the current session

SET commands

dBASE IV is configured by the manufacturer for stand-ard circumstances. As we have seen in chapter 3, you can adapt these settings to your own work situation. This can be done in two ways: you can switch the indi-vual settings on or off, and you can alter the system par-ameters. The commands used to do these are as fol-lows:

```
SET setting ON/OFF
SET system parameter TO value
```

Examples:

```
SET BELL ON/OFF
```
This command is used to switch on/off the acoustic sig-nal which you receive with an error message or when the maximum field length is exceeded. The default set-ting is ON.

```
SET MARGIN TO 10
```
This left margin for printer output is set to 10.

A survey of the most important SET commands is shown is appendix A.

SET using menu support

If you wish to alter a system setting but you are no longer sure of how this is done exactly, give the follow-ing command:

```
SET
```

A menu line appears on the screen. The *Options* menu is activated.

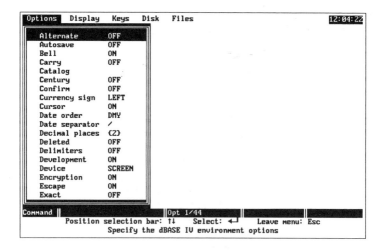

```
Options  Display  Keys  Disk  Files                              12:04:22
  Alternate      OFF
  Autosave       OFF
  Bell           ON
  Carry          OFF
  Catalog
  Century        OFF
  Confirm        OFF
  Currency sign  LEFT
  Cursor         ON
  Date order     DMY
  Date separator /
  Decimal places {2}
  Deleted        OFF
  Delimiters     OFF
  Development    ON
  Device         SCREEN
  Encryption     ON
  Escape         ON
  Exact          OFF
Command                              Opt 1/44
       Position selection bar: ↑↓    Select: ←┘    Leave menu: Esc
                    Specify the dBASE IV environment options
```

Changing settings using the Options menu

Imagine that you wish to switch off the acoustic signal
which is given when the maximum field length is exceeded. Proceed as follows:

Using the Cursor Down key, go to the *Bell ON* option in
the *Options* menu. By pressing Enter, the setting will
switch from ON to OFF and back again.

You can gain help information about any individual point
by pressing F1.

The Display menu

By pressing Cursor Right when in the *Options* menu,
you will open the *Display* menu.

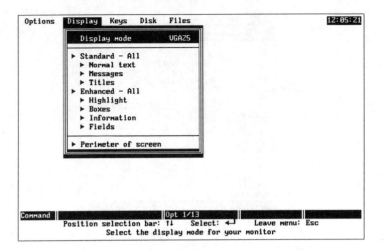

Using this menu, you can specify the colours for all parts of the dBASE screen if you have a colour monitor, or the screen attributes if you have a monochrome screen. To do this, go to the option which you wish to alter using the cursor keys, and then examine all the possibilities by pressing the spacebar or Enter.

The Keys menu

You can alter the definition of the function keys using the *Keys* menu. The F1 function key is reserved for the help function and cannot be altered. Function keys F2 to F10 have been assigned default definitions, but these may be altered if required. The figure below shows the default definition.

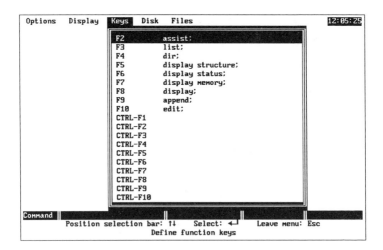

Example:

You wish to assign the text CLEAR; (the semicolon represents Enter) to function key F3. Activate the *Keys* menu using Cursor Right and then go to the existing definition of F3 using Cursor Down. Press Enter. Type CLEAR;, confirm this using Enter and quit the SET menu using Esc.

If you now press F3, the screen is cleared. This will remain so until you ascribe a different definition to F3 or quit dBASE.

You may also assign several command words to one function key as long as the total number of characters does not exceed 30. Each word must be separated from the next by a semi-colon. For instance:

```
CLEAR;LIST;STATUS;
```

13.2 Editing the CONFIG.DB configuration file

dBASE stores the default system settings in the CONFIG.DB configuration file. This is a normal ASCII text file which you can edit using a word processor or an editor.

When a standard installation has been carried out, the following commands (among others) are located in CONFIG.DB:

```
COMMAND = ASSIST
STATUS = ON
```

In addition, CONFIG.DB contains the defintions for the printer, the screen type and the directory for SQL files.

The command STATUS = ON results in the status line being shown at the bottom of the screen. COMMAND = ASSIST means that the Control Center is activated directly at the beginning of the dBASE program.

Example:

We shall now make some changes to the CONFIG.DB file in order to alter the dBASE configuration. We shall do this by means of the editor integrated in dBASE. Give the following command to load the configuration file:

```
. MODIFY COMMAND config.db
```

The following now appears on the screen:

```
 Layout   Words   Go To   Print   Exit
█······▼1·····•··▼··2····▼····3··▼·•····4▼·······▼5·····•··▼··6····▼····7··▼·•·····
✳
✳       dBASE IV Configuration File
✳   Written by Install.exe on 13/5/93
✳
COLOR OF NORMAL       = N+/BG
COLOR OF HIGHLIGHT    = RG+/W
COLOR OF MESSAGES     = W/B
COLOR OF TITLES       = W+/BG
COLOR OF BOX          = W+/B
COLOR OF INFORMATION = BG+/B
COLOR OF FIELDS       = W+/N
DISPLAY               = VGA25
COMMAND               = ASSIST
EXCLUSIVE             = ON
STATUS                = ON
SQLDATABASE           = SAMPLES
SQLHOME               = C:\DBASE\SQLHOME
CURRENCY              = "£"
DATE                  = DMY
HOURS                 = 24
Program ║C:\dbase\CONFIG            ║Line:1 Col:1    ║          ║          ║    Ins
```

In the editor, you can use the normal keys:

cursor key	moving the cursor
Ins	inserting
Del	deletes one character
Ctrl-Y	deletes one line
Ctrl-N	insert a blank line
Ctrl-A	one word to the left
Ctrl-F	one word to the right
Ctrl-W	end

Now delete the COMMAND = ASSIST and STATUS = ON lines using the key combination Ctrl-Y and then add the following new lines:

```
F3 = "CLEAR;"
F4 = "SET STATUS OFF;"
F5 = "SET COLOR TO /GR,/W,G;"
F6 = "MODIFY COMMAND;"
TEDIT = Q
SET MARGIN TO 6
COMMAND = CLEAR
```

The significance of the new lines is:

The first four lines assign new functions to the function keys F3 to F6.

The CLEAR command clears the screen. The semi-colon represents a keystroke on Enter. Thus, you can always clear the screen using F3 (even if you are working in the prompt mode).

The SET STATUS OFF command suppresses the display of status information and message lines at the bottom of the screen.

The SET COLOR command in the third line regulates the colour for the dBASE screen. If you are using a monochrome screen, you can omit this line.

By assigning the MODIFY COMMAND instruction to F6, you are able to activate the dBASE editor with one keystroke in order to edit a program.

The fifth command, TEDIT = Q, installs an alternative editor (in this case the shareware editor QEdit) instead of the editor integrated in dBASE. You can use this command if you are writing a great deal of texts and/or lengthy programs and you prefer to work with a certain editor or word processor. Then replace the Q in the above command with the command by which you normally activate the required program (for instance, WP for WordPerfect, WORD for Microsoft Word etc.). The command may also refer to a batch file.

The editor which has been installed by TEDIT = is automatically activated by the MODIFY COMMAND instruction. Keep in mind that the editor must be located in the same directory as dBASE and that your computer must have sufficient memory available.

The SET MARGIN TO 6 command sets the left margin to 6 for all printer output.

The COMMAND = CLEAR line ensures that the screen is automatically cleared each time dBASE is activated.

Appendix A
List of dBASE commands

We shall deal briefly with the most well-used dBASE commands in this appendix. A complete list would require dozens of extra pages. If you wish to know more about a certain command, refer to the index and look up the appropriate passage in the book. The dBASE help function (F1) provides information concerning the syntax and parameters. Commands originating in the more recent versions of dBASE, will not apply to older versions.

*	Precedes a comment line in the program.
$	Relational operator (comparison) for character fields.
&	Indicates the contents of a memory variable.
?	Display of a (list of) variable(s) on the following line.
??	Display of a (list of) variable(s) on the current line.
@ x,y GET	Displays data on a specified position on the screen ###; they may be subsequently modified.
@ x,y SAY	Displays data on a specified position on the screen or printer.
@ x1,y1 TO x2,y2	Draws a frame.
@-FUNCTION	Formatting function.

ABS()	Calculates the absolute value.
ACCEPT	Stores a string in a character variable in memory.
APPEND	Adds records to the end of a database.
APPEND FROM	Adds records from other files to the end of a database. By applying an extra option, data can be imported from files originating in other programs.
ASC()	Converts a character to the corresponding ASCII code.
ASSIST	Activates the Control Center.
AT	Defines the starting position of a string within another string.
AVERAGE()	Calculates the average of a range of values.
BOF()	Returns .T. if the record pointer is at the beginning of a database file.
BROWSE	Activates the page-oriented edit mode.
CALL	Used with a LOAD command, executes a binary file.
CANCEL	Discontinues the execution of a program, closes the .PRG file and returns to the dBASE prompt or the Control Center.
CASE	Tests against one condition in a DO CASE construction.

CDOW()	Produces the day of the week as text.
CHANGE	Activates the edit mode for individual records and fields in a database.
CHR()	Converts an ASCII code to the corresponding character.
CLEAR	Clears the screen.
CLEAR ALL	Closes all files and deletes all memory variables.
CLEAR FIELDS	Deletes all fields from the SET FIELDS list in the current work area.
CLEAR GETS	Makes all current GET variables invisible to the screen-oriented READ command.
CLEAR MEMORY	Clears all memory variables.
CLEAR TYPEAHEAD	Clears the keyboard buffer.
CLOSE	Closes all or the specified files types.
CMONTH()	Produces the current month as text.
COL()	Returns the current column position on the screen.
CONTINUE	Places the record pointer at the next record which satisfies the conditions specified in the previous LOCATE command.

COPY	Copies the opened database to a new database.
COPY FILE	Copies a chosen file (similar to DOS COPY).
COPY STRUCTURE	Copies the structure of the opened database to a new database.
COUNT()	Returns the number of records which fulfil the specified range clause.
CREATE	Creates a new database.
CREATE FROM	Creates a new database from a file which was created using using COPY STRUCTURE EXTENDED.
CREATE LABEL	Makes a Label file.
CREATE QUERY	Creates a Query file.
CREATE REPORT	Creates a Report file.
CREATE SCREEN	Creates a screen file, a format file and a database if required.
CREATE VIEW	Creates a View file.
CTOD()	Converts a character field to a date field.
DATE()	Returns the system date.
DAY()	Returns the day of the month from a date expression.
DBF()	Returns the name of the current database file.

DEBUG   Gives you access to the pro-
                                gram debugger to rectify pro-
                                gramming errors.

DEFINE   Used to define certain options.

DEFINE BAR   Used along with line number
                                OF popup name to define a
                                single option in a popup menu.

DEFINE MENU   Used along with the menu
                                name and the DEFINE PAD
                                command to define a menu.

DELETE   Assigns a deletion mark to rec-
                                ords.

DELETED()   Returns a true (.T.) if the rec-
                                ord in question is marked for
                                deletion.

DIR   Displays a list of files in the cur-
                                rent or in a specified directory.

DISKSPACE()   Returns the number of free
                                bytes on the default diskdrive.

DISPLAY   Shows records and fields on
                                the screen.

DISPLAY HISTORY   Displays a list of the last com-
                                mands specified.

DISPLAY MEMORY   Displays a list of the current
                                memory variables.

DISPLAY STATUS   Displays information concern-
                                ing the opened files and the
                                system settings.

DISPLAY   Shows the structure of the cur-
  STRUCTURE   rent database on the screen.

DO	Executes a program or a procedure.
DO CASE	Constructs a multiple choice process.
DO WHILE	Constructs a loop with a starting condition.
DO WITH	Activates a program or a procedure with parameters.
DOW()	Returns the day of the week as a number.
DTOC()	Converts a date field to a character field.
EDIT	Activates the record-oriented edit mode.
EJECT	Sends a Form Feed to the printer.
ELSE	Constructs the second branch of a double selection process.
ENDCASE	Ends a DO CASE construction.
ENDDO	Ends a DO WHILE construction.
ENDIF	Ends an IF construction.
ENDTEXT	Ends the display of a text which was preceded by the TEXT command. Provides a convenient way of writing text to the output device.

EOF()   Returns a true (.T.) if the rec-
                               ord pointer is placed at the end
                               of the file.

ERASE   Deletes one or more records
                               from the disk.

ERROR()   Returns an error number for an
                               ON ERROR test.

EXIT   Quits a DO WHILE loop pre-
                               maturely.

EXP()   Calculates powers of e (the
                               natural logarithm base).

EXPORT   Exports dBASE files to other
                               specified file formats, such as
                               Framework and dBASE II.

FIELD()   Returns the name of a certain
                               field in a database.

FLDCOUNT()   Counts the number of fields in
                               an open database file.

FILE(0   Checks whether a certain file is
                               present.

FIND   Places the record pointer on a
                               record whose index key corre-
                               sponds to a specified string.

FKLABEL()   Returns the names of the func-
                               tion keys.

FKMAX()   Returns the maximum number
                               of function keys.

FOUND()   Determines whether the pre-
                               vious search action in the data-
                               base was successful.

GETENV()	Returns the contents of the operating system environment variables.
GO/GOTO	Places the record pointer directly on a certain record.
HELP	Accesses the menu-operated help system.
IF	Constructs a single or double selection process.
IIF()	Constructs a one-lined selection process in which the value of one of two expressions is assigned to a variable.
IMPORT	Imports files in certain file formats such as Framework and dBASE II into dBASE files.
INDEX	Generates an index file.
INKEY()	Keyboard input during a program.
INPUT	Stores the value of an expression in a variable.
INSERT	Adds data to a database.
INT()	Displays only integers (no decimals).
ISALPHA()	Checks whether a variable contains text.
ISCOLOR()	Checks whether dBASE is running in the colour mode.

ISLOWER()	Checks whether a variable contains a small letter.
ISMOUSE ()	Returns a logical true (.T.) if a mouse driver is installed.
ISUPPER()	Checks whether a variable contains a capital letter.
JOIN	Links specified records and fields from two databases.
LABEL	Displays data in label format using the specified Label file.
LEFT()	Returns the left part of a string.
LEN()	Returns the length of a string.
LIST	Displays records and fields on the screen.
LIST HISTORY	Shows a list of the last specified commands.
LIST MEMORY	Shows a list of the memory variables.
LIST STATUS	Displays information concerning the opened files and the system settings.
LIST STRUCTURE	Displays a survey of the file structure.
LOAD	Loads a binary module in memory. The module can then be activated using CALL.
LOCATE	Places the record pointer on a record to which the specified condition applies.

LOG()	Calculates the natural logarithm (base e) of a number.
LOOP	Jumps to the beginning of a DO WHILE loop.
LOWER()	Convert capitals to small letters.
LTRIM()	Remove spaces at the beginning of a string.
LUPDATE()	Returns the date to the previous database update.
MAX()	Returns the larger of two values.
MESSAGE()	Returns the error message for the last error.
MIN()	Returns the smaller of two values.
MOD()	Calculates the remainder from a division of two numeric expressions.
MODIFY COMMAND	Activates the internal editor or the external editor specified by TEDIT, in order to modify a program file.
MODIFY LABEL	Edits a Label file.
MODIFY QUERY	Edits a Query file.
MODIFY REPORT	Edits a Report file.
MODIFY SCREEN	Edits a SCREEN file, a format file and a database if required.

MODIFY STRUCTURE   Enables you to alter the struc-
                   ture of the database.

MODIFY VIEW   Edits a View file.

MONTH()   Returns the current month as a
                   number.

NDX()   Returns the name of the
                   opened index files.

NOTE   Precedes a comment line in a
                   program.

ON ERROR/ESCAPE   Enables you to react to three
/KEY   possibilities in your programs:
                   the occurrence of an error, to
                   press the Esc key or to press a
                   random key.

ORDER   Activates an index of a multiple
                   index file.

OTHERWISE   Provides an alternative if none
                   of the CASE conditions lead to
                   a DO CASE construction.

OS()   Returns the name of the opera-
                   ting system.

PACK   Removes all records which
                   have been marked for deletion
                   from the current file.

PARAMETERS   Defines the memory variables
                   which are to contain the data
                   which are passed on via a DO
                   WITH command.

PCOL()   Returns the current column po-
                   sition on the printer.

PRIVATE | Renders a variable invisible to program files at higher levels.

PROCEDURE | Marks the beginning of a procedure in a procedure file.

PROW() | Returns the current row position on the printer.

PUBLIC | Defines a variable as being public, in other words, available at all levels.

QUIT | Closes all files and ends dBASE.

READ | Reads data into GET fields or variables.

READKEY() | Returns a number which represents the key pressed to exit from a full-screen editing mode.

RECALL | Recalls deleted records.

RECCOUNT() | Returns the number of records in a database.

RECNO() | Returns the number of the current record.

RECSIZE() | Returns the size of a record.

REINDEX | Rebuilds all active index and multiple index files in the current work area.

RELEASE | Deletes the current variables from memory.

REMARK

Precedes comment which is to appear on screen during the execution of a program.

RENAME

Renames a file.

REPLACE

Enters new data in fields. The old data are lost.

REPORT

Displays a report.

RESTORE

Reads in variables which have been stored in a disk file.

RESUME

Resumes a program which was discontinued using SUS-PEND.

RETRY

Returns to the activating pro-gram and executes the same command once again.

RETURN

Returns to the activating pro-gram and executes the next command.

RIGHT()

Displays the right part of the string.

ROUND()

Rounds off numeric values.

ROW()

Returns the current row posi-tion on the screen.

RTRIM()

Removes spaces at the end of a string.

RUN

Executes an external program. Behind RUN, specify the start command as you would do be-hind the DOS prompt.

SAVE

Saves the current memory variables in a disk file.

SEEK

Places the record pointer on a record whose index key corresponds to the specified expression.

SELECT

Selects one of the ten dBASE work areas. A different file can be opened in each work area by giving the command USE.

SET

Activates the menu-operated SET command.

SET ALTERNATE
ON/OFF

Transports all displayed data simultaneously to a file. The default setting is OFF.

SET ALTERNATE TO

Creates a file which will contain all displayed data.

SET BELL ON/OFF

Switches on or off the acoustic signal which is given in the case of errors or when the limits of the fields are exceeded during input. The default setting is ON.

SET BORDER TO
SINGLE/DOUBLE/
PANEL/NONE

Defines the way in which frames are displayed.

SET CARRY ON/OFF

Carries forwards changes made in the contents of the last record during APPEND and IN-SERT. The default setting is OFF.

SET CATALOG
ON/OFF

Adds files to the opened catalog. The default setting is OFF.

SET CATALOG TO   Creates a new catalog, opens
                        an existing catalog or closes
                        the current catalog.

SET CENTURY   Displays the century in a date
ON/OFF   field. The default setting is
                        OFF.

SET COLOR ON/OFF   Switches between colour and
                        monochrome display. The de-
                        fault setting depends on the
                        situation when dBASE is acti-
                        vated.

SET COLOR TO   Determines the colours to be
                        used or the screen attributes.

SET CONFIRM   Determines whether it is
ON/OFF   necessary to press Enter when
                        a field is completely filled with
                        data. The default setting is
                        OFF.

SET CONSOLE   Determines whether data
ON/OFF   should be displayed on the
                        screen. The default setting is
                        ON.

SET DATE   Determines which format is
                        used to display calender data.

SET DEBUG ON/OFF   Determines whether the data
                        passed on by ECHO should
                        also be printed. The default
                        setting is OFF.

SET DECIMALS TO   Defines the number of deci-
                        mals in the output of numeric
                        data.

SET DEFAULT TO   Defines the current drive.

SET DELETED
ON/OFF

Determines whether records with a deletion mark should be displayed in data survey. The default setting is OFF.

SET DELIMITERS
ON/OFF

Determines whether the separators specified by SET DELIMITERS TO should be used. The default setting is OFF.

SET DELIMITERS TO

Defines the limiting characters for page-oriented display of field contents and variables.

SET DESIGN

Protects design screens so that users cannot alter the layout.

SET DEVICE TO
SCREEN/PRINT

Determines whether the output from @SAY commands is transported to the screen or the printer. The default setting is SCREEN.

SET DISPLAY TO

Enables you to specify a colour or monochrome monitor and the number of lines your screen is to display.

SET DOHISTORY
ON/OFF

Determines whether command files should be stored in HISTORY. The default setting is OFF.

SET ECHO ON/OFF

Determines whether command lines are displayed on the screen during execution. The default setting is OFF.

SET ESCAPE ON/OFF Determines whether the program can be discontinued
using the Esc key. The default
setting is ON.

SET EXACT ON/OFF Determines whether exact
correspondence should occur
in the comparison of character
fields or whether correspondence of the first characters is
sufficient. The default setting is
OFF.

SET FIELDS ON/OFF Determines whether dBASE
should take into account the
fields list defined by SET
FIELDS TO. The default setting is OFF.

SET FIELDS TO   Defines which fields of the current database can be edited.

SET FILTER TO   Renders all records invisible
which do not fulfil a specified
condition.

SET FIXED ON/OFF   Defines the decimal display.
The default setting is OFF.

SET FORMAT TO   Opens a form file for data
input.

SET FUNCTION TO   Defines the significance of the
function keys.

SET HEADING   Determines whether the field
  ON/OFF   names should appear as column headings above the data
when LIST and DISPLAY are
used. The default setting is
ON.

SET HELP ON/OFF	Determines whether the help system should be automatically activated when an error occurs. The default setting is ON.
SET HISTORY ON/OFF	Determines whether the last specified commands should be memorized. The default setting is ON.
SET HISTORY TO	Defines the number of commands to be memorized in the SET HISTORY ON setting.
SET INDEX TO	Opens the specified index files.
SET INTENSITY ON/OFF	Determines whether the display should be more resolute. The default setting is ON.
SET MARGIN TO	Defines the left-hand margin for printer output.
SET MEMOWIDTH TO	Defines the column width for the output of memo fields.
SET MENU ON/OFF	Determines whether a menu is displayed during the execution of page-oriented commands. The default setting is ON.
SET MESSAGE TO	Displays the specified message on the screen.
SET MOUSE ON/OFF	Enables or disables the mouse cursor.
SET ORDER TO	Activates a chosen opened single index file.

SET ORDER TO TAG   Activates an index from an opened multiple index file.

SET PATH TO   Defines the search path for files.

SET PRINT ON/OFF   Determines whether all displayed data should be transported to the printer. The default setting is OFF.

SET PRINTER TO   Transports all printer output to
<DOS device>   the specified device.

SET PROCEDURE TO   Opens the specified procedure file.

SET RELATION TO   Links two databases via a key field.

SET SAFETY ON/OFF   Switches on or off the warning that a file may be overwritten. The default setting is ON.

SET SCOREBOARD   Determines whether dBASE
ON/OFF   messages should appear in the status line. The default setting is ON.

SET STATUS ON/OFF   Determines whether the status and message lines should be visible on the screen. The default setting is ON.

SET STEP ON/OFF   Determines whether dBASE should pause after each program line while executing programs. The default setting is OFF.

SET TALK ON/OFF   Determines whether the result
                         of all commands should be
                         shown on the screen. The de-
                         fault setting is ON.

SET TITLE ON/OFF   Determines whether dBASE
                         should request a description
                         when adding a file to a catalog.
                         The default setting is ON.

SET TYPEAHEAD TO   Defines the size of the key-
                         board buffer.

SET UNIQUE ON/OFF   Displays either only the first
                         record (ON) or all records with
                         identical keys in an index file
                         (OFF). The default setting is
                         OFF.

SET VIEW TO   Opens a View file.

SKIP   Moves a specified number of
                         records backwards or forwards
                         from the current record.

SORT   Creates a sorted version of the
                         current database.

SPACE()   Generates a string consisting
                         of a specified number of blank
                         spaces.

SQRT()   Calculates the square root of a
                         number.

STORE   Stores the value of an expres-
                         sion in a variable.

STR()   Converts numeric fields to
                         character fields.

STUFF()	Replaces a part of a string with another string.
SUBSTR()	Displays a part of a string.
SUM	Calculates the sum of a series of values and saves the result in a variable.
SUSPEND	Interrupts a program temporarily. The execution can be continued using RESUME.
TAG	Identifies an index in a multiple index file.
TEDIT	Defines an external editor to be used instead of the internal dBASE editor.
TEXT	Precedes the display of a lengthy passage of text. The display is ended using END-TEXT.
TIME()	Returns the system time as a string.
TOTAL	Calculates the sum of the numeric fields in a database and writes them in a new file.
TRANSFORM	Displays a character or number in the specified PICTURE format.
TRIM()	Removes spaces at the end of a string.
TYPE()	Checks the validity of expressions.

UPDATE	Updates a database using a mutation file.
UPPER()	Converts small letters to capitals.
USE	Opens or closes a database in the current work area.
VAL()	Converts character fields to numeric fields.
VERSION()	Shows the dBASE version number.
WAIT	Interrupts the execution of a program until a random key is pressed.
YEAR()	Returns the current year.
ZAP	Removes all records from the current file.

Appendix B
dBASE-related files

.ACC	access file (network)
.APP	program file (application)
.BAK	backup of a file
.BAR	bar menu
.BCH	batch file for application generator
.BIN	binary file for LOAD and CALL
.CAC	Cache file (becomes .EXE at installation)
.CAT	catalog file
.CHT	CHART MASTER file
.COD	template source file
.COM	executable DOS program
.CPT	coded memo file
.CRP	coded data file
.DB	configuration file
.DB2	dBASE II data file
.DBF	dBASE III, III+ or IV data file
.DBO	compiled program file or procedure file
.DBT	memo file
.DEF	definition file for the selector
.DIF	standard format for exchange of data between various programs (Data Interchange Format: VisiCalc, Open Access)
.DOC	documentation file of the application generator
.ERR	file containing errors which have arisen when creating forms
.EXE	executable DOS program
.FIL	list of files from the application generator
.FMO	compiled mask file
.FMT	mask file as source code
.FNL	report from Binary named list (BNL-file)
.FR3	former dBASE III report file (.FRG)
.FRG	report file as source code
.FRM	report file
.FRO	compiled report file

.FW2, FW3, FW4	Framework file
.GEN	template file for generators
.GRP	group file for dBase IV under MS-Windows
.HLP	help texts
.ICO	icon file for dBASE IV under MS-Windows
.KEY	keyboard macro file
.LB3	former dBASE III label file (.LBG)
.LBG	label file in source code
.LBL	label file
.LBO	compiled label file
.LNL	label from Binary named list (BNL file)
.LOG	log file for transactions
.MBK	backup of index file for several dBASE IV indexes
.MDX	index file for several dBASE IV indexes
.MEM	variables file
.OVL	overlay file
.PIF	file containing program information for MS-Windows
.POP	pop-up menu file for the application generator
.PR2	printer driver
.PRF	file for the printer settings
.PRG	program and procedure file as source code
.PRS	dBASE/SQL program and procedure file
.PRT	printer output file
.QBE	vision filter
.QBO	compiled vision filter
.QRY	view file
.RES	resource file
.RPD	RapidFile file
.SC3	former dBASE III mask file (.SCR)
.SCR	dBASE IV mask file
.SNL	screen from Binary named list file (BNL file)
.STR	structure list for application generator
.TBK	backup of .DBT memo file
.T44, W44	temporary file for sorting and indexing
.TXT	text output file
.UPD	mutation filter
.UPO	compiled .UPD file

.VAL	object file for Values menu in the application generator
.VUE	dBASE III view file
.WIN	file with opened logical windows
.WKS	file in the Lotus 1-2-3 version 1 format
.WK1	file in the Lotus 1-2-3 version 2 format

Appendix C
ASCII table

Dec	Hex	Chr	Dec	Hex	Chr	Dec	Hex	Chr	Dec	Hex	Chr
0	0		32	20		64	40	@	96	60	`
1	1	☺	33	21	!	65	41	A	97	61	a
2	2	☻	34	22	"	66	42	B	98	62	b
3	3	♥	35	23	#	67	43	C	99	63	c
4	4	♦	36	24	$	68	44	D	100	64	d
5	5	♣	37	25	%	69	45	E	101	65	e
6	6	♠	38	26	&	70	46	F	102	66	f
7	7	•	39	27	'	71	47	G	103	67	g
8	8		40	28	(	72	48	H	104	68	h
9	9	○	41	29	)	73	49	I	105	69	i
10	A		42	2A	*	74	4A	J	106	6A	j
11	B	♂	43	2B	+	75	4B	K	107	6B	k
12	C	♀	44	2C	,	76	4C	L	108	6C	l
13	D	♪	45	2D	-	77	4D	M	109	6D	m
14	E	♫	46	2E	.	78	4E	N	110	6E	n
15	F	☼	47	2F	/	79	4F	O	111	6F	o
16	10	►	48	30	0	80	50	P	112	70	p
17	11	◄	49	31	1	81	51	Q	113	71	q
18	12	↕	50	32	2	82	52	R	114	72	r
19	13	‼	51	33	3	83	53	S	115	73	s
20	14	¶	52	34	4	84	54	T	116	74	t
21	15	§	53	35	5	85	55	U	117	75	u
22	16	▬	54	36	6	86	56	V	118	76	v
23	17	↨	55	37	7	87	57	W	119	77	w
24	18	↑	56	38	8	88	58	X	120	78	x
25	19	↓	57	39	9	89	59	Y	121	79	y
26	1A	→	58	3A	:	90	5A	Z	122	7A	z
27	1B	←	59	3B	;	91	5B	[	123	7B	{
28	1C	∟	60	3C	<	92	5C	\	124	7C		
29	1D	↔	61	3D	=	93	5D	]	125	7D	}
30	1E	▲	62	3E	>	94	5E	^	126	7E	~
31	1F	▼	63	3F	?	95	5F	_	127	7F	⌂

Dec	Hex	Chr	Dec	Hex	Chr	Dec	Hex	Chr	Dec	Hex	Chr
128	80	Ç	160	A0	á	192	C0	└	224	E0	α
129	81	ü	161	A1	í	193	C1	┴	225	E1	ß
130	82	é	162	A2	ó	194	C2	┬	226	E2	Γ
131	83	â	163	A3	ú	195	C3	├	227	E3	π
132	84	ä	164	A4	ñ	196	C4	─	228	E4	Σ
133	85	à	165	A5	Ñ	197	C5	┼	229	E5	σ
134	86	å	166	A6	ª	198	C6	╞	230	E6	μ
135	87	ç	167	A7	º	199	C7	╟	231	E7	τ
136	88	ê	168	A8	¿	200	C8	╚	232	E8	Φ
137	89	ë	169	A9	⌐	201	C9	╔	233	E9	Θ
138	8A	è	170	AA	¬	202	CA	╩	234	EA	Ω
139	8B	ï	171	AB	½	203	CB	╦	235	EB	δ
140	8C	î	172	AC	¼	204	CC	╠	236	EC	∞
141	8D	ì	173	AD	¡	205	CD	═	237	ED	ø
142	8E	Ä	174	AE	«	206	CE	╬	238	EE	∈
143	8F	Å	175	AF	»	207	CF	╧	239	EF	∩
144	90	É	176	B0	░	208	D0	╨	240	F0	≡
145	91	æ	177	B1	▒	209	D1	╤	241	F1	±
146	92	Æ	178	B2	▓	210	D2	╥	242	F2	≥
147	93	ô	179	B3	│	211	D3	╙	243	F3	≤
148	94	ö	180	B4	┤	212	D4	╘	244	F4	⌠
149	95	ò	181	B5	╡	213	D5	╒	245	F5	⌡
150	96	û	182	B6	╢	214	D6	╓	246	F6	÷
151	97	ù	183	B7	╖	215	D7	╫	247	F7	≈
152	98	ÿ	184	B8	╕	216	D8	╪	248	F8	°
153	99	Ö	185	B9	╣	217	D9	┘	249	F9	∙
154	9A	Ü	186	BA	║	218	DA	┌	250	FA	·
155	9B	¢	187	BB	╗	219	DB	█	251	FB	√
156	9C	£	188	BC	╝	220	DC	▄	252	FC	ⁿ
157	9D	¥	189	BD	╜	221	DD	▌	253	FD	²
158	9E	₧	190	BE	╛	222	DE	▐	254	FE	■
159	9F	ƒ	191	BF	┐	223	DF	▀	255	FF	

Index